W9-BOL-938

Shakespeare's

Hamlet

Edited by Sidney Lamb

Associate Professor of English

Sir George Williams University, Montreal

Complete Text + Commentary + Glossary

Commentary by Terri Mategrano, Ph.D.

IDG Books Worldwide, Inc.

An International Data Group Company

Foster City, CA • Chicago, IL • Indianapolis, IN • New York, NY

CLIFFSCOMPLETE

Shakespeare's

Hamlet

About the Author

Terri Mategrano earned her Ph.D. at Northern Illinois University in Dekalb, Illinois, where she is presently a Visiting Assistant Professor. Her dissertation, "*Shrouded Behind the Arras:* The Shadow of Shakespeare in the First Quarto of *Hamlet*," is under consideration for publication. Professor Mategrano received the Dissertation Completion Award from the Graduate School at Northern Illinois University for her groundbreaking work on the publication of this early Shakespearean text. She is currently continuing her research involving an in-depth study of the publishers and printers in Elizabethan and Jacobean London who published Shakespeare's play texts.

Publisher's Acknowledgments

Editorial

Project Editor: Joan Friedman

Acquisitions Editor: Gregory W. Tubach

Copy Editor: Linda S. Stark

Illustrator: DD Dowden

Editorial Manager: Kristin A. Cocks

Special Help: Laura Jefferson

Production

Indexer: Liz Cunningham

Proofreader: Ethel M. Winslow

IDG Books Indianapolis Production Department

CliffsComplete *Hamlet*

Published by
IDG Books Worldwide, Inc.
An International Data Group Company
919 E. Hillsdale Blvd.
Suite 400
Foster City, CA 94404
www.idgbooks.com (IDG Books Worldwide Web site)
www.cliffsnotes.com (CliffsNotes Web site)

Note: If you purchased this book without a cover you should be aware that this book is stolen property. It was reported as "unsold and destroyed" to the publisher, and neither the author nor the publisher has received any payment for this "stripped book."

Copyright © 2000 IDG Books Worldwide, Inc. All rights reserved. No part of this book, including interior design, cover design, and icons, may be reproduced or transmitted in any form, by any means (electronic, photocopying, recording, or otherwise) without the prior written permission of the publisher.

Library of Congress Catalog Card No.: 00-101842

ISBN: 0-7645-8568-1

Printed in the United States of America

10 9 8 7 6 5 4 3 2

1O/QU/QV/QQ/IN

Distributed in the United States by IDG Books Worldwide, Inc.

Distributed by CDG Books Canada Inc. for Canada; by Transworld Publishers Limited in the United Kingdom; by IDG Norge Books for Norway; by IDG Sweden Books for Sweden; by IDG Books Australia Publishing Corporation Pty. Ltd. for Australia and New Zealand; by TransQuest Publishers Pte Ltd. for Singapore, Malaysia, Thailand, Indonesia, and Hong Kong; by Gotop Information Inc. for Taiwan; by ICG Muse, Inc. for Japan; by Intersoft for South Africa; by Eyrolles for France; by International Thomson Publishing for Germany, Austria and Switzerland; by Distribuidora Cuspide for Argentina; by LR International for Brazil; by Galileo Libros for Chile; by Ediciones ZETA S.C.R. Ltda. for Peru; by WS Computer Publishing Corporation, Inc., for the Philippines; by Contemporanea de Ediciones for Venezuela; by Express Computer Distributors for the Caribbean and West Indies; by Micronesia Media Distributor, Inc. for Micronesia; by Chips Computadoras S.A. de C.V. for Mexico; by Editorial Norma de Panama S.A. for Panama; by American Bookshops for Finland.

For general information on IDG Books Worldwide's books in the U.S., please call our Consumer Customer Service department at 800-762-2974. For reseller information, including discounts and premium sales, please call our Reseller Customer Service department at 800-434-3422.

For information on where to purchase IDG Books Worldwide's books outside the U.S., please contact our International Sales department at 317-596-5530 or fax 317-572-4002.

For consumer information on foreign language translations, please contact our Customer Service department at 1-800-434-3422, fax 317-572-4002, or e-mail rights@idgbooks.com.

For information on licensing foreign or domestic rights, please phone +1-650-653-7098.

For sales inquiries and special prices for bulk quantities, please contact our Order Services department at 800-434-3422 or write to the address above.

For information on using IDG Books Worldwide's books in the classroom or for ordering examination copies, please contact our Educational Sales department at 800-434-2086 or fax 317-572-4005.

For press review copies, author interviews, or other publicity information, please contact our Public Relations department at 650-653-7000 or fax 650-653-7500.

For authorization to photocopy items for corporate, personal, or educational use, please contact Copyright Clearance Center, 222 Rosewood Drive, Danvers, MA 01923, or fax 978-750-4470.

LIMIT OF LIABILITY/DISCLAIMER OF WARRANTY: THE PUBLISHER AND AUTHOR HAVE USED THEIR BEST EFFORTS IN PREPARING THIS BOOK. THE PUBLISHER AND AUTHOR MAKE NO REPRESENTATIONS OR WARRANTIES WITH RESPECT TO THE ACCURACY OR COMPLETENESS OF THE CONTENTS OF THIS BOOK AND SPECIFICALLY DISCLAIM ANY IMPLIED WARRANTIES OF MERCHANTABILITY OR FITNESS FOR A PARTICULAR PURPOSE. THERE ARE NO WARRANTIES WHICH EXTEND BEYOND THE DESCRIPTIONS CONTAINED IN THIS PARAGRAPH. NO WARRANTY MAY BE CREATED OR EXTENDED BY SALES REPRESENTATIVES OR WRITTEN SALES MATERIALS. THE ACCURACY AND COMPLETENESS OF THE INFORMATION PROVIDED HEREIN AND THE OPINIONS STATED HEREIN ARE NOT GUARANTEED OR WARRANTED TO PRODUCE ANY PARTICULAR RESULTS, AND THE ADVICE AND STRATEGIES CONTAINED HEREIN MAY NOT BE SUITABLE FOR EVERY INDIVIDUAL. NEITHER THE PUBLISHER NOR AUTHOR SHALL BE LIABLE FOR ANY LOSS OF PROFIT OR ANY OTHER COMMERCIAL DAMAGES, INCLUDING BUT NOT LIMITED TO SPECIAL, INCIDENTAL, CONSEQUENTIAL, OR OTHER DAMAGES.

Trademarks: Cliffs, CliffsNotes, and all related logos and trade dress are registered trademarks or trademarks of CliffsNotes, Inc. in the United States and other countries. All other brand names and product names used in this book are trade names, service marks, trademarks, or registered trademarks of their respective owners. IDG Books Worldwide, Inc. and CliffsNotes, Inc. are not associated with any product or vendor mentioned in this book.

is a registered trademark under exclusive license to IDG Books Worldwide, Inc. from International Data Group, Inc. in the United States and/or other countries.

CLIFFSCOMPLETE

Shakespeare's

Hamlet

CONTENTS AT A GLANCE

CLIFFSCOMPLETE

Shakespeare's

Hamlet

TABLE OF CONTENTS

Shakespeare's
HAMLET

INTRODUCTION TO WILLIAM SHAKESPEARE

William Shakespeare, or the "Bard" as people fondly call him, permeates almost all aspects of our society. He can be found in our classrooms, on our televisions, in our theatres, and in our cinemas. Speaking to us through his plays, Shakespeare comments on his life and culture, as well as our own. Actors still regularly perform his plays on the modern stage and screen. The 1990s, for example, saw the release of cinematic versions of *Romeo and Juliet, Hamlet, Othello, A Midsummer Night's Dream,* and many more of his works.

In addition to the popularity of Shakespeare's plays as he wrote them, other writers have modernized his works to attract new audiences. For example, *West Side Story* places *Romeo and Juliet* in New York City, and *A Thousand Acres* sets *King Lear* in Iowa corn country. Beyond adaptations and productions, his life and works have captured our cultural imagination. The twentieth century witnessed the production of a play and film about two minor characters from Shakespeare's *Hamlet* in *Rosencrantz and Guildenstern are Dead* and a fictional movie about Shakespeare's early life and poetic inspiration in *Shakespeare in Love.*

Despite his monumental presence in our culture, Shakespeare remains enigmatic. He does not tell us which plays he wrote alone, on which plays he collaborated with other playwrights, or which versions of his plays to read and perform. Furthermore, with only a handful of documents available about his life, he does not tell us much about Shakespeare the person, forcing critics and scholars to look to historical references to uncover the true-life great dramatist.

Anti-Stratfordians — modern scholars who question the authorship of Shakespeare's plays — have used this lack of information to argue that William Shakespeare either never existed or, if he did exist, did not write any of the plays we attribute to him. They believe that another historical figure, such as Francis Bacon or Queen Elizabeth I, used the name as a cover. Whether or not a man named William Shakespeare ever actually existed is ultimately secondary to the recognition that the group of plays bound together by that name does exist and continues to educate, enlighten, and entertain us.

An engraved portrait of Shakespeare by an unknown artist, ca. 1607.
Culver Pictures, Inc./SuperStock

Family life

Though scholars are unsure of the exact date of Shakespeare's birth, records indicate that his parents — Mary and John Shakespeare — baptized him on April 26, 1564, in the small provincial town of Stratford-upon-Avon — so named because it sat on the banks of the Avon river. Because common practice was to baptize infants a few days after they were born, scholars generally recognize April 23, 1564 as Shakespeare's birthday. Coincidentally, April 23 is the day of St. George, the patron saint of England, as well as the day upon which Shakespeare would die 52 years later. William was the third of Mary and John's eight children and the first of four sons. The house in which scholars believe Shakespeare was born stands on Henley Street and, despite many modifications over the years, you can still visit it today.

Shakespeare's father

Prior to William Shakespeare's birth, John Shakespeare lived in Snitterfield, where he married Mary Arden, the daughter of his landlord. After moving to Stratford in 1552, he worked as a glover, a money-lender, and a dealer in agricultural products such as wool and grain. He also pursued public office and achieved a variety of posts including bailiff, Stratford's highest elected position — equivalent to a small town's mayor. At the height of his career, sometime near 1576, he petitioned the Herald's Office for a coat of arms and thus the right to be a gentleman. But the rise from the middle class to the gentry did not come right away, and the costly petition expired without being granted.

About this time, John Shakespeare mysteriously fell into financial difficulty. He became involved in serious litigation, was assessed heavy fines, and even lost his seat on the town council. Some scholars suggest that this decline could have resulted from religious discrimination because the Shakespeare family may have supported Catholicism, the practice of which was illegal in England. However, other scholars point out that not all religious dissenters (both Catholics and radical Puritans) lost their posts due to their religion. Whatever the cause of his decline, John did regain some prosperity toward the end of his life. In 1596, the Herald's Office granted the Shakespeare family a coat of arms at the petition of William, by then a successful playwright in London. And John, prior to his death in 1601, regained his seat on Stratford's town council.

Childhood and education

Our understanding of William Shakespeare's childhood in Stratford is primarily speculative because children do not often appear in the legal records from which many scholars attempt to reconstruct Shakespeare's life. Based on his father's local prominence, scholars speculate that Shakespeare most likely attended King's New School, a school that usually employed Oxford graduates and was generally well respected. Shakespeare would have started *petty school* — the rough equivalent to modern preschool — at the age of four or five. He would have learned to read on a *hornbook*, which was a sheet of parchment or paper on which the alphabet and the Lord's Prayer were written. This sheet was framed in wood and covered with a transparent piece of horn for durability. After two years in petty school, he would have transferred to grammar school, where his school day would have probably lasted from 6 or 7 o'clock in the morning (depending on the time of year) until 5 o'clock in the evening, with only a handful of holidays.

While in grammar school, Shakespeare probably studied primarily Latin, reciting and reading the works of classical Roman authors such as Plautus, Ovid, Seneca, and Horace. Traces of these authors' works can be seen in his dramatic texts. Toward his last years in grammar school, Shakespeare would have acquired some basic skills in Greek as well. Thus the remark made by Ben Jonson, Shakespeare's well-educated friend and contemporary playwright, that Shakespeare knew "small Latin and less Greek" is accurate. Jonson is not saying that when Shakespeare

*Shakespeare's birthplace in Stratford-upon-Avon.
SuperStock*

left grammar school he was only semi-literate; he merely indicates that Shakespeare did not attend university, where he would have gained more Latin and Greek instruction.

Wife and children

When Shakespeare became an adult, the historical records documenting his existence began to increase. In November 1582, at the age of 18, he married 26-year-old Anne Hathaway from the nearby village of Shottery. The disparity in their ages, coupled with the fact that they baptized their first daughter, Susanna, only six months later in May 1583, has caused a great deal of modern speculation about the nature of their relationship. However, sixteenth-century conceptions of marriage differed slightly from our modern notions. Though all marriages needed to be performed before a member of the clergy, many of Shakespeare's contemporaries believed that a couple could establish a relationship through a premarital contract by exchanging vows in front of witnesses. This contract removed the social stigma of pregnancy before marriage. (Shakespeare's plays contain instances of marriage prompted by pregnancy, and *Measure for Measure* includes this kind of premarital contract.) Two years later, in

February 1585, Shakespeare baptized his twins Hamnet and Judith. Hamnet would die at the age of 11 when Shakespeare was primarily living away from his family in London.

For seven years after the twins' baptism, the records remain silent on Shakespeare. At some point, he traveled to London and became involved with the theatre, but he could have been anywhere between 21 and 28 years old when he did. Though some have suggested that he may have served as an assistant to a schoolmaster at a provincial school, it seems likely that he went to London to become an actor, gradually becoming a playwright and gaining attention.

The plays: On stage and in print

The next mention of Shakespeare comes in 1592 by a university wit named Robert Greene when Shakespeare apparently was already a rising actor and playwright for the London stage. Greene, no longer a successful playwright, tried to warn other university wits about Shakespeare. He wrote:

> *For there is an upstart crow, beautified with our feathers, that with his "Tiger's heart wrapped in a player's hide" supposes he is as well able to bombast out a blank verse as the best of you, and, being an absolute Johannes Factotum, is in his own conceit the only Shake-scene in a country.*

This statement comes at a point in time when men without a university education, like Shakespeare, were starting to compete as dramatists with the university wits. As many critics have pointed out, Greene's statement recalls a line from *3 Henry VI*, which reads, "O tiger's heart wrapped in a woman's hide!" (I.4.137). Greene's remark does not indicate that Shakespeare was generally disliked. On the contrary, another university wit, Thomas Nashe, wrote of the great theatrical success of *Henry VI*, and Henry Chettle, Greene's publisher, later printed a flattering apology to Shakespeare. What Greene's statement does show us is that Shakespeare's reputation for poetry had enough prominence to provoke the envy of a failing competitor.

In the following year, 1593, the government closed London's theatres due to an outbreak of the bubonic plague. Publication history suggests that during this closure, Shakespeare may have written his two narrative poems, *Venus and Adonis,* published in 1593, and *The Rape of Lucrece,* published in 1594. These are the only two works that Shakespeare seems to have helped into print; each carries a dedication by Shakespeare to Henry Wriothesley, Earl of Southampton.

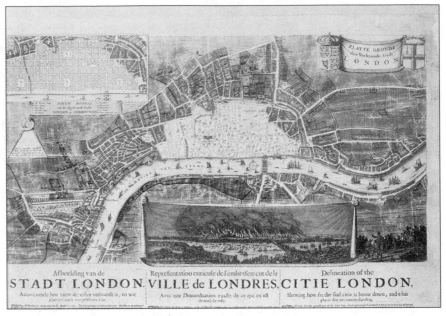

A ground plan of London after the fire of 1666, drawn by Marcus Willemsz Doornik. Guildhall Library, London/AKG, Berlin/SuperStock

Stage success

When the theatres reopened in 1594, Shakespeare joined the Lord Chamberlain's Men, an acting company. Though uncertain about the history of his early dramatic works, scholars believe that by this point he had written *The Two Gentlemen of Verona, The Taming of the Shrew,* the *Henry VI* trilogy, and *Titus Andronicus.* During his early years in the theatre, he primarily wrote history plays, with his romantic comedies emerging in the 1590s. Even at this early stage in his career, Shakespeare was a success. In 1597, he was able to purchase New Place, one of the two largest houses in Stratford, and secure a coat of arms for his family.

In 1597, the lease expired on the Lord Chamberlain's playhouse, called The Theatre. Because the owner of The Theatre refused to renew the lease, the acting company was forced to perform at various playhouses until the 1599 opening of the now famous Globe theatre, which was literally built with lumber from The Theatre. (The Globe, later destroyed by fire, has recently been reconstructed in London and can be visited today.)

Recent scholars suggest that Shakespeare's great tragedy *Julius Caesar* may have been the first of Shakespeare's plays performed in the original Globe theatre. When this open-air theatre on the Thames River opened, financial papers list Shakespeare's name as one of the principal investors. Already an actor and a playwright, Shakespeare was now becoming a "Company Man." This new status allowed him to share in the profits of the theatre rather than merely getting paid for his plays, some of which publishers were beginning to release in quarto format.

Publications

A *quarto* was a small, inexpensive book typically used for leisure books such as plays; the term itself indicates that the printer folded the paper four times. The modern day equivalent of a quarto would be a paperback. In contrast, the first collected works of Shakespeare were in folio format, which means that the printer folded each sheet only once. Scholars call the collected edition of Shakespeare's works the *First Folio*. A folio was a larger and more prestigious book than a quarto, and printers generally reserved the format for works such as the Bible.

No evidence exists that Shakespeare participated in the publication of any of his plays. Members of Shakespeare's acting company printed the First Folio seven years after Shakespeare's death. Generally, playwrights wrote their works to be performed on stage, and publishing them was an innovation at the time. Shakespeare probably would not have thought of them as books in the way we do. In fact, as a principal investor in the acting company (which purchased the play as well as the exclusive right to perform it), he may not have even thought of them as his own. He probably would have thought of his plays as belonging to the company.

For this reason, scholars have generally characterized most quartos printed before the First Folio as "bad" by arguing that printers pirated the plays and published them illegally. How would a printer have received a pirated copy of a play? The theories range from someone stealing a copy to an actor (or actors) selling the play by relating it from memory to a printer. Many times, major differences exist between a quarto version of the play and a folio version, causing uncertainty about which is Shakespeare's true creation. *Hamlet,* for example, is almost twice as long in the Folio as in quarto versions. Recently, scholars have come to realize the value of the different versions. The *Norton Shakespeare,* for example, includes all three versions of *King Lear* — the quarto, the folio, and the *conflated* version (the combination of the quarto and folio).

Prolific productions

The first decade of the 1600s witnessed the publication of additional quartos as well as the production of most of Shakespeare's great tragedies, with *Julius*

Caesar appearing in 1599 and *Hamlet* in 1600–1601. After the death of Queen Elizabeth in 1603, the Lord Chamberlain's Men became the King's Men under James I, Elizabeth's successor. Around the time of this transition in the English monarchy, the famous tragedy *Othello* (1603–1604) was most likely written and performed, followed closely by *King Lear* (1605–1606), *Antony and Cleopatra* (1606), and *Macbeth* (1606) in the next two years.

Shakespeare's name also appears as a major investor in the 1609 acquisition of an indoor theatre known as the Blackfriars. This last period of Shakespeare's career, which includes plays that considered the acting conditions both at the Blackfriars and the open-air Globe theatre, consists primarily of romances or tragicomedies such as *The Winter's Tale* and *The Tempest*. On June 29, 1613, during a performance of *All is True*, or *Henry VIII*, the thatching on top of the Globe caught fire and the playhouse burned to the ground. After this incident, the King's Men moved solely into the indoor Blackfriars theatre.

Final days

During the last years of his career, Shakespeare collaborated on a couple of plays with contemporary dramatist John Fletcher, even possibly coming out of retirement — which scholars believe began sometime in 1613 — to work on *The Two Noble Kinsmen* (1613–1614). Three years later, Shakespeare died on April 23, 1616. Though the exact cause of death remains unknown, a vicar from Stratford in the mid-seventeenth-century wrote in his diary that Shakespeare, perhaps celebrating the marriage of his daughter, Judith, contracted a fever during a night of revelry with fellow literary figures Ben Jonson and Michael Drayton. Regardless, Shakespeare may have felt his death was imminent in March of that year because he altered his will. Interestingly, his will mentions no book or theatrical manuscripts, perhaps indicating the lack of value that he put on printed versions of his dramatic works and their status as company property.

Seven years after Shakespeare's death, John Heminge and Henry Condell, fellow members of the King's Men, published his collected works. In their preface, they claim that they are publishing the true versions of Shakespeare's plays partially as a response to the previous quarto printings of 18 of his plays, most of these with multiple printings. This Folio contains 36 plays to which scholars generally add *Pericles* and *The Two Noble Kinsmen*. This volume of Shakespeare's plays began the process of constructing Shakespeare not only as England's national poet but also as a monumental figure whose plays would continue to captivate imaginations at the end of the millenium with no signs of stopping. Ben Jonson's prophetic line about Shakespeare in the First Folio — "He was not of an age, but for all time!" — certainly holds true.

Chronology of Shakespeare's plays

1590–1591	*The Two Gentlemen of Verona*
	The Taming of the Shrew
1591	*2 Henry VI*
	3 Henry VI
1592	*1 Henry VI*
	Titus Andronicus
1592–1593	*Richard III*
	Venus and Adonis
1593–1594	*The Rape of Lucrece*
1594	*The Comedy of Errors*
1594–1595	*Love's Labour's Lost*
1595	*Richard II*
	Romeo and Juliet
	A Midsummer Night's Dream
1595–1596	*Love's Labour's Won*
	(This manuscript was lost.)
1596	*King John*
1596–1597	*The Merchant of Venice*
	1 Henry IV
1597–1598	*The Merry Wives of Windsor*
	2 Henry IV
1598	*Much Ado About Nothing*

1598–1599	*Henry V*
1599	*Julius Caesar*
1599–1600	*As You Like It*
1600–1601	*Hamlet*
1601	*Twelfth Night,* or *What You Will*
1602	*Troilus and Cressida*
1593–1603	*Sonnets*
1603	*Measure for Measure*
1603–1604	*A Lover's Complaint*
	Othello
1604–1605	*All's Well That Ends Well*
1605	*Timon of Athens*
1605–1606	*King Lear*
1606	*Macbeth*
	Antony and Cleopatra
1607	*Pericles*
1608	*Coriolanus*
1609	*The Winter's Tale*
1610	*Cymbeline*
1611	*The Tempest*
1612–1613	*Cardenio* (with John Fletcher; this manuscript was lost.)
1613	*All is True (Henry VIII)*
1613–1614	*The Two Noble Kinsmen* (with John Fletcher)

This chronology is derived from Stanley Wells' and Gary Taylor's *William Shakespeare: A Textual Companion,* which is listed in the "Works consulted" section on the next page.

A note on Shakespeare's language

Readers encountering Shakespeare for the first time usually find Early Modern English difficult to understand. Yet, rather than serving as a barrier to Shakespeare, the richness of this language should form part of our appreciation of the Bard.

One of the first things readers usually notice about the language is the use of pronouns. Like the King James Version of the Bible, Shakespeare's pronouns are slightly different from our own and can cause confusion. Words like "thou" (you), "thee" and "ye" (objective cases of you), and "thy" and "thine" (your/yours) appear throughout Shakespeare's plays. You may need a little time to get used to these changes. You can find the definitions for other words that commonly cause confusion in the glossary column on the right side of each page in this edition.

Iambic pentameter

Though Shakespeare sometimes wrote in prose, he wrote most of his plays in poetry, specifically blank verse. Blank verse consists of lines in unrhymed *iambic pentameter*. *Iambic* refers to the stress patterns of the line. An *iamb* is an element of sound that consists of two beats — the first unstressed (da) and the second stressed (DA). A good example of an iambic line is Hamlet's famous line "To be or not to be," in which you do not stress "to," "or," and "to," but you do stress "be," "not," and "be." *Pentameter* refers to the *meter* or number of stressed syllables in a line. *Penta*-meter has five stressed syllables. Juliet's line "But soft, what light through yonder window breaks?" (II.2.2) is a good example of iambic pentameter.

Wordplay

Shakespeare's language is also verbally rich as he, along with many dramatists of his period, had a fondness for wordplay. This wordplay often takes the forms of *puns,* where a word can mean more than one thing in a given context. Shakespeare often employs puns as a way of illustrating the distance between what is on the surface — *apparent* meanings — and what meanings lie underneath. Though recognizing these puns may be difficult at first, the glosses (definitions) in the right column point many of them out to you.

If you are encountering Shakespeare's plays for the first time, the following reading tips may help ease you into the plays. Shakespeare's lines were meant to be spoken; therefore, reading them aloud or speaking them should help with comprehension.

Also, though most of the lines are poetic, do not forget to read complete sentences — move from period to period as well as from line to line. Although Shakespeare's language can be difficult at first, the rewards of immersing yourself in the richness and fluidity of the lines are immeasurable.

Works consulted

For more information on Shakespeare's life and works, see the following:

Bevington, David, ed. *The Complete Works of Shakespeare*. New York: Longman, 1997.

Evans, G.Blakemore, ed. *The Riverside Shakespeare*. Boston: Houghton Mifflin Co., 1997.

Greenblatt, Stephen, ed. *The Norton Shakespeare*. New York: W.W. Norton and Co., 1997.

Kastan, David Scott, ed. *A Companion to Shakespeare*. Oxford: Blackwell, 1999.

McDonald, Russ. *The Bedford Companion to Shakespeare: An Introduction with Documents*. Boston: Bedford-St. Martin's Press, 1996.

Wells, Stanley and Gary Taylor. *William Shakespeare: A Textual Companion*. New York: W.W. Norton and Co., 1997.

INTRODUCTION TO EARLY MODERN ENGLAND

William Shakespeare (1564–1616) lived during a period in England's history that people have generally referred to as the English Renaissance. The term *renaissance*, meaning rebirth, was applied to this period of English history as a way of celebrating what was perceived as the rapid development of art, literature, science, and politics: in many ways, the rebirth of classical Rome.

Recently, scholars have challenged the name "English Renaissance" on two grounds. First, some scholars argue that the term should not be used because women did not share in the advancements of English culture during this time period; their legal status was still below that of men. Second, other scholars have challenged the basic notion that this period saw a sudden explosion of culture. A rebirth of civilization suggests that the previous period of time was not civilized. This second group of scholars sees a much more gradual transition between the Middle Ages and Shakespeare's time.

Some people use the terms *Elizabethan* and *Jacobean* when referring to periods of the sixteenth and seventeenth centuries. These terms correspond to the reigns of Elizabeth I (1558–1603) and James I (1603–1625). The problem with these terms is that they do not cover large spans of time; for example, Shakespeare's life and career spans both monarchies.

Scholars are now beginning to replace Renaissance with the term Early Modern when referring to this time period, but people still use both terms interchangeably. The term *Early Modern* recognizes that this period established many of the foundations of our modern culture. Though critics still disagree about the exact dates of the period, in general, the dates range from 1450 to 1750. Thus, Shakespeare's life clearly falls within the Early Modern period.

Shakespeare's plays live on in our culture, but we must remember that Shakespeare's culture differed greatly from our own. Though his understanding of human nature and relationships seems to apply to our modern lives, we must try to understand the world he lived in so we can better understand his plays. This introduction helps you do just that. It examines the intellectual, religious, political, and social contexts of Shakespeare's work before turning to the importance of the theatre and the printing press.

Intellectual context

In general, people in Early Modern England looked at the universe, the human body, and science very differently from the way we do. But while we do not share their same beliefs, we must not think of people during Shakespeare's time as lacking in intelligence or education. Discoveries made during the Early Modern period concerning the universe and the human body provide the basis of modern science.

Cosmology

One subject we view very differently than Early Modern thinkers is cosmology. Shakespeare's contemporaries believed in the astronomy of Ptolemy, an intellectual from Alexandria in the second century A.D. Ptolemy thought that the earth stood at the center of the universe, surrounded by nine concentric rings. The celestial bodies circled the earth in the following order: the moon, Mercury, Venus, the sun, Mars, Jupiter, Saturn, and the stars. The entire system was controlled by the *primum mobile,* or Prime Mover, which initiated and maintained the movement of the celestial bodies. No one had yet discovered the last three planets in our solar system, Uranus, Neptune, and Pluto.

In 1543, Nicolaus Copernicus published his theory of a sun-based solar system, in which the sun stood at the center and the planets revolved around it. Though this theory appeared prior to Shakespeare's birth, people didn't really start to change their minds until 1610, when Galileo used his telescope to confirm Copernicus's theory. David Bevington asserts in the general introduction to his edition of Shakespeare's works that during most of Shakespeare's writing career, the cosmology of the universe was in question, and this sense of uncertainty influences some of his plays.

Universal hierarchy

Closely related to Ptolemy's hierarchical view of the universe is a hierarchical conception of the Earth (sometimes referred to as the Chain of Being). During the Early Modern period, many people believed that all of creation was organized hierarchically. God existed at the top, followed by the angels, men, women, animals, plants, and rocks. (Because all women were thought to exist below all men on the chain, we can easily imagine the confusion that Elizabeth I caused when she became Queen of England. She was literally "out of order," an expression that still exists in our society.) Though the concept of this hierarchy is a useful one when beginning to study Shakespeare, keep in mind that distinctions in this hierarchical view were not always clear and that we should not reduce all Early Modern thinking to a simple chain.

Elements and humors

The belief in a hierarchical scheme of existence created a comforting sense of order and balance that carried over into science as well. Shakespeare's contemporaries generally accepted that four different elements composed everything in the universe: earth, air, water, and fire. People associated these four elements with four qualities of being. These qualities — hot, cold, moist, and dry — appeared in different combinations in the elements. For example, air was hot and moist; water was cold and moist; earth was cold and dry; and fire was hot and dry.

In addition, people believed that the human body contained all four elements in the form of *humors* — blood, phlegm, yellow bile, and black bile — each of which corresponded to an element. Blood corresponded to air (hot and moist), phlegm to water (cold and moist), yellow bile to fire (hot and dry), and black bile to earth (cold and dry). When someone was sick, physicians generally believed that the patient's humors were not in the proper balance. For example, if someone were diagnosed with an abundance of blood, the physician would bleed the patient (by using leeches or cutting the skin) in order to restore the balance.

Shakespeare's contemporaries also believed that the humors determined personality and temperament. If a person's dominant humor was blood, he was considered light-hearted. If dominated by yellow bile (or choler), that person was irritable. The dominance of phlegm led a person to be dull and kind. And if black bile prevailed, he was melancholy or sad. Thus, people of Early Modern England often used the humors to explain behavior and emotional outbursts. Throughout Shakespeare's plays, he uses the concept of the humors to define and explain various characters.

For example, Hamlet is said to suffer from melancholy. The first time we see him, he is dressed in black and unable to join in the festivities at court. Hamlet's father died recently and his mother, Gertrude, married his father's brother less than two months later. To Hamlet, the situation is unbearable. His uncle and mother believe that Hamlet is grieving too long over the death of his father, and Gertrude asks her son to "cast thy nighted colour off" (I.2.68). Hamlet indicates that the color of his clothes reflects the black shadow of doubt and depression that afflict his soul. He says his garments are "but the trappings and the suits of woe" (I.2.86). Hamlet's black mood and black clothing tell us that melancholy, the result of a dominance of black bile, has overtaken his spirit.

Religious context

Shakespeare lived in an England full of religious uncertainty and dispute. From the Protestant Reformation to the translation of the Bible into English, the Early Modern era is punctuated with events that have greatly influenced modern religious beliefs.

The Reformation

Until the Protestant Reformation, the only Christian church in western Europe was the Catholic, or "universal," church. Beginning in the early sixteenth century, religious thinkers such as Martin Luther and John Calvin, who claimed that the Roman Catholic

Church had become corrupt and was no longer following the word of God, began what has become known as the Protestant Reformation. The Protestants ("protestors") believed in salvation by faith rather than works. They also believed in the primacy of the Bible and advocated giving all people access to reading the Bible.

Many English people initially resisted Protestant ideas. However, the Reformation in England began in 1527 during the reign of Henry VIII, prior to Shakespeare's birth. In that year, Henry VIII decided to divorce his wife, Catherine of Aragon, for her failure to produce a male heir. (Only one of their children, Mary, survived past infancy.) Rome denied Henry's petitions for a divorce, forcing him to divorce Catherine without the Church's approval, which he did in 1533.

A portrait of King Henry VIII, artist unknown, ca. 1542. National Portrait Gallery, London/SuperStock

The Act of Supremacy

The following year, the Pope excommunicated Henry VIII while Parliament confirmed his divorce and the legitimacy of his new marriage through the *Act of Succession*. Later in 1534, Parliament passed the *Act of Supremacy,* naming Henry the "Supreme Head of the Church in England." Henry persecuted both radical Protestant reformers and Catholics who remained loyal to Rome.

Henry VIII's death in 1547 brought Edward VI, his 10-year-old son by Jane Seymour (the king's third wife), to the throne. Edward's succession gave Protestant reformers the chance to solidify their break with the Catholic Church. During Edward's reign, Archbishop Thomas Cranmer established the foundation for the Anglican Church through his 42 articles of religion. He also wrote the first *Book of Common Prayer*, adopted in 1549, which was the official text for worship services in England.

Bloody Mary

Catholics continued to be persecuted until 1553, when the sickly Edward VI died and was succeeded by Mary, his half-sister and the Catholic daughter of Catherine of Aragon. The reign of Mary witnessed the reversal of religion in England through the restoration of Catholic authority and obedience to Rome. Protestants were executed in large numbers, which earned the monarch the nickname *Bloody Mary*. Many Protestants fled to Europe to escape persecution.

Elizabeth, the daughter of Henry VIII and Anne Boleyn, outwardly complied with the mandated Catholicism during her half-sister Mary's reign, but she restored Protestantism when she took the throne in 1558 after Mary's death. Thus, in the space of a single decade, England's throne passed from Protestant to Catholic to Protestant, with each change carrying serious and deadly consequences.

Though Elizabeth reigned in relative peace from 1558 to her death in 1603, religion was still a serious concern for her subjects. During Shakespeare's life, a great deal of religious dissent existed in England.

Many Catholics, who remained loyal to Rome and their church, were persecuted for their beliefs. At the other end of the spectrum, the Puritans were persecuted for their belief that the Reformation was not complete. (The English pejoratively applied the term *Puritan* to religious groups that wanted to continue purifying the English church by such measures as removing the *episcopacy*, or the structure of bishops.)

The Great Bible

One thing agreed upon by both the Anglicans and Puritans was the importance of a Bible written in English. Translated by William Tyndale in 1525, the first authorized Bible in English, published in 1539, was known as the Great Bible. This Bible was later revised during Elizabeth's reign into what was known as the Bishop's Bible. As Stephen Greenblatt points out in his introduction to the *Norton Shakespeare,* Shakespeare would probably have been familiar with both the Bishop's Bible, heard aloud in Mass, and the Geneva Bible, which was written by English exiles in Geneva. The last authorized Bible produced during Shakespeare's lifetime came within the last decade of his life when James I's commissioned edition, known as the King James Bible, appeared in 1611.

Political context

Politics and religion were closely related in Shakespeare's England. Both of the monarchs under whom Shakespeare lived had to deal with religious and political dissenters.

Elizabeth I

Despite being a Protestant, Elizabeth I tried to take a middle road on the religious question. She allowed Catholics to practice their religion in private as long as they outwardly appeared Anglican and remained loyal to the throne.

Elizabeth's monarchy was one of absolute supremacy. Believing in the divine right of kings, she styled herself as being appointed by God to rule England. To oppose the Queen's will was the equivalent of opposing God's will. Known as *passive obedience,* this doctrine did not allow any opposition even to a tyrannical monarch because God had appointed the king or queen for reasons unknown to His subjects on earth. However, as Bevington notes, Elizabeth's power was not as absolute as her rhetoric suggested. Parliament, already well established in England, reserved some power, such as the authority to levy taxes, for itself.

Elizabeth I lived in a society that restricted women from possessing any political or personal autonomy and power. As queen, Elizabeth violated and called into question many of the prejudices and practices against women. In a way, her society forced her to "overcome" her sex in order to rule effectively. However, her position did nothing to increase the status of women in England.

A portrait of Elizabeth I by George Gower, ca. 1588. National Portrait Gallery, London/SuperStock

One of the rhetorical strategies that Elizabeth adopted in order to rule effectively was to separate her position as monarch of England from her natural body — to separate her *body politic* from her *body natural*. In addition, throughout her reign, Elizabeth brilliantly negotiated between domestic and foreign factions — some of whom were anxious about a female monarch and wanted her to marry — appeasing both sides without ever committing to one.

She remained unmarried throughout her 45-year reign, partially by styling herself as the Virgin Queen whose purity represented England herself. Her refusal to marry and her habit of hinting and promising marriage with suitors both foreign and domestic helped Elizabeth maintain internal and external peace. Not marrying allowed her to retain her independence, but it left the succession of the English throne in question. In 1603, on her deathbed, she named James VI, King of Scotland and son of her cousin Mary, as her successor.

James I

When he assumed the English crown, James VI of Scotland became James I of England. (Some historians refer to him as James VI and I.) Like Elizabeth, James was a strong believer in the divine right of kings and their absolute authority.

Upon his arrival in London to claim the English throne, James made his plans to unite Scotland and England clear. However, a long-standing history of enmity existed between the two countries. Partially as a result of this history and the influx of Scottish courtiers into English society, anti-Scottish prejudice abounded in England. When James asked Parliament for the title of "King of Great Britain," he was denied.

As scholars such as Bevington have pointed out, James was less successful than Elizabeth was in negotiating between the different religious and political factions in England. Although he was a Protestant, he began to have problems with the Puritan sect of the House of Commons, which ultimately led to a rift between the court (which also started to have Catholic sympathies) and the Parliament. This rift between the monarchy and Parliament eventually escalated into the civil war that would erupt during the reign of James's son, Charles I.

In spite of its difficulties with Parliament, James's court was a site of wealth, luxury, and extravagance. James I commissioned elaborate feasts, masques, and pageants, and in doing so he more than doubled the royal debt. Stephen Greenblatt suggests that Shakespeare's *The Tempest* may reflect this extravagance through Prospero's magnificent banquet and accompanying masque. Reigning from 1603 to 1625, James I remained the King of England throughout the last years of Shakespeare's life.

Social context

Shakespeare's England divided itself roughly into two social classes: the aristocrats (or nobility) and everyone else. The primary distinctions between these two classes were ancestry, wealth, and power. Simply put, the aristocrats were the only ones who possessed all three.

Aristocrats were born with their wealth, but the growth of trade and the development of skilled professions began to provide wealth for those not born with it. Although the notion of a middle class did not begin to develop until after Shakespeare's death, the possibility of some social mobility did exist in Early Modern England. Shakespeare himself used the wealth gained from the theatre to move into the lower ranks of the aristocracy by securing a coat of arms for his family.

Shakespeare was not unique in this movement, but not all people received the opportunity to increase their social status. Members of the aristocracy feared this social movement and, as a result, promoted harsh laws of apprenticeship and fashion, restricting certain styles of dress and material. These laws dictated that only the aristocracy could wear certain articles of clothing, colors, and materials. Though enforcement was a difficult task, the Early Modern aristocracy considered dressing above one's station a moral and ethical violation.

The status of women

The legal status of women did not allow them much public or private autonomy. English society functioned on a system of patriarchy and hierarchy (see "Universal Hierarchy" earlier in this introduction), which means that men controlled society beginning with the individual family. In fact, the family metaphorically corresponded to the state. For example, the husband was the king of his family. His authority to control his family was absolute and based on divine right, similar to that of the country's king. People also saw the family itself differently than today, considering apprentices and servants part of the whole family.

The practice of *primogeniture* — a system of inheritance that passed all of a family's wealth through the first male child — accompanied this system of patriarchy. Thus, women did not generally inherit their family's wealth and titles. In the absence of a male heir, some women, such as Queen Elizabeth, did. But after women married, they lost almost all of their already limited legal rights, such as the right to inherit, to own property, and to sign contracts. In all likelihood, Elizabeth I would have lost much of her power and authority if she married.

Furthermore, women did not generally receive an education and could not enter certain professions, including acting. Instead, society relegated women to the domestic sphere of the home.

In *Hamlet,* Ophelia and Gertrude are frequently motivated by Early Modern attitudes toward women. Gertrude was married to Hamlet's father, the King of Denmark. After his death, she quickly married the dead king's brother, Claudius. Had she remained the widow of the king, she would have been excluded from society and confined to a small household where she would be a dowager queen. But as the new wife of Claudius, her life changes very little from its previous status. Although the wedding occurs before the play opens, we can deduce that Gertrude's decision to remarry was probably motivated by her reluctance to retire from society.

Ophelia is a good example of the position of young unmarried women during this time period. She is utterly dependent on her father, Polonius, and obligated to him as her primary source of support. In the social hierarchy explained above, unmarried daughters were expected to be obedient to their fathers above all others. Ophelia obeys her father by rejecting Hamlet's overtures. She obeys him again when she sets Hamlet up so Polonius and the king can spy on him. Although we may interpret her actions as a betrayal of Hamlet, Ophelia actually behaves in a moral and responsible way. Her inner loyalty to Hamlet seems clear, but because she and Hamlet are not married, she must obey Polonius. Like Gertrude, she does what is necessary to adhere to the rules of the patriarchal society.

Daily life

Daily life in Early Modern England began before sunup — exactly how early depended on one's station in life. A servant's responsibilities usually included preparing the house for the day. Families usually possessed limited living space; even among wealthy families, multiple family members tended to share a small number of rooms, suggesting that privacy may not have been important or practical.

Working through the morning, Elizabethans usually had lunch about noon. This midday meal was the primary meal of the day, much like dinner is for modern families. The workday usually ended around sundown or 5 p.m., depending on the season. Before an early bedtime, Elizabethans usually ate a light repast and then settled in for a couple of hours of reading (if the family members were literate and could bear the high cost of books) or socializing.

Mortality rates

Mortality rates in Early Modern England were high compared to our standards, especially among infants. Infection and disease ran rampant because physicians did not realize the need for antiseptics and sterile equipment. As a result, communicable diseases often spread very rapidly in cities, particularly London.

In addition, the bubonic plague frequently ravaged England, with two major outbreaks — from 1592–1594 and in 1603 — occurring during Shakespeare's lifetime. People did not understand the plague and generally perceived it as God's punishment. (We now know that the plague was spread by fleas and could not be spread directly from human to human.) Without a cure or an understanding of what transmitted the disease, physicians could do nothing to stop the thousands of deaths that resulted from each outbreak. These outbreaks had a direct effect on Shakespeare's career, because the government often closed the theatres in an effort to impede the spread of the disease.

London life

In the sixteenth century, London, though small compared to modern cities, was the largest city of Europe, with a population of about 200,000 inhabitants in the city and surrounding suburbs. London was a crowded city without a sewer system, which facilitated epidemics such as the plague. In addition, crime rates were high in the city due to inefficient law enforcement and the lack of street lighting.

Despite these drawbacks, London was the cultural, political, and social heart of England. As the home of the monarch and most of England's trade, London was a bustling metropolis. Not surprisingly, a young Shakespeare moved to London to begin his professional career.

The theatre

Most theatres were not actually located within the city of London. Rather, theatre owners built them on the south bank of the Thames River (in Southwark) across from the city in order to avoid the strict regulations that applied within the city's walls. These restrictions stemmed from a mistrust of public performances as locations of plague and riotous behavior. Furthermore, because theatre performances took place during the day, they took laborers away from their jobs. Opposition to the theatres also came from Puritans who believed that they fostered immorality. Therefore, theatres moved out of the city, to areas near other sites of restricted activities, such as dog fighting, bear- and bull-baiting, and prostitution.

Despite the move, the theatre was not free from censorship or regulation. In fact, a branch of the government known as the Office of the Revels attempted to ensure that plays did not present politically or socially sensitive material. Prior to each performance, the Master of the Revels would read a complete text of each play, cutting out offending sections or, in some cases, not approving the play for public performance.

The recently reconstructed Globe theatre.
Chris Parker/PAL

Performance spaces

Theatres in Early Modern England were quite different from our modern facilities. They were usually open-air, relying heavily on natural light and good weather. The rectangular stage extended out into an area that people called the *pit* — a circular, uncovered area about 70 feet in diameter. Audience members had two choices when purchasing admission to a theatre. Admission to the pit, where the lower classes (or *groundlings*) stood for the performances, was the cheaper option. People of wealth could purchase a seat in one of the three covered tiers of seats that ringed the pit. At full capacity, a public theatre in Early Modern England could hold between 2,000 and 3,000 people.

A scene from Shakespeare in Love *shows how the interior of the Globe would have appeared.*
Everett Collection

The stage, which projected into the pit and was raised about five feet above it, had a covered portion called the *heavens*. The heavens enclosed theatrical equipment for lowering and raising actors to and from the stage. A trapdoor in the middle of stage provided theatrical graves for characters such as Ophelia and also allowed ghosts, such as Hamlet's father, to rise from the earth. A wall separated the back of the stage from the actors' dressing room, known as the *tiring house*. At each end of the wall stood a door for major entrances and exits. Above the wall and doors stood a gallery directly above the stage, reserved for the wealthiest spectators. Actors occasionally used this area when a performance called for a difference in height — for example, to represent Juliet's balcony or the walls of a besieged city. A good example of this type of theatre was the original Globe theatre in London in which Shakespeare's company, The Lord Chamberlain's Men (later the King's Men), staged its plays. However, indoor theatres, such as the Blackfriars, differed slightly because the pit was filled with chairs that faced a rectangular stage. Because only the wealthy could afford the cost of admission, the public generally considered these theatres private.

The original Globe theatre in London was the arena in which Shakespeare's company staged his plays. Several different scenes in *Hamlet* make direct references to the theatre. For example, in Act II, Scene 2, Hamlet tells Rosencrantz and Guildenstern that "this goodly frame, the earth, / seems to me a sterile promontory; this most excellent / canopy, the air, look you, this brave o'erhanging / firmament, this majestical roof fretted with golden / fire, why, it appears no other thing to me but a foul / and pestilent congregation of vapors" (303–307). The Early Modern audience probably picked up immediately that the stage is the "earth," which thrusts forward into the pit (hence "promontory"). The canopied ceiling of the Globe was brightly painted with stars, planets, and suns, which explains the "roof fretted with golden fire."   At the end of these lines, the actors probably heard snickers from the groundlings because of the "vapors" that surely emanated up onto the stage from their unwashed bodies and the urine that they freely deposited in a drain around the periphery of the pit.

Actors and staging

Performances in Shakespeare's England do not appear to have employed scenery. However, theatre companies developed their costumes with great care and expense. In fact, a playing company's costumes were its most valuable items. Extravagant costumes were the object of much controversy because some aristocrats feared that the actors could use them to disguise their social status on the streets of London.

Costumes also disguised a player's gender. All actors on the stage during Shakespeare's lifetime were men. Young boys whose voices had not reached maturity played female parts. This practice no doubt influenced Shakespeare's and his contemporary playwrights' thematic explorations of cross-dressing.

Though historians have managed to reconstruct the appearance of the Early Modern theatre, such as the recent construction of the Globe in London, much of the information regarding how plays were performed during this era has been lost. Scholars of Early Modern theatre have turned to the scant external and internal stage directions in manuscripts in an effort to find these answers. While a hindrance for modern critics and scholars, the lack of detail about Early Modern performances has allowed modern directors and actors a great deal of flexibility and room to be creative.

Hamlet's advice to the players who visit Elsinore offers interesting insight into Elizabethan acting techniques. In Act II, Scene 2, Hamlet remarks to one young player, whose voice appears to be changing, "Pray God, your voice, like a piece of / uncurrent gold, be not cracked within the ring" (430–431). The advice indicates that the young man may be outgrowing his ability to portray female

characters effectively. In Act III, Scene 2, Hamlet tells the players, "Speak the speech, I pray you, as I / pronounced it to you, trippingly on the tongue" (1–2). Hamlet plays the director in this scene, coaching the players to perform their parts well, without overacting or bombastic speech. From his advice, we can deduce some of Shakespeare's own criticisms of some Early Modern players.

The printing press

If not for the printing press, many Early Modern plays may not have survived until today. In Shakespeare's time, printers produced all books by *sheet* — a single large piece of paper that the printer would fold in order to produce the desired book size. For example, a folio required folding the sheet once, a quarto four times, an octavo eight, and so on. Sheets would be printed one side at a time; thus, printers had to simultaneously print multiple nonconsecutive pages.

In order to estimate what section of the text would be on each page, the printer would *cast off* copy. After the printer made these estimates, *compositors* would set the type upside down, letter by letter. This process of setting type produced textual errors, some of which a proofreader would catch. When a proofreader found an error, the compositors would fix the piece or pieces of type. Printers called corrections made after printing began *stop-press* corrections because they literally had to stop the press to fix the error. Because of the high cost of paper, printers would still sell the sheets printed before they made the correction.

Printers placed frames of text in the bed of the printing press and used them to imprint the paper. They then folded and grouped the sheets of paper into gatherings, after which the pages were ready for sale. The buyer had the option of getting the new play bound.

The printing process was crucial to the preservation of Shakespeare's works, but the printing of drama in Early Modern England was not a standardized practice. Many of the first editions of Shakespeare's plays appear in quarto format and, until recently, scholars regarded them as "corrupt." In fact, scholars still debate how close a relationship exists between what appeared on the stage in the sixteenth and seventeenth centuries and what appears on the printed page. The inconsistent and scant appearance of stage directions, for example, makes it difficult to determine how close this relationship was.

We know that the practice of the theatre allowed the alteration of plays by a variety of hands other than the author's, further complicating any efforts to extract what a playwright wrote and what was changed by either the players, the printers, or the government censors. Theatre was a collaborative environment. Rather than lament our inability to determine authorship and what exactly Shakespeare wrote, we should work to understand this collaborative nature and learn from it.

Shakespeare wrote his plays for the stage, and the existing published texts reflect the collaborative nature of the theatre as well as the unavoidable changes made during the printing process. A play's first written version would have been the author's *foul papers,* which invariably consisted of blotted lines and revised text. From there, a scribe would recopy the play and produce a *fair copy*. The theatre manager would then copy out and annotate this copy into a playbook (what people today call a *prompt-book*).

At this point, scrolls of individual parts were copied out for actors to memorize. (Due to the high cost of paper, theatre companies could not afford to provide their actors with a complete copy of the play.) The government required the company to send the playbook to the Master of the Revels, the government official who would make any necessary changes or mark any passages considered unacceptable for performance.

Printers could have used any one of these copies to print a play. We cannot determine whether a printer used the author's version, the modified theatrical version, the censored version, or a combination when printing a given play. Refer back to the "Publications" section of the "Introduction to William Shakespeare" for further discussion of the impact printing practices has on our understanding of Shakespeare's works.

Hamlet is a good example of a typical Shakespeare play, because it exists in three very different published versions: The First Quarto, printed in 1603; the Second Quarto, printed in 1604; and the text included in the Folio edition of Shakespeare's plays, printed in 1623.

The First Quarto was previously designated the "bad" quarto because scholars believed that it was reconstructed from an actor's memory and sold to a publisher without Shakespeare's knowledge or consent. This theory is now being challenged on several fronts. The order of the scenes and the language of the First Quarto are significantly different from the other two versions, but the play works well onstage. Some actors, in fact, *prefer* this version to the other versions. One current theory holds that the First Quarto reflects the *Hamlet* that was performed during Shakespeare's lifetime.

The Second Quarto is a more literary version of the play; its length would probably have precluded it from being performed in seventeenth-century London. The Folio version reflects qualities of both previous versions and is regarded as more theatrically viable than the Second Quarto.

Works cited

For more information regarding Early Modern England, consult the following works:

Bevington, David. "General Introduction." *The Complete Works of William Shakespeare*. Updated Fourth edition. New York: Longman, 1997.

Greenblatt, Stephen. "Shakespeare's World." *Norton Shakespeare*. New York: W.W. Norton and Co., 1997.

Kastan, David Scott, ed. *A Companion to Shakespeare*. Oxford: Blackwell, 1999.

McDonald, Russ. *The Bedford Companion to Shakespeare: An Introduction with Documents*. Boston: Bedford-St. Martin's Press, 1996.

INTRODUCTION TO *HAMLET*

Hamlet is the most widely produced Shakespearean play. In spite of the nearly 400 years that have passed since it was first staged, *Hamlet* continues to intrigue and attract theatrical and literary audiences. As a result, it is also the most widely critiqued Shakespearean play.

The story of *Hamlet* contains all the elements necessary for a good tragedy. The protagonist is a young prince of Denmark who is caught between his desire for revenge and the dictates of his conscience. His uncle Claudius has killed Hamlet's father, and the ghost of the old king has appeared to Hamlet and demanded revenge for his "foul and most unnatural murder" (I.5.25). To complicate the story further, Claudius has married his brother's widow and Hamlet's mother, Gertrude. Hamlet's dilemma constitutes the focal point of the action and, in turn, the language of the play, which is some of the most poignant and profound of any that Shakespeare wrote.

We have a difficult time dating *Hamlet* definitively because there are references to a *Hamlet* being staged in London as early as 1589. Scholars traditionally have believed that this version of the play, called the *Ur-Hamlet* (meaning the first or earliest version), was written by Thomas Kyd. But because the evidence connecting Kyd to the *Ur-Hamlet* is sketchy and speculative, some scholars are now questioning that theory. In light of recent studies, it seems more likely that Shakespeare wrote the early *Hamlet*, possibly in 1586 or 1587. Among his connections to the story, Shakespeare was intimately familiar with the name of Hamlet. He named his son Hamnet after his best friend in Stratford, Hamnet Sadler. Hamnet is a variation on the name Hamlet.

Shakespeare's sources

Shakespeare's sources for *Hamlet* are undoubtedly those found in the stories of François de Belleforest's *Histoires Tragique*, published in 1570 when Shakespeare was six years old. Belleforest's version was based on the legend of the Danish prince named Amleth. In the twelfth century, the historian Saxo Grammaticus compiled several old Danish legends and wrote them down in Latin in a book titled *Historica Danicae* or *The History of the Danes,* published in Paris in 1514. Books 3 and 4 of this compilation include the story of Amleth, a story with all the basic plot lines found in Shakespeare's play.

Saxo Grammaticus

In *The History of the Danes,* Amleth's father, King Horwendil of Denmark, is killed by his brother Feng. Feng subsequently marries Gerutha, who is Horwendil's widow and Amleth's mother. Amleth secretly vows to take revenge on Feng. Amleth, whose name means "simpleton," must pretend to be mad as he plots his revenge; if Feng feels threatened by Amleth, he may kill him.

Other similarities between Saxo's story and Shakespeare's play include the young woman sent by Feng to try to ferret out Amleth's secrets and the conversation that Amleth has with his mother in her bedchamber. One of the king's councilors hides himself under the bed in order to eavesdrop on Amleth and Gerutha. He is discovered and subsequently killed by Amleth. Feng sends Amleth to England accompanied by two members of the court with a letter demanding Amleth's death at the hands of the King of England. Amleth substitutes a letter requesting that the courtiers be killed instead. Amleth then returns to Denmark, kills the king, and is elected to the throne.

François de Belleforest

Belleforest includes all these plot elements in his French prose translation, but he gives the characters added depth, thereby providing a starting point for the character development that Shakespeare would complete in his play. Belleforest expands upon Saxo's reference to the battle with the Norwegian king, thus creating an opportunity for the introduction of the character of young Fortinbras. In addition, Belleforest writes about Amleth's relationship with a young woman who has loved him since they were children and about the dead king's "shade" (or ghost) demanding revenge from his living son. All these elements reappear in some form in Shakespeare's *Hamlet*, but Hamlet's internal dialogues, punning riddles, and wordplay are purely Shakespearean innovations.

Synopsis of the play

Hamlet is a play as associated with tragedy as its protagonist is associated with black. As the play opens, soldiers on guard duty have seen a ghost and have asked Hamlet's friend, the scholar Horatio, to verify what they have seen. The ghost is the spirit of Hamlet's father. Hamlet is summoned, and the ghost tells his horrified son that he

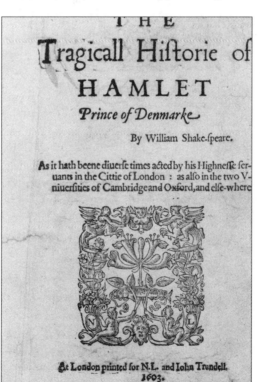

Title page or frontispiece for the 1603 version of Hamlet.
The Huntington Library/SuperStock

was murdered by his brother Claudius, the man who now wears the crown of Denmark. Hamlet vows to avenge his father's death, and the rest of the play revolves around this vow. Before the play ends, Hamlet discovers that revenge is easier said than done.

A guilty conscience

Claudius struggles with uncertainty and guilt because of his crime. He has won the throne and the queen, but his nephew, Hamlet, poses a threat to the king's security. When Hamlet begins to act as if he has lost his mind (in order to disguise his intention to exact revenge), Claudius doubts that the madness is legitimate. In an attempt to discover Hamlet's true state of mind, Claudius employs two of the prince's boyhood companions, Rozencrantz and Guildenstern, to spy on the prince.

Obedient Ophelia

The king and queen confide their fears about Hamlet to their chief councilor, Polonius, who is also the father of Laertes and Ophelia. Polonius is an interfering, garrulous old man obsessed with his own importance; he has little genuine regard for his children. Polonius spies on Hamlet for the royal couple and tells his obedient daughter, Ophelia, to help him.

Ophelia ends her relationship with Hamlet on her father's orders, although she clearly still loves the prince. Her primary obligation is to her father, and she does as he asks. During the Early Modern Era, women were obligated to obey their fathers until they married, at which time their loyalty shifted to their husbands. Ophelia is a perfect example of the dutiful daughter.

Setting a snare

Hamlet struggles with his vengeful duty. He must fulfill his father's request, but he is not convinced that killing Claudius is the right thing to do. When a troupe of players comes to Elsinore, Hamlet uses them to verify Claudius's guilt. A play staged at Hamlet's request convinces Hamlet that the ghost spoke the truth about the crime against his father.

After the play, Hamlet discovers Claudius in a position of prayer. The audience realizes that Claudius cannot truly repent, because doing so would require him to give up his throne and Gertrude, something he knows he cannot do. Claudius realizes that he is damned. Hamlet draws his dagger to kill Claudius, but he hesitates. To kill the king at prayer would be to send him straight to heaven — a privilege his own father did not receive from Claudius. Hamlet decides that the time is not right. He wants to kill Claudius when the king is steeped in sin. Only then will the revenge be complete.

Confronting Gertrude

In a very powerful and troubling scene, Hamlet is summoned to Gertrude's bedchamber. Gertrude greets her son with angry words about his behavior toward Claudius at the play. Hamlet can no longer restrain himself and attacks Gertrude verbally, forcing her to look at the truth of her hasty marriage to Claudius. Polonius, who has hidden himself behind a curtain to spy on Hamlet, cries out when he hears Hamlet's angry words. Thinking that the voice belongs to the king, Hamlet kills the old man through the curtain.

Hamlet continues to berate his mother until he is stopped suddenly by a second apparition of his father's ghost. The ghost reminds Hamlet not to raise his hand to Gertrude. Hamlet stops his barrage and,

after receiving Gertrude's promise to repent and reform her life, he drags the body of Polonius from the room.

Claudius enters soon after Hamlet departs, and when he hears what has happened, he makes up his mind to eliminate the threat that Hamlet poses. Under the pretense that Hamlet has committed a crime and must leave the country for his own safety, he sends Hamlet to England in the company of Rozencrantz and Guildenstern.

The gravediggers

Hamlet escapes the death order that Claudius sends with him to England and finds a way to return to Denmark. Approaching Elsinore, Hamlet, accompanied by Horatio, stops at the sight of two gravediggers toiling over a new grave. Hamlet's exchange with the first gravedigger is one of the best known scenes in the play, for good reason. It is a delightful moment of wit and wisdom shared between the educated prince and the hard working and probably illiterate gravedigger.

In this scene, Shakespeare creates a pattern of contrasts. Life merges with death, and illusion merges with reality. As he contemplates the inevitability of death, Hamlet is interrupted by the approach of a funeral procession. To Hamlet's amazement, the funeral is for Ophelia. Driven to the brink of madness by Hamlet's rejection, Ophelia could not bear the news of her father's death at Hamlet's hands.

Revenge for all

Ophelia's brother Laertes had returned from France at the news of his father's death. When he loses his sister as well, he vows to revenge both by killing Hamlet. Claudius uses Laertes's passionate hatred to his own advantage. He convinces Laertes to challenge Hamlet to a duel. Laertes, outdoing even Claudius in evil intent, tips the scales in his favor by using a poisoned rapier as his weapon.

At the duel, Gertrude is the first casualty. She dies accidentally after drinking a cup of poisoned wine that Claudius had intended for Hamlet. The action of the duel itself is quick and aggressive. Out of turn, Laertes delivers a superficial wound with the poisoned weapon to Hamlet. Hamlet fights with renewed fury, and in a heated scuffle, the two men exchange weapons. Hamlet attacks his opponent with a final lunge. Laertes confesses to Hamlet that they are both dying because of the poison that has now killed the Queen as well.

Mark Rylance as Hamlet in a Royal Shakespeare Company touring production, 1988. Clive Barda/PAL

With the king's full treachery revealed, Hamlet finally kills Claudius. Losing strength, Hamlet turns to Horatio, his truest friend, and asks him to spread the story of all that has happened. As Hamlet dies, young Fortinbras enters the court with his troops and surveys a scene of tragic devastation. The entire royal family of Denmark has been destroyed by the crime of one man.

Shakespeare's techniques

Shakespeare lived and wrote during a time when elocution, memory, writing, and drama were taught as elemental parts of grammar school education. He learned techniques that we do not emphasize in our curricula today. For example, his understanding of the classics, the Greek and Roman authors who lived and wrote long before the time of Christ, far surpassed what we are taught today. He was expected to memorize long passages from Seneca, Virgil, Plautus, and other ancient authors. He learned the classical format for plays and poetry. He understood the nature of comedy and the nature of tragedy as the classical authors viewed them. Comedy allows us to see human nature with all of its flaws and foibles and helps us to laugh at ourselves. Tragedy deals with the extreme emotions of life. In a tragedy, one man reaches the pinnacle of success, only to fall down to utter defeat and death. Shakespeare patterned his tragedies after those of the Roman author Seneca, but then he expanded on the formulaic pattern to create a richer, more insightful story. Shakespearean tragedies expose the intimacies of the human mind and explore the workings of human behavior and human relationships.

Hamlet fits this pattern perfectly. He is a great nobleman, and the well-being of the state is dependent on his well-being. He is a Renaissance prince; he is a scholar, a swordsman, a lover of the arts, a wit, and an athlete. He is concerned with the welfare of the people of Denmark, and he is aware of his responsibilities. Hamlet must make a moral choice in response to the evil actions of his uncle. He knows that the choice he makes will ultimately mean his own destruction. Neverthe-less, he takes the moral high ground, sacrificing his own desires for the greater good of doing what is right. The result is catastrophic for Hamlet and his family, but in another sense, Hamlet restores order in a universe turned upside down by the actions of the king.

Classical elements

Shakespeare has written this play in such a way that the audience cannot help but respond both individually and collectively. In that way, the audience shares fully in the tragic emotions of the play. As Aristotle taught, effective tragedy allows *catharsis;* that is, through the action of the play, the audi-ence is able to experience all the emotions of pity and sympathy, fear and horror, tremendous grief and exhilarating happiness that are inherent in human life.

In classical tragedy, the hero is greater or larger than life. *Hamlet* varies from that pattern of tragedy in that the *protagonist,* or hero, is a man of inner greatness. His choices, like his internal dialogues, are not clear-cut. It takes him a long time to decide what his action should be, and even then, he is not sure how to accomplish his goal. These very human qual-ities allow the audience to relate to Hamlet. We can understand this kind of hero and sympathize deeply with his plight.

Shakespeare stocked this play with believable characters and realistic action. Intrigue, denied love,

Mel Gibson and Glenn Close in the 1990 film directed by Franco Zeffirelli. *Everett Collection*

secret murder, preparations for war, drinking, traveling players, references to far-off places like Paris, Witten-berg, and England all con-tribute to the colorful, exciting, and unpredictable nature of the drama.

Shakespeare did not divide this play into acts and scenes. Theatrical practi-tioners added those ele-ments in 1676. The divisions help to clarify the action and the shifts in place and mood. There are three main kinds of scenes in *Hamlet:* court scenes, domestic or family scenes, and Hamlet's soliloquies, where he muses on life, the nature of man, and the dilemmas posed by fate.

Anachronism

An *anachronism* occurs when a character is placed in a place or a situation that could not be possible dur-ing that person's lifetime. For example, if one were to write a story of a person living in the twentieth century who meets Shakespeare, the story would be anachronistic. Shakespeare did not spend much time making sure that dates and people in his plays fit where he put them. For example, Hamlet lived in seventh-century Denmark, but Shakespeare has him studying at Wittenberg, a university founded in 1502. This reference helped Shakespeare's audience to identify with the play and its characters. The audience would recognize that Hamlet is a scholar, that he is probably a Protestant, and that he would most likely be a skeptic — not a believer in spirits and ghosts.

Imagery

Shakespeare conveys much of his meaning by planting patterns of images in the minds of his audience members. Denmark under the rule of Claudius is repeatedly associated with corruption and disease. Hamlet wears an "inky cloak" that connects him with the black cloud of grief. Feeling betrayed by Gertrude and Ophelia, Hamlet associates all women with makeup, or the artificial appearance that hides their true faces. Ophelia is linked to the image of violets, and her destroyed relationship with Hamlet is linked to weeds.

Irony

Irony is essentially the use of words or actions that simultaneously convey a literal meaning and its opposite. We are most familiar with *verbal irony:* the use of words or phrases that convey these multiple meanings. The gravedigger scene at the opening of Act V contains many instances of verbal irony. But actions can also convey irony with great effect. For example, when Hamlet discovers Claudius at prayer, he believes that he sees Claudius making his peace with God. This belief halts his action and changes the course of the play. The irony inherent in this scene is that Claudius cannot pray. He puts on the show of prayer but finds that he is not fully repentant. His action contains both the appearance of prayer and the inability to pray.

Dramatic irony is another device that Shakespeare uses to draw the audience in. Dramatic irony occurs when one character knows more than another does, and/or when the audience knows more than the characters do. From its privileged position, the audience can interpret an otherwise innocent sounding remark and realize its full meaning. For example, when Hamlet witnesses the funeral procession in Act V, he naively remarks that the "maimed rites" indicate the person being buried took her own life (V.1.229). His remarks are casual, and yet they evoke great emotion in the audience, which already knows that the funeral is for Ophelia. Hamlet's soliloquies are a great source of dramatic irony, because they allow the audience to know more than the other characters about Hamlet's state of mind.

Shakespeare's language

Shakespeare wrote his plays in a combination of verse (rhythmic patterned lines, both rhymed and unrhymed) and prose (sentences that are neither rhythmic nor rhymed, such as those I am writing right now). In Shakespeare's time, the Doctrine of Decorum was a formula that writers were expected to follow. The Doctrine had to do with the accepted hierarchical view of society. Highly ranked characters, such as kings, nobles, bishops, and gods, spoke in verse. Lowly ranked characters, such as clowns, laborers, and mad people, spoke in prose.

Blank verse

Shakespeare's use of *blank verse,* or unrhymed iambic pentameter, is an important element of his plays. In rhymed verse, the words that fall at the end of lines sound very similar, like "love" and "dove," or "moon" and "june." Shakespeare sometimes uses rhyming couplets in his plays, which are two consecutive lines of rhyming verse. An example would be "Indeed this counsellor / Is now most still, most secret, and most grave, / Who was in life a foolish prating knave" (III.4.213–215).

Blank verse, on the other hand, has no rhyme, but it has a definite rhythm created by the careful structuring of *iambic feet* — patterns of stressed and unstressed syllables. One poetic foot is a single unit that is repeated to give a steady rhythm to a line of verse (whether rhymed or unrhymed). The iambic foot (or iamb) consists of an unstressed syllable followed by a stressed syllable, like "inSIST" or "reSIST." Iambic pentameter was the standard format used primarily in English drama and often in English poetry during the Early Modern period. The Earl of Surrey was the first to use it in his translation of Virgil's *Aeneid*. Blank verse is sometimes referred to as "Marlowe's mighty line," because the playwright Christopher Marlowe adapted it to the English stage. Shakespeare, however, carried it forward and developed it most brilliantly.

Shifts

Hamlet, like all of Shakespeare's plays, contains both verse and prose. For the most part, it follows the Doctrine of Decorum. The gravediggers speak in prose. Hamlet's mad scenes are all written in prose, as are Ophelia's (with the exception of her bawdy songs). But *Hamlet* does not always follow expectations. Shakespeare was flexible with his language, and if a certain style fit a certain mood, he did not hesitate to break the rules. For example, the soldiers, who are certainly not noble, speak in beautiful blank verse. Also, Hamlet sometimes speaks in prose when he is neither mad nor comic. Shakespeare tempers his early adherence to form with a more mature voice in *Hamlet*. Compare the player's speech about Pyrrhus (II.2.448–513), written in a very structured style, with Hamlet's soliloquy (II.2.543–601) that ends the same scene. The voices are distinct and indicate Shakespeare's dexterity with both formulaic and more flexible language.

Paul Freeman and David Ryall in the RSC 1997 production.
Clive Barda/PAL

Theatrical and critical history

Fortunately, the stage history of *Hamlet* is well documented, beginning with the previously mentioned references to the earliest productions staged in London during Shakespeare's life. We also have the 1603 Quarto. Although the text was previously maligned as a "bad" quarto — a stolen and illegally reproduced text — scholars now generally recognize it as the printed text of the promptbook of the play as staged by Shakespeare's company. Thus, the 1603 Quarto stands as most representative of the earliest staged *Hamlet*. The stage history is so long and complicated that it can only be briefly described here.

First performances

The first documented connection between *Hamlet* and Shakespeare appears in 1594 in a book titled *Henslowe's Diary*. Philip Henslowe was the owner of the Rose Theatre. He kept a meticulous ledger in which he recorded a performance of *Hamlet* by the Lord Chamberlain's Men, whose members included a 30-year-old player named William Shakespeare. Theatrical tradition claims that Shakespeare played the role of the ghost in these early productions.

One of Shakespeare's fellows, the player Richard Burbage (1567?–1619), first acted the role of Hamlet. From all reports, Burbage's Hamlet was more elemental — that is, less thoughtful and more eager to carry out his mission of revenge — than the "melancholy Dane" to which modern audiences have become accustomed.

Burbage was a player with Shakespeare in both the Lord Chamberlain's Men and the company that later became the King's Men. The two men were also *sharers,* or co-owners, in the Globe theatre, where *Hamlet* must have been frequently performed. We do not have documented evidence of performances at the Globe, but the play itself contains several references to the theatre.

Hamlet must have been an extremely popular play. Other well-known playwrights such as Robert Greene, Thomas Lodge, and Thomas Nashe wrote about the staged version of *Hamlet* in pamphlets and books as early as 1589. The play text was published as a book in 1603, and then a longer version of the play was published in 1604–1605. *Hamlet* continued in the repertoire of playing companies until 1642, when the Puritan Commonwealth government finally closed the theatres.

Puritan influence

The Puritans viewed theatres as places of corruption. Plays were staged in the daytime during the week, drawing apprentices and workmen away from their places of business. The theatres also attracted prostitutes and vagabonds, because a quick pound or shilling could be made off of the crowd. To the Puritans, the theatre encouraged a dissolute and irresponsible lifestyle. Puritans also considered acting a form of deception and lies.

London city officials did not disagree with the Puritans, because the large crowds that the theatres drew threatened the general populace in times of plague. City officials and Puritans alike thought it better to close the theatres and destroy the buildings. Given the fact that they did exactly that in 1642 after the English monarchy was replaced by a Puritan government (called the Commonwealth), we are fortunate that any plays survived the period. When the monarchy was restored in 1660, the theatres reopened, and *Hamlet* was one of the first of Shakespeare's plays to be resurrected.

Actors' interpretations

Since 1660, *Hamlet* has continuously been produced and reinterpreted. Every actor who has taken on the part has brought something of him or herself to the role. (Some productions have cast a woman in the title role, the most famous being the nineteenth-century actress Sarah Bernhardt.) Some actors have

The Death of Ophelia *by Eugene Delacroix, 19th century.*
Musee de Louvre, Paris/ET Archive, London/SuperStock

even published what are known as *acting editions* of their plays — printed versions that reflect the actor's interpretations.

Some of the best actors of their day have taken on the role of Hamlet. The famous eighteenth-century actor David Garrick tackled it, as did John Philip Kemble, Charles Kean, Edwin Booth, Henry Irving, and Johnston Forbes-Robertson, just to name a few. The most enduring and popular Hamlets during the twentieth century were John Barrymore, John Gielgud, Laurence Olivier, and, most recently, Mel Gibson and Kenneth Branagh. *Hamlet* continues to be staged and reinterpreted and remains one of the most popular and well-known plays in the world.

Critical responses

Critical reception has been as varied as the play's production history. *Hamlet* is surely the most widely discussed of Shakespeare's plays. Most libraries have several shelves dedicated solely to books written about *Hamlet.* One of the first and most important of these works was written by Samuel Johnson (1709–1784) in 1765. This work does not praise *Hamlet* but rather conveys Johnson's strong opinion that the play is a failure. Samuel Taylor Coleridge (1772–1834) thought that Hamlet was essentially impotent, incapable of acting on his father's demand for revenge. The Romantics, members of a literary and philosophical movement popular in the eighteenth century, embraced the idea of Hamlet as the "melancholy Dane," a term first coined by Johann von Goethe (1749–1832). This interpretation of an introspective, indecisive Hamlet was reinforced by

maudlin theatrical interpretations in the nineteenth century.

Not until the twentieth century did critics begin to reevaluate Hamlet. This reevaluation has come about largely because of radical new theatrical experiments using the 1603 printed text. The 1603 Quarto was lost sometime early in the seventeenth century and not rediscovered until 1823. Until then, and for another hundred years after, performances were based only on the Second Quarto and the Folio editions of the work. Because of the significant differences in language, scene order, and length, the 1603 Quarto was rejected as a non-Shakespearean work. Although one theatrical director, William Poel, staged *Hamlet* based on the First Quarto in 1881 and again in 1900, his productions did not receive positive reviews and the text continued to be overlooked in favor of the two more familiar versions. Critics and theatrical practitioners did not recognize that the First Quarto preserved many of the play's original Elizabethan trappings.

Although Poel's productions were not successful, the First Quarto reemerged in the last third of the twentieth century. Since then, the 1603 version has been produced in its entirety and in combination with the Second Quarto and Folio editions of the play. The theatre community has accepted it as a part of the play's history, and now scholars are beginning to recognize its validity as well.

CHARACTERS IN THE PLAY

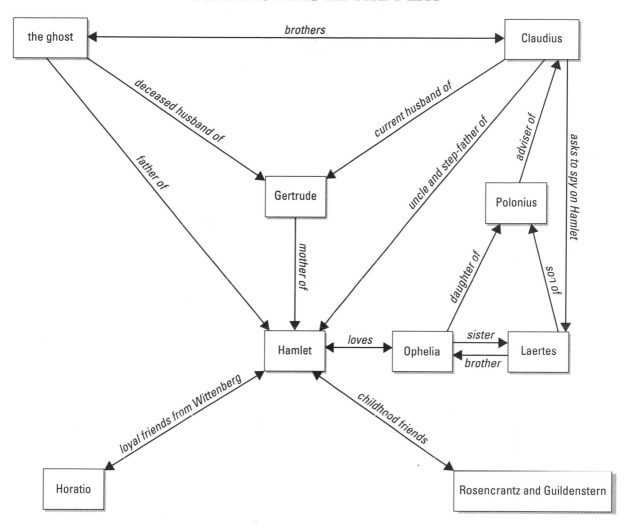

CLIFFSCOMPLETE

HAMLET
ACT I

Hamlet *Oh God! God!*

> *How weary, stale, flat, and unprofitable*
> *Seem to me all the uses of this world.*
> *Fie on 't! Ah fie! 'tis an unweeded garden,*
> *That grows to seed; things rank and gross in nature*
> *Possess it merely.*

Act 1, Scene 1

On the castle battlements of Elsinore in Denmark, two soldiers, Marcellus and Bernardo, have asked Horatio, a friend of the Danish prince Hamlet, to stand their watch with them. The men have seen a ghost and think that it may be the spirit of Hamlet's father, the former king. Prince Fortinbras of Norway has been threatening to attack Denmark, and Horatio thinks that the spirit may be an omen of trouble. Horatio decides to tell Hamlet.

ACT I, SCENE 1
Elsinore. A platform before the castle.

[FRANCISCO at his post. Enter to him BERNARDO]

Bernardo Who's there?

Francisco Nay, answer me. Stand and unfold yourself.

Bernardo Long live the king?

Francisco Bernardo?

Bernardo He.　　　　　　　　　　　　　　　　　　　　　　　　　5

Francisco You come most carefully upon your hour.

Bernardo 'Tis now struck twelve; get thee to bed, Francisco.

Francisco For this relief much thanks; 'tis bitter cold,
　And I am sick at heart.

Bernardo Have you had quiet guard?

Francisco　　　　　　　　　　　　　　Not a mouse stirring.　　10

Bernardo Well, good-night.
　If you do meet Horatio and Marcellus,
　The rivals of my watch, bid them make haste.

Francisco I think l hear them. Stand, ho! Who is there?

[Enter HORATIO and MARCELLUS]

Horatio Friends to this ground.

Marcellus　　　　　　　　　　　And liegemen to the Dane.　　15

Francisco Give you good-night.

Marcellus　　　　　　　　　　Oh! farewell, honest soldier:
　Who hath reliev'd you?

Francisco　　　　　　　　　　Bernardo has my place.
　Give you good-night. *[Exit]*

NOTES

s.d. *Elsinore:* the capitol of Denmark and the castle where the action of *Hamlet* takes place.

2. *unfold:* reveal who you are.

6. *most carefully upon your hour:* exactly when you were expected.

13. *rivals:* partners.

15. *liegemen:* loyal subjects.
the Dane: the King of the Danes.

Marcellus   Holla! Bernardo!

Bernardo Say, what! is Horatio there?

Horatio   A piece of him.

Bernardo Welcome, Horatio; welcome, good Marcellus.   20

Horatio What! has this thing appear'd again to-night ?

Bernardo I have seen nothing.

Marcellus Horatio says 'tis but our fantasy,
And will not let belief take hold of him
Touching this dreaded sight twice seen of us: 25
Therefore I have entreated him along
With us to watch the minutes of this night;
That if again this apparition come,
He may approve our eyes and speak to it.

Horatio Tush, tush! 'twill not appear.

Bernardo   Sit down awhile,   30
And let us once again assail your ears,
That are so fortified against our story,
What we two nights have seen.

Horatio   Well, sit we down,
And let us hear Bernardo speak of this.

Bernardo Last night of all,   35
When yond same star that's westward from the pole
Had made his course to illume that part of heaven
Where now it burns, Marcellus and myself,
The bell then beating one, —

[Enter GHOST]

Marcellus Peace! break thee off; look, where it comes again!40

Bernardo In the same figure like the king that's dead.

Marcellus Thou art a scholar; speak to it, Horatio.

Bernardo Looks it not like the king? mark it, Horatio.

Horatio Most like: it harrows me with fear and wonder.

Bernardo It would be spoke to.

Marcellus   Question it, Horatio.   45

---

23.   *fantasy:* imagination.

25.   *of:* by.

29.   *approve our eyes:* verify what we ourselves see.

36.   *pole:* Polaris, the North Star, long used by navigators as a reliable point of reference.

37.   *illume:* illuminate, light up.

39.   *beating:* tolling

42.   *scholar:* having the necessary knowledge of Latin to exorcise a spirit. This was a common Elizabethan belief.

43.   *mark:* look!

45.   *Question it, Horatio:* The belief was that a ghost could not open a conversation.

Horatio What art thou that usurp'st this time of night,
Together with that fair and war-like form
In which the majesty of buried Denmark
Did sometimes march? by heaven I charge thee, speak!

Marcellus It is offended.

Bernardo   See! it stalks away.   50

Horatio Stay! speak, speak! I charge thee, speak!
[Exit GHOST]

Marcellus 'Tis gone, and will not answer.

Bernardo How now, Horatio! you tremble and look pale:
Is not this something more than fantasy?
What think you on't?   55

Horatio Before my God, I might not this believe
Without the sensible and true avouch
Of mine own eyes.

Marcellus   Is it not like the king?

Horatio As thou art to thyself:
Such was the very armour he had on   60
When he the ambitious Norway combated;
So frown'd he once, when in an angry parle
He smote the sledded Polacks on the ice.
'Tis strange.

Marcellus Thus twice before, and jump at this dead hour,   65
With martial stalk hath he gone by our watch.

Horatio In what particular thought to work I know not:
But in the gross and scope of my opinion,
This bodes some strange eruption to our state.

Marcellus Good now, sit down, and tell me, he that   70
    knows,
Why this same strict and most observant watch
So nightly toils the subject of the land,
And why such daily cast of brazen cannon,
And foreign mart for implements of war,
Why such impress of shipwrights, whose sore task   75
Does not divide the Sunday from the week,
What might be toward, that this sweaty haste
Doth make the night joint-labourer with the day:
Who is't that can inform me?

48.	*the . . . Denmark:* the late King of Denmark.
55.	*on't:* on it, of it.
57.	*avouch:* avouchment, verification.
61.	*Norway:* King of Norway. In Shakespeare's day, a ruler was often referred to by the name of his or her country or territory.
62.	*parle:* parley, meeting.
63.	*sledded Polacks:* the Polish army traveling on sleighs or sleds.
65.	*jump:* precisely.
68.	*gross and scope:* general meaning.
69.	*eruption:* upheaval.
72.	*toils:* wearies.
	subject: subjects.
73.	*cast:* casting.
74.	*foreign mart:* marketing (purchasing) abroad.
76.	*divide:* distinguish.
77.	*toward:* on foot, coming.

Horatio   That can I;

At least, the whisper goes so. Our last king,   80
Whose image even but now appear'd to us,
Was, as you know, by Fortinbras of Norway,
Thereto prick'd on by a most emulate pride,
Dar'd to the combat; in which our valiant Hamlet —
For so this side of our known world esteem'd him —   85
Did slay this Fortinbras; who, by a seal'd compact,
Well ratified by law and heraldry,
Did forfeit with his life all those his lands
Which he stood seiz'd of, to the conqueror;
Against the which, a moiety competent   90
Was gaged by our king; which had return'd
To the inheritance of Fortinbras,
Had he been vanquisher; as, by the same co-mart,
And carriage of the article design'd,
His fell to Hamlet. Now, sir, young Fortinbras,   95
Of unimproved mettle hot and full,
Hath in the skirts of Norway here and there
Shark'd up a list of lawless resolutes
For food and diet to some enterprise
That hath a stomach in 't; which is no other —   100
As it doth well appear unto our state —
But to recover of us, by strong hand
And terms compulsative, those foresaid lands
So by his father lost. And this, I take it,
Is the main motive of our preparations,   105
The source of this our watch and the chief head
Of this post-haste and romage in the land.

Bernardo I think it be no other but e'en so;
Well may it sort that this portentous figure
Comes armed through our watch, so like the king   110
That was and is the question of these wars.

Horatio A mote it is to trouble the mind's eye.
In the most high and palmy state of Rome,
A little ere the mightiest Julius fell,
The graves stood tenantless, and the sheeted dead   115
Did squeak and gibber in the Roman streets;
As stars with trains of fire and dews of blood,
Disasters in the sun; and the moist star

---

83. *prick'd:* spurred.

emulate: envious.

86–95. It had been agreed prior to the combat that the victor was to have the other's lands.

86. *seal'd compact:* formal agreement.

89. *seized of:* a legal term for owned.

90. *moiety competent:* sufficient portion.

91. *gaged:* pledged.

94. *carriage . . . design'd:* carrying out of the agreement.

96. *unimproved mettle:* untested strength.

97. *skirts:* outlying parts.

98. *Shark'd:* gathered indiscriminately.

lawless resolutes: desperadoes.

100. *hath . . . in't:* calls for courage.

103. *terms compulsative:* forced terms.

106. *chief head:* main purpose.

107. *romage:* rummage, bustle.

109. *Well . . . sort::* It may turn out.

111. *question:* subject.

112. *mote:* speck of dust.

113–120. Compare *Julius Caesar,* I.3.10–32, and II.1.16–23. Julius Caesar was assassinated by people who were afraid that he might proclaim himself emperor.

113. *palmy:* flourishing.

115. *sheeted:* shrouded.

118. *Disasters:* ominous signs like sun spots or solar flares.

moist star: moon.

Upon whose influence Neptune's empire stands
Was sick almost to doomsday with eclipse;　　　　　120
And even the like precurse of fierce events,
As harbingers preceding still the fates
And prologue to the omen coming on,
Have heaven and earth together demonstrated
Unto our climatures and countrymen.　　　　　125
[Re-enter GHOST]
But, soft! behold! lo! where it comes again.
I'll cross it, though it blast me. Stay, illusion!
If thou hast any sound, or use of voice,
Speak to me:
If there be any good thing to be done,　　　　　130
That may to thee do ease and grace to me,
Speak to me:
If thou art privy to thy country's fate,
Which happily foreknowing may avoid,
O! speak!　　　　　135
Or if thou hast uphoarded in thy life
Extorted treasure in the womb of earth,
For which, they say, you spirits oft walk in death,
Speak of it: stay, and speak! *[Cock crows]* Stop it,
　　Marcellus.

Marcellus Shall I strike at it with my partisan?　　　　　140

Horatio Do, if it will not stand.

Bernardo　　　　　　　　　　'Tis here!

Horatio　　　　　　　　　　　　'Tis here!

[Exit GHOST]

Marcellus 'Tis gone!
　We do it wrong, being so majestical,
　To offer it the show of violence;
　For it is, as the air, invulnerable,　　　　　145
　And our vain blows malicious mockery.

Bernardo It was about to speak when the cock crew.

Horatio And then it started like a guilty thing
　Upon a fearful summons. I have heard,
　The cock, that is the trumpet to the morn,　　　　　150
　Doth with his lofty and shrill-sounding throat
　Awake the god of day; and at his warning,

120.　*doomsday:* the end of the world.

121.　*precurse:* sign, indication.

122.　*harbingers:* messengers announcing forthcoming events.

123.　*omen:* the ominous event or disaster.

125.　*climatures:* regions.

127.　*I'll cross it, though it blast me:* A common Elizabethan belief held that to cross the path of a ghost was to put one's self in its power.

133.　*privy to:* possessed of secret (private) knowledge of.

134.　*happily:* either perchance (haply) or luckily.

137.　*Extorted:* wrongfully acquired.

140.　*partisan:* long-handled spear carried by foot soldiers.

143.　*majestical:* majestic.

Whether in sea or fire, in earth or air,
Th' extravagant and erring spirit hies
To his confine; and of the truth herein 155
This present object made probation.

Marcellus It faded on the crowing of the cock.
Some say that ever 'gainst that season comes
Wherein our Saviour's birth is celebrated,
The bird of dawning singeth all night long; 160
And then, they say, no spirit dare stir abroad;
The nights are wholesome; then no planets strike,
No fairy takes, nor witch hath power to charm,
So hallow'd and so gracious is that time.

Horatio So have I heard and do in part believe it. 165
But look, the morn in russet mantle clad
Walks o'er the dew of yon high eastern hill;
Break we our watch up; and by my advice
Let us impart what we have seen to-night
Unto young Hamlet; for, upon my life, 170
This spirit, dumb to us, will speak to him.
Do you consent we shall acquaint him with it,
As needful in our loves, fitting our duty?

Marcellus Let's do't, I pray; and I this morning know
Where we shall find him most conveniently. 175

[Exeunt]

154. *extravagant and erring:* vagrant and wandering (both used in their original Latin sense — a common device used by Shakespeare).

155. *confine:* prison.

156. *probation:* proof.

158. *'gainst:* in preparation for.

162. *strike:* exert a malignant influence — a common belief of the times.

163. *No fairy takes:* It was believed that fairies stole children.

166. *russet:* To the Elizabethan, this meant the warm gray tone of homespun cloth.

COMMENTARY

The play opens at night, on the cold, dark castle battlements of Elsinore in Denmark. A lone sentinel and "honest soldier," Francisco, hears a noise, and he challenges the intruder (16). Tired and cold, he is relieved to hear the voices of his comrades. Francisco's lonely depression is apparent ("I am sick at heart") and sets the scene for what we discover later is the cause of Hamlet's melancholy (8). All is not well in this place.

Awaiting the apparition

The soldiers Marcellus and Bernardo identify themselves to the jumpy Francisco. They enter the scene accompanied by Horatio, a visitor and friend of "the Dane," Hamlet (15). Marcellus and Bernardo have seen an apparition twice, and they have asked Horatio to help verify and perhaps explain the meaning of the specter. Horatio will act as messenger for the soldiers, for the spirit, and, as we will see, ultimately for Hamlet.

As a scholar, Horatio is skeptical about ghosts, and this attitude distinguishes him from the uneducated and superstitious soldiers. Most people during Shakespeare's time still believed in ghosts and evil spirits. The Renaissance had not yet changed superstitious ideas among the general populace. In the societal hierarchy still prevalent during the Early Modern era, Horatio is positioned above the soldiers. His actual social standing is never made clear, but because he is a scholar and a friend to the prince, the men defer to his judgment.

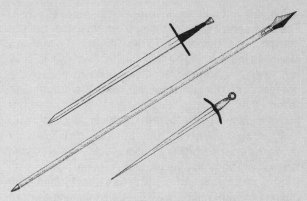

The play opens with the soldiers on guard outside Elsinore.

They also trust that if the ghost reappears, Horatio will be able to speak to it. They believe that the ghost may need to be addressed in Latin, the language of scholars.

Horatio questions the men. He wants to know how often they have seen the ghost, and when and where it appeared. Bernardo's allusions to the expected sights and sounds of the night — such as one star's firelike qualities and its regular and predictable movements, as dependable as the "bell then beating one" — stand in stark contrast to the irregularity of the ghost (39).

Keep in mind that Shakespeare crafted highly figurative language to create specific moods and themes in the Elizabethan theatre, whereas modern theatre or cinema would use visual effects for this purpose. *Hamlet*, like all Elizabethan plays, was staged in broad daylight, in the middle of the afternoon, outside. Yet the audience had to perceive this scene as taking place on a cold battlement sometime after midnight (the time when ghosts are most likely to appear).

A specter dressed in armor

Suddenly, the ghost appears. The much-anticipated event is now upon them and the soldiers, though fearful, watch for Horatio's reaction. Horatio's doubts are dispelled when he sees the ghostly figure dressed in armor, as if ready for battle. The fact that the skeptical Horatio is now convinced validates the ghost for the soldiers as well as the audience, although they cannot be sure that it is not an evil spirit.

Horatio attempts to speak to the ghost again, but it turns away and departs, regal, soldierly, and proud.

Horatio calls after it. He wants to hear the ghost's reasons for walking the night. Perhaps the ghost is offended because it is addressed in terms that imply it is a fraud, and it departs without speaking.

Early Modern belief held that ghosts could only speak (or communicate in some way) to the person for whom a message was intended. Not seeing that person, the spirit disappears, leaving Horatio shaken and the soldiers excited but puzzled. They look to Horatio for an answer, and Horatio gives the men the only explanation that he can think of. Their dialogue reveals their confusion, but it serves a definite theatrical purpose. The exchange helps the audience to understand and accept the appearance of the ghost. In addition, Horatio's description of the affairs of state explains what has happened between Denmark and Norway and sets the scene for the appearance of Fortinbras. Horatio's explanation also provides a possible and logical reason for the apparition: Norway may be mobilizing for war with Denmark. Young Fortinbras wants to avenge the death of his father, who was killed in battle by the now dead King Hamlet. Here we have the first mention of revenge, the primary motif (or theme) of the play.

The ethics of revenge tragedies

Three families will ultimately be involved with revenge in this play: Fortinbras for his father, Hamlet for his father, and Laertes for his father and sister. Shakespeare's audiences knew that staging a revenge play like *Hamlet* would always mean a tragic and probably bloody end. This did not discourage audiences from seeing these plays; in fact, revenge tragedies were among the more popular plays in England (and Europe) in the sixteenth and seventeenth centuries. Like horror or "slasher" movies today, revenge tragedies drew enthusiastic audiences because of, rather than in spite of, their violence.

The tragic endings of revenge plays were preordained by church and state expectations. Plays were often censored during Shakespeare's time if they carried a negative message to the community. Revenge was considered morally acceptable only if the protagonist (the person seeking revenge) died at the end of the play. Only by dying could someone be forgiven for the immoral and illegal act of revenge.

Understanding this helps to understand why Shakespeare would write his tragedies the way he did. Remember, too, that these kinds of plays were very popular with Elizabethan audiences, so they were good moneymakers. Several other playwrights of the era wrote similar kinds of plays. *Hamlet* provided good competition for the other bloody revenge tragedies that were being staged at the same time.

Interpreting the unknown

No one yet knows the true reason for the apparition. Horatio refers to the death of Caesar, which occurred at a time, it was believed, when there were strange disturbances in the universe. (See Act I, Scene 3 of Shakespeare's *Julius Caesar*.) This notion reflects the accepted wisdom of the day.

Norway may be preparing to invade Denmark. The men believe that spirits usually mean trouble, and they believe that this particular spirit may either be the ghost of their dead king or an evil spirit disguised as the king. The soldiers are cold and tired and afraid. That the ghost is an omen, or a sign of trouble for Denmark, seems possible and their anxiety increases.

Without warning, the ghost reappears. Horatio is more deferential this time. He begs the spirit to speak to him, but once again, it departs without a response. The soldiers try to stop it with their weapons, but the ghost is not of this world. To their dismay, the men are reminded that nothing earthly can interfere with it. They are awed and amazed this time, overwhelmed in the presence of the supernatural, and their language reflects their almost spiritual mood. Marcellus's description of the dawn (lines 158–164) is one of the most beautiful passages in the play. Horatio's response has been called the most perfect line of blank verse in the English language: "So I have heard and do in part believe it" (165). The language of the play has transformed from the talk of wary soldiers — clipped lines and hurried questions — to an almost lyrical, musical movement.

Horatio reflects on the apparition. The vision resembled the old king, and Horatio believes that it is trying to find Hamlet. Like all ghosts, this one has disappeared with the coming of dawn — another common Early Modern belief about the limits placed on spirits. Horatio is convinced that the specter will return night after night, persevering until it communicates with the prince. The spirit refused to speak to him or the soldiers, but it will surely speak to Hamlet. Horatio decides that Hamlet must be told.

Act I, Scene 2

This scene introduces the new Danish king, Claudius, his new wife, Gertrude, and Gertrude's son, Hamlet, the prince of Denmark. Hamlet's father has been dead for less than two months, and his mother is already remarried to her late husband's brother. Hamlet is depressed and angry at this turn of events. Horatio, Marcellus, and Bernardo tell Hamlet what they have seen.

ACT I, SCENE 2
The council chamber.

[Enter CLAUDIUS, King of Denmark, GERTRUDE, the Queen, Councillors, POLONIUS and his son LAERTES, VOLTIMAND and CORNELIUS, HAMLET and Attendants]

King Though yet of Hamlet our dear brother's death
  The memory be green, and that it us befitted
  To bear our hearts in grief, and our whole kingdom
  To be contracted in one brow of woe,
  Yet so far hath discretion fought with nature   5
  That we with wisest sorrow think on him,
  Together with remembrance of ourselves.
  Therefore our sometime sister, now our queen,
  Th' imperial jointress to this war-like state,
  Have we, as 'twere with a defeated joy,   10
  With one auspicious and one dropping eye,
  With mirth in funeral and with dirge in marriage,
  In equal scale weighing delight and dole,
  Taken to wife: nor have we herein barr'd
  Your better wisdoms, which have freely gone   15
  With this affair along: for all, our thanks.
  Now follows, that you know, young Fortinbras,
  Holding a weak supposal of our worth,
  Or thinking by our late dear brother's death
  Our state to be disjoint and out of frame,   20
  Colleagued with the dream of his advantage,
  He hath not fail'd to pester us with message,
  Importing the surrender of those lands
  Lost by his father, with all bands of law,
  To our most valiant brother. So much for him.   25
  Now for ourself and for this time of meeting.
  Thus much the business is: we have here writ

NOTES

2.   *green:* fresh.

4.   *in one brow of woe:* Everyone in the kingdom ought to mourn.

5.   *discretion:* common sense.

    nature: natural sorrow.

6–7. *That we . . . ourselves:* While we mourn the departed king, we must not forget the welfare of the state.

8.   *sometime:* former.

    sister: sister-in-law.

9.   *jointress:* partner.

10. *defeated:* spoiled, marred.

11. *one . . . eye:* rejoicing and sorrowing at the same time.

13. *dole:* grief.

14. *barr'd:* excluded, forbidden expression of.

15–16. *freely . . . along:* approved the proceedings.

17. *that you know:* that (which) you know.

18. *weak supposal:* poor opinion.

20. *disjoint . . . frame:* disjointed and in shambles.

21. *Colleagued . . . advantage:* together with the hope of what he might gain.

23. *Importing:* concerning.

26. *ourself:* royal plural, used throughout the king''s speeches.

To Norway, uncle of young Fortinbras,
Who, impotent and bed-rid, scarcely hears
Of this his nephew's purpose, to suppress   30
His further gait herein; in that the levies,
The lists and full proportions, are all made
Out of his subject; and we here dispatch
You, good Cornelius, and you, Voltimand,
For bearers of this greeting to old Norway,   35
Giving to you no further personal power
To business with the king more than the scope
Of these delated articles allow.
Farewell and let your haste commend your duty.

Cornelius and Voltimand In that and all things will we
show our duty.   40

King We doubt it nothing: heartily farewell.
[Exeunt VOLTIMAND and CORNELIUS]
And now, Laertes, what's the news with you?
You told us of some suit; what is 't, Laertes?
You cannot speak of reason to the Dane,
And lose your voice; what wouldst thou beg, Laertes,   45
That shall not be my offer, not thy asking?
The head is not more native to the heart,
The hand more instrumental to the mouth,
Than is the throne of Denmark to thy father.
What wouldst thou have, Laertes?

Laertes   Dread my lord,   50
Your leave and favour to return to France;
From whence though willingly I came to Denmark,
To show my duty in your coronation,
Yet now, I must confess, that duty done,
My thoughts and wishes bend again toward France   55
And bow them to your gracious leave and pardon.

King Have you your father's leave? What says Polonius?

Polonius He hath, my lord, wrung from me my slow leave
By laboursome petition, and at last
Upon his will I seal'd my hard consent: 60
I do beeseech you, give him leave to go.

31.	*gait:* progress.
31–33.	*levies . . . subject:* the King of Norway's army is made up of his subjects.
37.	*scope:* limit.
38.	*delated articles:* detailed provisions set forth in their instructions.
39.	*let haste . . . duty:* display your zeal for duty by performing it quickly.
43.	*suit:* petition.
44.	*of reason:* with reason.
	the Dane: the king
45.	*lose your voice:* speak in vain.
46.	*That . . . asking?:* that I am not ready to give without being asked.
47.	*native:* closely related or from the same country.
48.	*instrumental:* serviceable.
49.	*the throne:* the king.
50.	*Dread:* dreaded.
56.	*pardon:* permission.
60.	*will:* desire.
	seal'd . . . consent: reluctantly agreed to let him go.

King Take thy fair hour, Laertes; time be thine,
And thy best graces spend it at thy will.
But now, my cousin Hamlet, and my son, —

Hamlet *[Aside]* A little more than kin, and less than kind.   65

King How is it that the clouds still hang on you?

Hamlet Not so, my lord; I am too much i' the sun.

Queen Good Hamlet, cast thy nighted colour off,
And let thine eye look like a friend on Denmark.
Do not for ever with thy vailed lids   70
Seek for thy noble father in the dust:
Thou know'st 'tis common; all that live must die,
Passing through nature to eternity.

Hamlet Ay, madam, it is common.

Queen   If it be,
Why seems it so particular with thee?   75

Hamlet Seems, madam! Nay, it is; I know not 'seems'.
'Tis not alone my inky cloak, good mother,
Nor customary suits of solemn black,
Nor windy suspiration of forc'd breath,
No, nor the fruitful river in the eye,   80
Nor the dejected haviour of the visage,
Together with all forms, modes, shows of grief,
That can denote me truly; these indeed seem,
For they are actions that a man might play:
But I have that within which passeth show;   85
These but the trappings and the suits of woe.

King 'Tis sweet and commendable in your nature, Hamlet,
To give these mourning duties to your father:
But, you must know, your father lost a father;
That father lost, lost his; and the survivor bound   90
In filial obligation for some term
To do obsequious sorrow; but to persever
In obstinate condolement is a course
Of impious stubbornness; 'tis unmanly grief:
It shows a will most incorrect to heaven,   95
A heart unfortified, a mind impatient,
An understanding simple and unschool'd:
For what we know must be and is as common
As any the most vulgar thing to sense,

62.	*Take . . . hour:* Enjoy life while you are young; and/or, go whenever you like.
63.	*best . . . will:* use your skills to spend your time as you desire.
64.	*cousin:* kinsman. This word was used for any near relation; here it would refer to nephew.
65.	*kin . . . kind:* Hamlet, in the bitterness of his mood, plays on the words kin and kind. The latter originated from the former and denoted the similarity of character, nature, or race within a family or tribe. Kind also could refer to natural affection between relatives.
67.	*sun:* a pun on *son*, again indicating Hamlet's dislike of the new relationship between himself and his uncle.
68.	*nighted:* black, signifying deep mourning.
70.	*vailed lids:* downcast eyes.
75.	*particular:* special concern.
79.	*windy . . . breath:* profound sighs.
81.	*dejected . . . visage:* downcast countenance.
83.	*seem:* merely appear.
84.	*play:* act, as in a play.
86.	*trappings:* ornaments.
92.	*obsequious sorrow:* mourning for the dead.
93.	*obstinate condolement:* grief that is contrary to the will of heaven.
96.	*unfortified:* not strengthened by religious consolation.
99.	*any . . . sense:* as any common thing we experience.

Why should we in our peevish opposition   100
Take it to heart? Fie! 'tis a fault to heaven,
A fault against the dead, a fault to nature,
To reason most absurd, whose common theme
Is death of fathers, and who still hath cried,
From the first corse till he that died to-day,   105
'This must be so.' We pray you, throw to earth
This unprevailing woe, and think of us
As of a father; for let the world take note,
You are the most immediate to our throne;
And with no less nobility of love   110
Than that which dearest father bears his son
Do I impart toward you. For your intent
In going back to school in Wittenberg,
It is most retrograde to our desire;
And we beseech you, bend you to remain   115
Here, in the cheer and comfort of our eye,
Our chiefest courtier, cousin, and our son.

Queen Let not thy mother lose her prayers, Hamlet:
I pray thee, stay with us; go not to Wittenberg.

Hamlet I shall in all my best obey you, madam.   120

King Why, 'tis a loving and a fair reply:
Be as ourself in Denmark. Madam, come;
This gentle and unforc'd accord of Hamlet
Sits smiling to my heart; in grace whereof,
No jocund health that Denmark drinks to-day,   125
But the great cannon to the clouds shall tell,
And the king's rouse the heavens shall bruit again,
Re-speaking earthly thunder. Come away.

[Exeunt all except HAMLET]

Hamlet O! that this too too solid flesh would melt,
Thaw and resolve itself into a dew;   130
Or that the Everlasting had not fix'd
His canon 'gainst self-slaughter! O God! God!
How weary, stale, flat, and unprofitable
Seem to me all the uses of this world.
Fie on 't! Ah fie! 'tis an unweeded garden,   135
That grows to seed; things rank and gross in nature
Possess it merely. That it should come to this!
But two months dead: nay, not so much, not two:

104. *still:* always.

105. *corse:* corpse, body.

107. *unprevailing:* futile.

112. *impart:* behave.

113. *school:* university.

114. *retrograde:* contrary.

115. *bend you:* incline yourself.

122. *Be as ourself in Denmark:* Claudius is extending to Hamlet all the special privileges and prerogatives belonging to a crowned prince.

126. *great cannon . . .tell:* It was a Danish custom to discharge a cannon when the king proposed a toast.

127. *rouse:* draught of liquor, toast.

bruit: proclaim.

130. *resolve:* dissolve.

132. *canon:* law; here refers to the sixth commandment in the Bible.

134. *uses:* usages, customs, and employment.

135. *Fie:* interjection expressing sense of outraged propriety.

136. *rank:* coarse.

137. *merely:* entirely.

So excellent a king; that was, to this,
Hyperion to a satyr; so loving to my mother　　　　　　140
That he might not beteem the winds of heaven
Visit her face too roughly. Heaven and earth!
Must I remember? why, she would hang on him,
As if increase of appetite had grown
By what it fed on; and yet, within a month,　　　　　145
Let me not think on't: Frailty, thy name is woman!
A little month; or ere those shoes were old
With which she follow'd my poor father's body,
Like Niobe, all tears; why she, even she, —
O God! a beast, that wants discourse of reason,　　　150
Would have mourn'd longer, — married with mine
　　　uncle,
My father's brother, but no more like my father
Than I to Hercules: within a month,
Ere yet the salt of most unrighteous tears
Had left the flushing in her galled eyes,　　　　　155
She married. O! most wicked speed, to post
With such dexterity to incestous sheets.
It is not nor it cannot come to good;
But break, my heart, for I must hold my tongue!

[Enter HORATIO, MARCELLUS and BERNARDO]

Horatio Hail to your lordship!

Hamlet　　　　　　　　　　　I am glad to see you well:　　160
Horatio, or I do forget myself.

Horatio The same, my lord, and your poor servant ever.

Hamlet Sir, my good friend; I'll change that name with you.
And what make you from Wittenberg, Horatio?
Marcellus?

Marcellus　　　My good lord, —　　　　　　　　165

Hamlet I am very glad to see you. *[To BERNARDO]*
Good even, sir.
But what, in faith, make you from Wittenberg?

Horatio A truant disposition, good my lord.

140.　*Hyperion:* a Titan often identified with the sun god.

　　　satyr: half goat, half man — an ugly and lecherous creature. Hamlet says that comparing his father to his uncle is like comparing Hyperion to a satyr.

Hamlet compares Claudius to a satyr.

141.　*beteem:* permit.

146.　*Frailty . . . woman:* Woman is the epitome of frailty.

149.　*Niobe:* in Greek mythology a woman turned to stone while weeping for slain children; hence an inconsolable woman.

150.　*wants:* lacks.

　　　discourse of reason: ability to reason.

153.　*Hercules:* in Greek mythology, a man possessed of superhuman strength.

154.　*unrighteous:* insincere.

155.　*flushing:* redness.

　　　galled: sore.

156.　*post:* hasten.

157.　*dexterity:* nimbleness.

　　　incestuous: Marriage to the brother of a dead husband was considered incestuous by both the Catholic and Protestant churches.

163.　*I'll change that name with you:* I am your servant.

164.　*make you from:* what is the news from?

Hamlet I would not hear your enemy say so,   170
   Nor shall you do mine ear that violence,
   To make it truster of your own report
   Against yourself; I know you are no truant.
   But what is your affair in Elsinore?
   We'll teach you to drink deep ere you depart.   175

Horatio My lord, I came to see your father's funeral.

Hamlet I pray thee, do not mock me, fellow-student;
   I think it was to see my mother's wedding.

Horatio Indeed, my lord, it follow'd hard upon.

Hamlet Thrift, thrift, Horatio! the funeral bak'd meats   180
   Did coldly furnish forth the marriage tables.
   Would I had met my dearest foe in heaven
   Or ever I had seen that day, Horatio!
   My father, methinks I see my father.

Horatio O! where, my lord?

Hamlet   In my mind's eye, Horatio.   185

Horatio I saw him once; he was a goodly king.

Hamlet He was a man, take him for all in all,
   I shall not look upon his like again.

Horatio My lord, I think I saw him yesternight.

Hamlet Saw who?   190

Horatio My lord, the king your father.

Hamlet   The king, my father!

Horatio Season your admiration for a while
   With an attent ear, till I may deliver,
   Upon the witness of these gentlemen,
   This marvel to you.

Hamlet   For God's love, let me hear.   195

Horatio Two nights together had these gentlemen,
   Marcellus and Bernardo, on their watch,
   In the dead vast and middle of the night,
   Been thus encounter'd: a figure like your father,
   Armed at point exactly, cap-a-pe,   200
   Appears before them, and with solemn march
   Goes slow and stately by them: thrice he walk'd

---

182.   *dearest:* most costly.

192.   *Season your admiration:* Moderate your wonder. Shakespeare frequently uses admiration in its original (Latin) sense of wonder.

193.   *attent:* attentive.

       deliver: report or express.

200.   *cap-a-pe:* fully armed from head to foot.

By their oppress'd and fear-surprised eyes,
Within his truncheon's length; whilst they, distill'd
Almost to jelly with the act of fear,   205
Stand dumb and speak not to him. This to me
In dreadful secrecy impart they did,
And I with them the third night kept the watch;
Where, as they had deliver'd, both in time,
Form of the thing, each word made true and good,   210
The apparition comes. I knew your father;
These hands are not more like.

Hamlet   But where was this?

Marcellus My lord, upon the platform where we
    watch'd.

Hamlet Did you not speak to it?

Horatio   My lord, I did;
  But answer made it none; yet once methought   215
  It lifted up its head and did address
  Itself to motion, like as it would speak;
  But even then the morning cock crew loud,
  And at the sound it shrunk in haste away
  And vanish'd from our sight.

Hamlet   'Tis very strange.   220

Horatio As I do live, my honour'd lord, 'tis true;
  And we did think it writ down in our duty
  To let you know of it.

Hamlet Indeed, indeed, sirs, but this troubles me.
  Hold you the watch to-night?

Marcellus and Bernardo   We do, my lord.   225

Hamlet Arm'd, say you?

Marcellus and Bernardo Arm'd, my lord.

Hamlet   From top to toe?

Marcellus and Bernardo My lord, from head to foot.

Hamlet Then saw you not his face?

Horatio O yes! my lord; he wore his beaver up.

Hamlet What! look'd he frowningly?   230

Horatio A countenance more in sorrow than in anger.

204. *truncheon:* a general's baton.

     distill'd: melted.

209. *deliver'd:* reported.

212. *These . . . like:* The apparition as closely resembled your father as my hands do each other.

229. *beaver:* the visor of the helmet, which could be lowered in battle.

Hamlet Pale or red?

Horatio Nay, very pale.

Hamlet   And fix'd his eyes upon you?

Horatio Most constantly.

Hamlet   I would I had been there.

Horatio It would have much amaz'd you.   235

Hamlet Very like, very like. Stay'd it long?

Horatio While one with moderate haste might tell
    a hundred.

Marcellus and Bernardo Longer, longer.

Horatio Not when I saw it.

Hamlet   His beard was grizzled, no?

Horatio It was, as I have seen it in his life,   240
   A sable silver'd.

Hamlet   I will watch to-night;
   Perchance 'twill walk again.

Horatio   I warrant it will.

Hamlet If it assume my noble father's person,
   I'll speak to it, though hell itself should gape
   And bid me hold my peace. I pray you all,   245
   If you have hitherto conceal'd this sight,
   Let it be tenable in your silence still;
   And whatsoever else shall hap to-night,
   Give it an understanding, but no tongue:
   I will requite your loves. So, fare you well.   250
   Upon the platform, 'twixt eleven and twelve,
   I'll visit you.

All Our duty to your honour.

Hamlet Your loves, as mine to you. Farewell.
   [Exeunt HORATIO, MARCELLUS, and BERNARDO]
   My father's spirit (in arms!) all is not well;
   I doubt some foul play: would the night were come!   255
   Till then sit still, my soul: foul deeds will rise,
   Though all the earth o'erwhelm them, to men's eyes. *[Exit]*

237.   *tell:* count to.

239.   *grizzled:* gray.

240.   *sable silver'd:* black streaked with white.

242.   *warrant:* guarantee.

244.   *gape:* open wide its mouth.

247.   *tenable:* held fast.

248.   *hap:* happen.

249.   *Give . . . no tongue:* Figure out the meaning of it for yourselves, but say nothing about it.

250.   *requite:* repay.

255.   *doubt:* suspect.

COMMENTARY

The brightness and warmth of the court stand in stark contrast to the bleak and gray castle walls in Scene 1. The overall impression of the court scene is one of extreme prosperity and comfort. Only the dark figure of Hamlet reminds us of the tension outside. He sits alone and downcast, dressed in black. The new king, Claudius, brother to the late king, thanks the court and the people assembled for joining in celebrating his marriage to the late king's wife (and Hamlet's mother), Gertrude.

Claudius holds court

King Claudius seems to be a large man (as expressed in IV.3.24 and III.4.182), probably opulently dressed, and we can imagine that his voice is both commanding and conciliatory. He handles the Fortinbras situation, as described by Horatio in the previous scene, with skillful diplomacy. His approach is quite unlike the warlike image we have of his late brother, King Hamlet. Claudius sends his ambassadors, Voltimand and Cornelius, to the old King of Norway to inform him of his nephew Fortinbras's preparations to invade Denmark. Claudius requests that the King of Norway do what he can to stop the impending war.

The parallel between the younger Hamlet and Fortinbras is notable in this scene. Norway, like Denmark, has an elected monarchy at this time. In Norway, just as in Denmark, the dead king has been succeeded by his brother (Old Norway) instead of his son (Fortinbras). In addition, Hamlet and Fortinbras have both lost their fathers, and each man will seek revenge. Their lives ultimately will intersect at the Danish throne.

State business complete, the king turns his attention to individual petitions — in this case a request from Laertes, the son of the court's chief advisor, Polonius. Laertes recently returned to Elsinore from Paris upon hearing of the death of King Hamlet. Now that the funeral (and subsequent wedding) is over, Laertes would like to return to his activities in France. When the king hears that Laertes has obtained his father's permission to leave for Paris, he does not hesitate to give his approval as well. The king probably does not care where Laertes goes, although he puts on a show of generosity and magnanimity: "Take thy fair hour, Laertes; time be thine, / And thy best graces spend it at thy will" (62–63).

Finally, the king addresses Hamlet and asks him why he remains in such deep mourning. Claudius explains that everyone must experience loss, but Hamlet's grief over the death of his father seems excessive. Hamlet's mother, Gertrude, joins her new husband in pleading with Hamlet to end this melancholy. Hamlet's response reveals his dismay and discontent. He appears to be the only one in court who remembers that the king died less than two months before. Gaiety is evident in court, and a wedding has just taken place between the king's widow and the king's brother, raising suspicions in Hamlet that the ghost will later confirm. Hamlet wants to return to his studies in Wittenberg, but Claudius asks him to stay, apparently for the sake of his mother who wants her son close by.

This scene brings up the following three questions:

1. **If Hamlet is the dead king's only son, how did the crown pass to the king's brother, Claudius?** Denmark had an elected monarchy. Although the crown usually passed from father to son, a formal election was held at the death of a Danish king. Claudius may have used his diplomatic skills even before the old king was dead to ensure his own popularity with the nobles, and thus his succession.

2. **If Claudius grieves for his brother, why has he married his brother's wife? How can he mourn with one eye weeping and the other eye smiling?** This reveals something about the duel nature of Claudius's personality; Hamlet must detest the hypocrisy he recognizes in his uncle.

3. **Are Claudius and Gertrude guilty of incest and adultery?** The adultery can only be presumed. Incest technically involves sex between blood relatives, and Claudius and Gertrude are not genetically related. However, during the sixteenth century, King Henry VIII divorced his wife, Catherine of Aragon, because she had been his brother's widow. Henry argued that their marriage constituted incest and a mortal sin, as evidenced by the fact that God punished them. (All but one of their children,

Mary, died in infancy and, as a result, Henry had no male heir.) Therefore, Elizabethan audiences may have viewed the marriage between Claudius and Gertrude as a form of incest.

Hamlet's discontent

Gertrude, in a worried motherly way, and Claudius, in a transparently phony and ostentatious way, try to reason with Hamlet. Gertrude gently reminds her son that life goes on — that death is merely another part of life. Hamlet will not listen to her. No matter what she and others might think, he is in mourning, and he is hurt by Gertrude's apparent lack of feeling for the man they both loved.

Hamlet does not trust or care for his uncle. The marriage of his mother to his uncle has left a bitter taste. Hamlet neither knows nor suspects his uncle's role in the death of the old king; his suspicions at this point are based largely on the hasty marriage and are directed largely towards his mother.

Hamlet uses witty puns to reveal the irony of the situation. For example, the line "I am too much i' the sun" has at least three possible meanings (67). Heard as "son," the line means "I am the son of the king and the son of the queen, and now my uncle calls me son, as well. That is one too many parents." The passage also refers to the sun because too much sun was thought to cause melancholy, a condition from which Hamlet is obviously suffering. One other way to interpret this line is to say that Hamlet is too much of a son to his father; he cannot forget his father's death so easily.

Hamlet displays the depth of his anger toward his mother and his disgust at her quick remarriage. He

wants to shame her somehow and make her realize that she has shamed him and the memory of his father. His "inky cloak" is just an outward symbol of the despair he feels (77). Hamlet clearly has a poetic and idealistic soul. He idolized his father and mother, and now his world has collapsed around him. Everything "seems"; nothing is as he thought it was (76).

The first soliloquy

After the court departs, Hamlet has time alone, and he voices his thoughts aloud in his first *soliloquy* — a speech given by a character who is, or believes himself to be, alone. In the 1948 film version of *Hamlet* starring Laurence Olivier, the soliloquies are delivered as voiceovers rather than as spoken lines. Hamlet is thinking out loud, as it were. Soliloquies usually function as a part of *dramatic irony;* the audience is let in on what is happening in the thoughts of a given character. Thereafter, the audience knows things that the other characters in the play are not aware of. Each line of Hamlet's first soliloquy builds upon the other, and each one reveals more about the past and the resultant situation in which the prince now finds himself.

Derek Jacobi, Kenneth Branagh, and Julie Christie star in the 1996 film version of Hamlet. *Everett Collection*

This soliloquy tells us much about Hamlet. It shows the extent of his disturbance prior to any revelations made by the ghost. Hamlet reveals the fury and shock that he is feeling, not because of his father's death, but because of his mother's marriage to his father's brother. This action is the crux of his exaggerated melancholy. The world is in chaos; everything feels wrong.

Ralph Fiennes as Hamlet in a 1997 Hackney Empire production.
Henrietta Butler/PAL

rapid-fire, staccato dialogue. *Stichomythia*, the technique in which two actors deliver speech in alternating lines, is a way to emphasize the importance of what is being discussed, and the scene gains force and excitement from it. Here, Horatio wants Hamlet to understand that the ghost of the old king has been seen and may appear again.

Hamlet is frustrated because he senses that something he does not understand is happening. He feels the presence of an evil that he cannot define or locate. He despises himself because he is the son of an unfaithful and disloyal mother. He displays all the characteristics of melancholy: He despises life, he wishes he were dead, and he feels that he has no control over himself or his surroundings. To increase his frustration, anger, and bitter despair, Hamlet must be silent. He cannot change the situation, but he cannot accept it either.

News of the apparition

The mood of the scene quickly changes as Horatio, Marcellus, and Bernardo enter. Hamlet extends to his friends a greeting that they receive with spontaneous and genuine pleasure. Now we see another aspect of Hamlet's multifaceted personality; this Hamlet contrasts dramatically with the Hamlet we have just seen. His enthusiasm and obvious happiness at the sight of Horatio betray his somewhat nervous vitality for life.

Horatio and Hamlet obviously have a strong bond. The extent of their friendship can be measured in their conversation and their quick understanding of each other. Horatio finds the perfect opportunity to tell Hamlet about the apparition. Initially, Hamlet is as skeptical as Horatio was the night before, and the two exchange

Hamlet, already frustrated, rejects the idea at first, but he questions Horatio, wanting to know every detail of the encounter. Whether this inquiry is Hamlet's way of reassuring himself that the spirit could be his father or an expression of the prince's disbelief is a matter of interpretation. But Hamlet's questions sound excited and hopeful. He is, at least for the time being, no longer melancholy.

Horatio holds steady throughout Hamlet's harangue. He answers Hamlet directly and calmly, telling him that the ghost looked like the old king. He says it was armed (meaning it was covered with armor "from head to foot"), and "he wore his beaver up" so that Horatio got a clear look at the spirit's face (227, 229). Hamlet tries to trip up Horatio in line 239, but again Horatio calmly answers with lines 240–241. Hamlet decides that Horatio and the soldiers have indeed seen a ghost, and because the form looks enough like Hamlet's father, Hamlet decides that he cannot afford to ignore the apparition. He will go and see it for himself, and perhaps he will find some answers to his troubling questions. However, he must wait until midnight when the ghost might walk again. For the characters as well as the audience, the suspense is almost unbearable.

Act I, Scene 3

Laertes bids farewell to his sister, Ophelia. Hamlet and Ophelia have been seeing each other romantically, and Laertes is concerned. He warns Ophelia not to give her love too freely. Their father, Polonius, hurries Laertes along to his departing ship and then tells Ophelia that he does not want her to see Prince Hamlet again. Ophelia promises to obey.

ACT I, SCENE 3
A room in Polonius's house.

[Enter LAERTES and OPHELIA]

Laertes My necessaries are embark'd; farewell:
  And, sister, as the winds give benefit
  And convoy is assistant, do not sleep,
  But let me hear from you.

Ophelia   Do you doubt that?

Laertes For Hamlet, and the trifling of his favour,   5
  Hold it a fashion and a toy in blood,
  A violet in the youth of primy nature,
  Forward, not permanent, sweet, not lasting,
  The perfume and suppliance of a minute;
  No more.

Ophelia   No more but so?

Laertes   Think it no more: 10
  For nature, crescent, does not grow alone
  In thews and bulk; but, as this temple waxes,
  The inward service of the mind and soul
  Grows wide withal. Perhaps he loves you now,
  And now no soil nor cautel doth besmirch   15
  The virtue of his will; but you must fear,
  His greatness weigh'd, his will is not his own,
  For he himself is subject to his birth;
  He may not, as unvalu'd persons do,
  Carve for himself, for on his choice depends   20
  The safety and the health of the whole state;
  And therefore must his choice be circumscrib'd
  Unto the voice and yielding of that body
  Whereof he is the head. Then if he says he loves you,

NOTES

1. *necessaries are inbarked:* Supplies and baggage are on board.

3. *convoy is assistant:* A means of conveyance is available.

6. *toy in blood:* trifling youthful passion.

7. *primy:* in its prime, youthful.

9. *suppliance of a minute:* a minute's pastime.

11. *crescent:* growing.

12. *temple:* body; the temple of the soul.

15. *cautel:* craft, deceit.

16. *will:* desire.

17. *His greatness weigh'd:* considering his high position.

18. *subject to:* controlled by.

20. *Carve:* choose.

22. *circumscrib'd:* restricted.

23. *voice and yielding:* approval and acquiescence.
    body: people of the state.

It fits your wisdom so far to believe it   25
As he in his particular act and place
May give his saying deed; which is no further
Than the main voice of Denmark goes withal.
Then weigh what loss your honour may sustain,
If with too credent ear you list his songs,   30
Or lose your heart, or your chaste treasure open
To his unmaster'd importunity.
Fear it, Ophelia, fear it, my dear sister;
And keep you in the rear of your affection,
Out of the shot and danger of desire.   35
The chariest maid is prodigal enough
If she unmask her beauty to the moon;
Virtue herself 'scapes not calumnious strokes;
The canker galls the infants of the spring
Too oft before their buttons be disclos'd,   40
And in the morn and liquid dew of youth
Contagious blastments are most imminent.
Be wary then; best safety lies in fear:
Youth to itself rebels, though none else near.

Ophelia I shall th' effect of this good lesson keep,   45
As watchman to my heart. But, good my brother,
Do not, as some ungracious pastors do,
Show me the steep and thorny way to heaven,
Whiles, like a puff'd and reckless libertine,
Himself the primrose path of dalliance treads,   50
And recks not his own rede.

Laertes   O! fear me not.
I stay too long; but here my father comes.
[Enter POLONIUS]
A double blessing is a double grace;
Occasion smiles upon a second leave.

Polonius Yet here, Laertes! aboard, aboard, for shame!   55
The wind sits in the shoulder of your sail,
And you are stay'd for. There, my blessing with thee!
And these few precepts in thy memory
Look thou character. Give thy thoughts no tongue,
Nor any unproportion'd thought his act.   60
Be thou familiar, but by no means vulgar;
The friends thou hast, and their adoption tried,
Grapple them to thy soul with hoops of steel;

25–28. *It fits your wisdom . . . withal:* Before you believe it, consider how far his position will allow him to carry out his promises. His actions are dependent on the public opinion in Denmark.

28. *withal:* with.

30. *credent:* credulous.

31. *chaste treasure:* precious chastity.

32. *unmaster'd importunity:* uncontrolled and determined wooing.

34–35. *keep you . . . danger of desire:* Don't allow your affections to get out of hand.

36. *chariest:* most modest and virtuous.

prodigal: wasteful, spendthrift.

39. *canker . . . spring:* The cankerworm damages the unopened buds.

40. *buttons:* buds.

disclos'd: opened.

42. *Contagious blastments:* destructive blights.

44. *Youth . . . near:* Youth tends to rebel, even if there's no temptation nearby.

47. *ungracious:* lacking grace. Protestant reformers believed that God extended grace even to unworthy sinners.

49. *puff'd:* panting.

libertine: unconstrained person.

50. *Himself . . . dalliance treads:* He enjoys all amorous pleasures.

51. *recks . . . rede:* doesn't listen to his own advice.

fear me not: don't be afraid for me.

54. *Occasion . . . second leave:* This happy circumstance allows us to say goodbye a second time.

57. *stay'd:* waited.

59. *character:* a pun on character in the sense of personal qualities.

60. *unproportion'd:* overly emotional, excessive.

61. *vulgar:* common.

62. *adoption tried:* friendship that has stood the test of time.

But do not dull thy palm with entertainment
Of each new-hatch'd, unfledg'd comrade. Beware   65
Of entrance to a quarrel, but, being in,
Bear 't that th' opposed may beware of thee.
Give every man thine ear, but few thy voice;
Take each man's censure, but reserve thy judgment.
Costly thy habit as thy purse can buy,   70
But not express'd in fancy; rich, not gaudy;
For the apparel oft proclaims the man,
And they in France of the best rank and station
Are most select and generous, chief in that.
Neither a borrower, nor a lender be;   75
For loan oft loses both itself and friend,
And borrowing dulls the edge of husbandry.
This above all: to thine own self be true,
And it must follow, as the night the day,
Thou canst not then be false to any man.   80
Farewell; my blessing season this in thee!

Laertes Most humbly do I take my leave, my lord.

Polonius The time invites you; go, your servants tend.

Laertes Farewell, Ophelia; and remember well
   What I have said to you.

Ophelia   'Tis in my memory lock'd,   85
And you yourself shall keep the key of it.

Laertes Farewell.
   [Exit]

Polonius What is 't, Ophelia, he hath said to you?

Ophelia So please you, something touching the Lord Hamlet.

Polonius Marry, well bethought: 90
   'Tis told me, he hath very oft of late
   Given private time to you; and you yourself
   Have of your audience been most free and bounteous.
   If it be so, — as so 'tis put on me,
   And that in way of caution, — I must tell you,   95
   You do not understand yourself so clearly
   As it behooves my daughter and your honour.
   What is between you? give me up the truth.

Ophelia He hath, my lord, of late made many tenders
   Of his affection to me.   100

64–65. *do not dull . . . unfledg'd comrade:* Don't lose your power of discrimination by entertaining (becoming friends with) every new acquaintance you make.

65. *unfledg'd:* literally, just out of the egg; immature.

69. *censure:* opinion

70. *habit:* dress.

71. *express'd in fancy:* showy.

73–74. *they in France . . . chief in that:* The French nobility display their taste and breeding particularly in their apparel.

77. *husbandry:* thrift.

81. *season:* ripen.

83. *tend:* attend, wait.

90. *Marry:* a common Elizabethan expletive for Mary, referring to the Virgin Mary.

94. *put on me:* reported to me.

97. *behooves:* fits.

99. *tenders:* tentative offers.

Polonius Affection! pooh! you speak like a green girl,
　Unsifted in such perilous circumstance.
　Do you believe his tenders, as you call them?

Ophelia I do not know, my lord, what I should think.

Polonius Marry, I'll teach you: think yourself a baby,　　　105
　That you have ta'en these tenders for true pay,
　Which are not sterling. Tender yourself more dearly;
　Or, — not to crack the wind of the poor phrase,
　Running it thus, — you'll tender me a fool.

Ophelia My lord, he hath importun'd me with love　　　110
　In honourable fashion.

Polonius Ay, fashion you may call it: go to, go to.

Ophelia And hath given countenance to his speech, my lord,
　With almost all the holy vows of heaven.

Polonius Ay, springes to catch woodcocks. I do know,　　　115
　When the blood burns, how prodigal the soul
　Lends the tongue vows: these blazes, daughter,
　Giving more light than heat, extinct in both,
　Even in their promise, as it is a-making,
　You must not take for fire. From this time　　　120
　Be somewhat scanter of your maiden presence;
　Set your entreatments at a higher rate
　Than a command to parley. For Lord Hamlet,
　Believe so much in him, that he is young,
　And with a larger tether may he walk　　　125
　Than may be given you: in few, Ophelia,
　Do not believe his vows, for they are brokers,
　Not of that dye which their investments show,
　But mere implorators of unholy suits,
　Breathing like sanctified and pious bonds,　　　130
　The better to beguile. This is for all:
　I would not, in plain terms, from this time forth,
　Have you so slander any moment's leisure,
　As to give words or talk with the Lord Hamlet
　Look to 't, I charge you; come your ways.　　　135

Ophelia I shall obey, my lord. *[Exeunt]*

101.　*green:* inexperienced or foolish.

102.　*Unsifted . . . circumstance:* untested in such a dangerous affair as courtship.

106–109.　*tenders . . . Tender:* Polonius makes a double pun. He first uses tenders to mean counters or poker chips, indicating value. The second use of tender means to show or offer.

107.　*sterling:* true currency (with the value of an English silver penny).

108.　*crack the wind of:* overwork. The phrase comes from working a horse so hard that it becomes winded.

111.　*fashion:* a whim, not lasting.

112.　*go to:* an expression of impatience, meaning "move along."

113.　*given . . . speech:* confirmed his words.

115.　*springes:* snares.

　　woodcocks: foolish birds that are easily caught.

116.　*blood burns:* passion is aroused.

　　prodigal: extravagantly.

117–120.　*Lends the tongue . . . take for fire:* These flashes (blazes) of passion must not be taken for true love (fire), because they are extinguished (extinct) as soon as they start.

122–123.　*Set . . . parley:* When he asks you for an interview (entreatments), don't consider it as a command to negotiate (parley).

125.　*larger tether:* greater freedom.

126.　*in few:* in short.

127–131.　*Do not believe . . . beguile:* His vows are not what they seem; they are designed to deceive you into doing something unholy.

127.　*brokers:* salesmen.

128.　*investments:* garments.

130.　*bonds:* marriage bonds.

131.　*beguile:* betray.

　　This is for all: to sum up.

133.　*slander . . . leisure:* abuse any moment of leisure.

135.　*come your ways:* come along.

COMMENTARY

Now the scene changes completely, and we enter an intimate family conversation between Polonius and his two children, Laertes and Ophelia.

This exchange offers a wonderful example of the way Shakespeare could draw on a domestic scene to introduce family dynamics as well as individual characteristics. Initially, we see Ophelia being lectured by her brother, Laertes, who is preparing to depart Elsinore for Paris. Before he leaves, Laertes wants to warn Ophelia about being in a relationship with Hamlet.

Laertes warns his sister in lines 4–10 that Hamlet is only trifling with her; because he is a prince, he will not be free to marry whom he chooses. In Shakespeare's time, marriages of heads of state were usually arranged. That meant that young men and women could be assigned a wife or a husband by their parents or by the state. Marriages were ways in which alliances could be made between countries. The unions also provided a means for one country to be guaranteed income from another country. It was not practical or realistic to think that members of the nobility could marry for something as unimportant as love.

Laertes reminds Ophelia of this truth when he says of Hamlet, "His greatness weighed, his will is not his own" (17). If Ophelia falls in love with Hamlet and loses her innocence (virginity) and therefore her honor, she will shame not only herself but also her entire family. Ophelia promises Laertes that she will be careful with Hamlet, but she chides Laertes, telling him that he shouldn't ask her to do what he himself does not do.

When Ophelia refers to Laertes as a "reckless libertine" and tells him that he follows the "path of dalliance," she reveals something about his character (49–50). Unlike Hamlet, who wants permission to leave Elsinore so that he can return to his studies at Wittenberg, Laertes wants to return to Paris for adventure and, probably, excitement with women. When Ophelia calls him on that fact, Laertes remembers suddenly that the time has come for him to leave.

At that moment Polonius enters. Polonius hurries Laertes along, but having noticed that his children were deep in conversation, he will later ask Ophelia what they were discussing. He will not be left out of their lives. Before that happens, he has to deliver his famous words of advice, called *precepts*, to Laertes in lines 59 through 79. The words that Polonius offers his son are a catalogue of hypocrisy, designed to keep up appearances but not backed by character or substance.

The family dynamic

Outwardly, Polonius and his children appear to be a caring and close family, but on closer inspection, we discover that father and son do not fully trust each other. Both men want to control Ophelia. When Ophelia tells her father of Laertes's advice, Polonius impulsively (as if to regain any control he has lost to Laertes) orders Ophelia to cease all contact with Hamlet.

Polonius and Laertes are much alike. In terms of their characters, Polonius and Laertes stand somewhere between Hamlet's ideal purity and Claudius's smiling villainy. Laertes judges Hamlet based on his own actions towards women, not based on Hamlet's behavior. Polonius already controls his daughter and does not trust Laertes's interference. Ophelia stands out in this family as an idealist, much like Hamlet. She is virtuous and, as expected of a young woman at the time, feels compelled to obey her father (110–111).

Polonius has no concern for his daughter's happiness and does not ask any significant questions about her feelings or desires. Ophelia is duty-bound to obey him, which she promises to do. She will not be trapped in Hamlet's "springes," or snares (115). This image will appear again at the end of the play (in V.2.310) when Laertes himself is trapped by his own treachery.

This domestic scene between Polonius and his children foreshadows much of what will happen to each of these characters by the end of the play. Polonius's meddling will bring about his own death; his death will, in turn, provoke Laertes's rage and desire to avenge his father's murder by killing Hamlet; and Ophelia's obedience to her father will destroy any chance for her happiness — a happiness that depends on her relationship with Hamlet.

Act I, Scene 4

Hamlet waits on the castle battlements for the ghost to appear. As Claudius's court drinks merrily within the castle, the ghost of the dead king reappears and beckons Hamlet to follow. Hamlet does so, despite the objections of Horatio and Marcellus.

ACT I, SCENE 4
The platform.

[Enter HAMLET, HORATIO, and MARCELLUS]

Hamlet The air bites shrewdly; it is very cold.

Horatio It is a nipping and an eager air.

Hamlet What hour now?

Horatio   I think it lacks of twelve.

Marcellus No, it is struck.

Horatio Indeed? I heard it not: then it draws near
     the season   5
   Wherein the spirit held his wont to walk.
   [A flourish of trumpets, and ordnance shot off, within]
   What does this mean, my lord?

Hamlet The king doth wake to-night and takes his rouse,
   Keeps wassail and the swaggering up-spring reels;
   And, as he drains his draughts of Rhenish down,   10
   The kettle-drum and trumpet thus bray out
   The triumph of his pledge.

Horatio   Is it a custom?

Hamlet Ay, marry, is 't:
   But to my mind, — though I am native here
   And to the manner born, — it is a custom   15
   More honour'd in the breach than the observance.
   This heavy-headed revel east and west
   Makes us traduc'd and tax'd of other nations;

NOTES

1.   *shrewdly:* bitterly.

2.   *eager:* sharp.

5.   *season:* time of night.

6.   *held . . . walk:* has been in the habit of walking.

8.   *wake:* hold a night of revel.

    rouse: a toast in which all glasses must be drained before lowering.

9.   *wassail:* revelry, carousing.

    up-spring: a high-kicking, wild German dance.

    reels: This is either a verb, of which up-spring is the subject, or a noun modified by up-spring.

10.   *Rhenish:* wine made in the Rhineland.

11.   *bray out:* celebrate.

12.   *The triumph of his pledge:* his drinking ability.

15.   *to the manner born:* accustomed to it since a child.

16.   *More honour'd . . . observance:* It is a custom that would bring us more honor if we disregarded rather than kept it.

17.   *heavy-headed:* a transferred epithet. Those who take part in the revel become heavy-headed (thick-headed).

18.   *traduc'd and tax'd:* defamed and censored.

    of: by.

They clepe us drunkards, and with swinish phrase
Soil our addition; and indeed it takes   20
From our achievements, though perform'd at height,
The pith and marrow of our attribute.
So, oft it chances in particular men,
That for some vicious mole of nature in them,
As, in their birth, — wherein they are not guilty,   25
Since nature cannot choose his origin, —
By the o'ergrowth of some complexion,
Oft breaking down the pales and forts of reason,
Or by some habit that too much o'er-leavens
The form of plausive manners; that these men,   30
Carrying, I say, the stamp of one defect,
Being nature's livery, or fortune's star,
His virtues else, be they as pure as grace,
As infinite as man may undergo,
Shall in the general censure take corruption   35
From that particular fault: the dram of evil
Doth all the noble substance often doubt,
To his own scandal.

[Enter GHOST]

Horatio   Look, my lord, it comes.

Hamlet Angels and ministers of grace defend us!
Be thou a spirit of health or goblin damn'd,   40
Bring with thee airs from heaven or blasts from hell,
Be thy intents wicked or charitable,
Thou com'st in such a questionable shape
That I will speak to thee: I'll call thee Hamlet,
King, father; royal Dane, O! answer me: 45
Let me not burst in ignorance; but tell
Why thy canoniz'd bones, hearsed in death,
Have burst their cerements; why the sepulchre,
Wherein we saw thee quietly inurn'd,
Hath op'd his ponderous and marble jaws,   50
To cast thee up again. What may this mean,
That thou, dead corse, again in complete steel
Revisits thus the glimpses of the moon,
Making night hideous; and we fools of nature
So horridly to shake our disposition   55
With thoughts beyond the reaches of our souls?
Say, why is this, wherefore? what should we do?

---

19. *clepe:* call.

19–20. *with swinish …addition:* They disgrace our honor by calling us swine.

20. *it:* refers to drunkenness.

21. *though . . . height:* though of the greatest merit.

22. *pith . . . attribute:* essential part of our reputation.

24. *mole:* blemish.

27–30. *By the o'ergrowth . . . plausive manners:* By the overdevelopment of some quality that breaks down the restraints of reason, or by the acquisition of some habit that sours (o'er-leavens — ferments) sweet (plausive — agreeable) manners.

32. *nature's livery, or fortune's star:* either inborn or the result of bad luck.

33. *His virtues else:* his other virtues.

34. *undergo:* sustain, or possess.

35. *general censure:* public's judgment.

36–38. *the dram . . . scandal:* a much-disputed passage. Perhaps a line is missing. The general meaning seems to be that it takes only a small portion of evil to bring a scandal on the entire substance, however noble it may otherwise be.

40. *spirit of health:* There are two possible meanings. First, a saved (healthy) soul, not a lost one. Second, a healing or beneficent spirit.

goblin damn'd: damned agent of the devil. Hamlet, from the very first, seems to question the authenticity of the ghost as the true spirit of his father.

43. *questionable:* inviting question.

47. *canoniz'd:* consecrated.

hearsed: buried.

48. *cerements:* winding-sheets.

49. *inurn'd:* buried.

52. *complete steel:* full armor.

54. *fools:* dupes. Nature hides supernatural truth from our eyes.

55. *disposition:* self-control.

[The Ghost beckons HAMLET]

Horatio It beckons you to go away with it,
As if it some impartment did desire
To you alone.

Marcellus   Look, with what courteous action   60
It waves you to a more removed ground:
But do not go with it.

Horatio   No, by no means.

Hamlet It will not speak; then, will I follow it.

Horatio Do not, my lord.

Hamlet   Why, what should be the fear?
I do not set my life at a pin's fee;   65
And for my soul, what can it do to that,
Being a thing immortal as itself?
It waves me forth again; I'll follow it.

Horatio What if it tempt you toward the flood, my lord,
Or to the dreadful summit of the cliff   70
That beetles o'er his base into the sea,
And there assume some other horrible form,
Which might deprive your sovereignty of reason
And draw you into madness? think of it;
The very place puts toys of desperation,   75
Without more motive, into every brain
That looks so many fathoms to the sea
And hears it roar beneath.

Hamlet It waves me still. Go on, I'll follow thee.

Marcellus You shall not go, my lord.

Hamlet   Hold off your hands!   80

Horatio Be rul'd; you shall not go.

Hamlet   My fate cries out,
And makes each petty artery in this body
As hardy as the Nemean lion's nerve. *[Ghost beckons]*
Still am I call'd. Unhand me, gentlemen,
[Breaking from them]
By heaven! I'll make a ghost of him that lets me: 85
I say, away! Go on, I'll follow thee.

[Exeunt Ghost and HAMLET]

59. *impartment:* communication.

65. *a pin's fee:* Hamlet considers his life of little value, less than that of a pin.

66–67. *it, itself:* both refer to the ghost.

69. *flood:* sea. Elsinore is situated on the Danish coast.

71. *beetles o'er:* overhangs.

73. *Which might . . .reason:* which might dethrone your reason (make you go crazy).

75. *toys of desperation:* desperate fancies or impulses — referring to the impulse to jump off a high place.

83. *hardy:* strong.

Nemean: the lion slain by Hercules.

nerve: sinew.

85. *lets:* hinders.

Horatio He waxes desperate with imagination.

Marcellus Let's follow; 'tis not fit thus to obey him.

Horatio Have after. To what issue will this come?

Marcellus Something is rotten in the state of Denmark.   90

Horatio Heaven will direct it.

Marcellus   Nay, let's follow him.

[Exeunt]

COMMENTARY

The action in this scene returns to the cold battlements. Again, Shakespeare contrasts neighboring scenes sharply, moving from a domestic scene to a military watch. The lateness of the hour and the cold make the anticipation of the ghost uncomfortable and more urgent. The mood is one of nervous anticipation as Hamlet, Horatio, and Marcellus wait.

The night watch

The men talk to each other to pass the time, just as regular people usually do in similar situations. The men discuss the weather, and they ask each other the time. Horatio thinks it is not yet 12 o'clock; Marcellus is sure that he heard the midnight bell. Shakespeare includes dialogue such as this within the structure of the play in order to set a specific tone or mood and also to describe what is happening on stage without the use of stage directions. Now the audience knows that the time is late at night, that the place is cold, and that the men are anxious.

Suddenly, an unexpected cannon shot and the sounds of trumpets startle the silence of the night. The mood is so tense that the entire theatre — actors and audience alike — are startled by the sound. The cannon does not signal danger; the artillery sound is merely the signal for the court to gather for drinking and carousing. We develop an idea of the luxurious excesses of Claudius's court, although Hamlet remarks that excessive drinking is a stereotypical trait of the Danes. Hamlet claims that his countrymen gained that reputation honestly.

In Viking days, the Mead Hall was an integral part of the warriors' daily lives. (The Old English poem *Beowulf* demonstrates this fact.) The warriors would gather to drink their favorite brew, *mead* (a form of beer fermented from honey instead of grain). Over time, the mead changed to a grain-based brew or wine ("draughts of Rhenish"), but the custom of drinking did not diminish (10). Claudius's court is no exception to this old custom; rather, it revels in it. Hamlet appears to be disgusted by the tradition.

This digression from the purpose at hand leads Hamlet to wonder about the nature of man and why some particular fault or another can destroy or corrupt an otherwise good person. Hamlet seeks truth, and these kinds of ruminations reveal his tendency to infer conclusions from his observations. He frequently moves from the specific to the general. (See, for example, I.2.23–38 and III.1.122–129, 136–142). Perhaps in this scene, Hamlet is questioning himself and his own motivations or weaknesses. But before he can contemplate his life further, the ghost appears.

The spirit returns

Again, the change in mood onstage is abrupt and unexpected. The dialogue concerning the Danish custom of drinking has made everyone temporarily forget that this exact moment is what they were awaiting. Horatio sees the spirit first and announces its presence to the others. Hamlet whispers a prayer, but he does not seem to fear any possible danger. He rushes forward impulsively to speak to the ghost, a figure he recognizes and calls, "King, father; royal Dane" (45).

Using powerful blank verse (in lines 40–55), Hamlet asks the ghost why he has left his grave to walk the earth and terrorize mere mortals "[w]ith thoughts beyond the reaches of our souls" (56). In other words, why is the ghost showing them sights that the living cannot possibly

The ghost appears dressed in armor.

understand? The ghost beckons, and Hamlet, heedless of any danger, starts after it. Marcellus warns Hamlet not to follow, and Horatio agrees. The men are fearful that the apparition will harm Hamlet in some way — perhaps kill him or drive him mad.

Hamlet ignores the men's entreaties. He is determined to follow; this may be the only chance he will ever have to connect with his father again. The ghost may be able to answer Hamlet's questions and put his mind at ease about his nagging feelings that something is horribly wrong. Hamlet considers this ghost to be a part of his destiny; nothing will prevent him from following it. He threatens to kill anyone who tries to stop him, and he commands the ghost to lead on.

Hamlet has not completely abandoned the possibility that the spirit may be Satan in disguise, but he throws caution to the wind. To Hamlet, the only thing that matters is settling the questions that have been overwhelming his psyche. This apparition, Hamlet thinks, may be able to satisfy him. He struggles against the restraining hands of the men, and we see that he is capable of great strength, determination, persistence, and courage. The Vikings, from whom the Danes evolved, had a spirit of comradeship that these men seem to have inherited. No Viking would ever leave his lord to face danger and possible death alone. This ingrained understanding among the soldiers makes it impossible for the men to abandon Hamlet. They refuse to follow orders, preferring to stay close to the prince and protect him, if possible.

Act I, Scene 5

Hamlet is alone with the spirit of his father. The ghost reveals the details of his murder at the hands of Hamlet's uncle, Claudius. Hamlet vows revenge. The spirit warns Hamlet not to hurt Gertrude. Horatio and Marcellus enter and find Hamlet a changed man. Hamlet makes the two men swear never to reveal what they have seen.

ACT I, SCENE 5
Another part of the platform.

[Enter Ghost and HAMLET]

Hamlet Whither wilt thou lead me? speak; I'll go no further.

Ghost Mark me.

Hamlet   I will.

Ghost   My hour is almost come,
When I to sulphurous and tormenting flames
Must render up myself.

Hamlet   Alas! poor ghost.

Ghost Pity me not, but lend thy serious hearing   5
To what I shall unfold.

Hamlet   Speak; I am bound to hear.

Ghost So art thou to revenge, when thou shalt hear.

Hamlet What?

Ghost I am thy father's spirit;
Doom'd for a certain term to walk the night,   10
And for the day confin'd to fast in fires,
Till the foul crimes done in my days of nature
Are burnt and purg'd away. But that I am forbid
To tell the secrets of my prison-house,
I could a tale unfold whose lightest word   15
Would harrow up thy soul, freeze thy young blood,
Make thy two eyes like stars start from their spheres,
Thy knotted and combined locks to part,
And each particular hair to stand on end,
Like quills upon the fretful porpentine: 20

NOTES

2.   *Mark me:* listen carefully to me.

6.   *bound:* obliged.

12. *nature:* natural life.

17. *spheres:* orbits.

18. *knotted and combined locks:* hair lying together in a mass.

19. *particular:* individual.

20. *porpentine:* porcupine.

The ghost says Hamlet's hair should rise like a porcupine's quills.

But this eternal blazon must not be
To ears of flesh and blood. List, list, O list!
If thou didst ever thy dear father love —

Hamlet O God!

Ghost Revenge his foul and most unnatural murder.   25

Hamlet Murder!

Ghost Murder most foul, as in the best it is;
But this most foul, strange, and unnatural.

Hamlet Haste me to know't, that I, with wings as swift
As meditation or the thoughts of love,   30
May sweep to my revenge.

Ghost   I find thee apt,
And duller shouldst thou be than the fat weed
That rots itself in ease on Lethe wharf,
Wouldst thou not stir in this. Now, Hamlet, hear:
'Tis given out, that sleeping in mine orchard,   35
A serpent stung me; so the whole ear of Denmark
Is by a forged process of my death
Rankly abus'd; but know, thou noble youth,
The serpent that did sting thy father's life
Now wears his crown.

Hamlet   O my prophetic soul!   40
My uncle?

Ghost Ay, that incestuous, that adulterate beast,
With witchcraft of his wit, with traitorous gifts, —
O wicked wit and gifts, that have the power
So to seduce! — won to his shameful lust   45
The will of my most seeming-virtuous queen.
O Hamlet! what a falling-off was there;
From me, whose love was of that dignity
That it went hand in hand even with the vow
I made to her in marriage; and to decline   50
Upon a wretch whose natural gifts were poor
To those of mine!
But virtue, as it never will be mov'd,
Though lewdness court it in a shape of heaven,
So lust, though to a radiant angel link'd,   55
Will sate itself in a celestial bed,
And prey on garbage.

21.	*eternal blazon:* description of eternity.
22.	*List:* listen.
27.	*in the best:* even for the best reason.
31.	*apt:* quick, ready.
32.	*fat:* thick, slimy, motionless.
33.	*in ease:* undisturbed.
	Lethe: the river of forgetfulness.
37.	*forged process:* false account.
38.	*Rankly abus'd:* greatly deceived.
42.	*adulterate:* adulterous.
43.	*wit:* cunning.
50.	*decline:* sink down both physically and morally.
52.	*To:* compared to.
54.	*lewdness:* sensuality, lust.

But, soft! methinks I scent the morning air;
Brief let me be. Sleeping within mine orchard,
My custom always of the afternoon,   60
Upon my secure hour thy uncle stole,
With juice of cursed hebona in a vial,
And in the porches of mine ears did pour
The leperous distilment; whose effect
Holds such an enmity with blood of man   65
That swift as quicksilver it courses through
The natural gates and alleys of the body,
And with a sudden vigour it doth posset
And curd, like eager droppings into milk,
The thin and wholesome blood: so did it mine;   70
And a most instant tetter bark'd about,
Most lazar-like, with vile and loathsome crust
All my smooth body.
Thus was I, sleeping, by a brother's hand,
Of life, of crown, of queen, at once dispatch'd;   75
Cut off even in the blossoms of my sin,
Unhousel'd, disappointed, unanel'd,
No reckoning made, but sent to my account
With all my imperfections on my head:
O, horrible! O, horrible! most horrible!   80
If thou hast nature in thee, bear it not;
Let not the royal bed of Denmark be
A couch for luxury and damned incest.
But, howsoever thou pursu'st this act,
Taint not thy mind, nor let thy soul contrive   85
Against thy mother aught; leave her to heaven,
And to those thorns that in her bosom lodge,
To prick and sting her. Fare thee well at once!
The glow-worm shows the matin to be near,
And 'gins to pale his uneffectual fire;   90
Adieu, adieu! Hamlet, remember me. *[Exit]*

Hamlet O all you host of heaven ! O earth! What else?
And shall I couple hell? O fie! Hold, hold, my heart!
And you, my sinews, grow not instant old,
But bear me stiffly up! Remember thee!   95
Ay, thou poor ghost, while memory holds a seat
In this distracted globe. Remember thee!
Yea, from the table of my memory

61. *secure:* careless, unguarded.

62. *hebona:* yew, a poisonous herb.

64. *leperous distilment:* a distilled liquid producing symptoms similar to leprosy.

68. *posset:* to thicken or allow to curdle.

69. *eager:* sour, acidic.

71. *instant:* immediate.

     tetter: skin eruption.

     bark'd about: encrusted, covered like bark on a tree.

72. *lazar-like:* like leprosy; from Lazarus, a leper in scripture.

76. *Cut off . . . my sin:* killed while in a state of sin and therefore in danger of eternal damnation.

77. *Unhousel'd:* not having received the sacrament of Eucharist, or Holy Communion.

     disappointed: ill-equipped, unprepared.

     unanel'd: unanointed, not having received Extreme Unction (the last anointment of the dying).

81. *nature:* natural feelings.

83. *luxury:* lust.

85. *contrive:* plot.

89. *matin:* morning prayers.

90. *'gins:* begins.

     uneffectual: The daylight makes it ineffectual, or cold.

97. *globe:* Hamlet's head, but also refers to the Globe theatre in which the play was probably performed.

98. *table:* tablet.

I'll wipe away all trivial fond records,
All saws of books, all forms, all pressures past   100
That youth and observation copied there;
And thy commandment all alone shall live
Within the book and volume of my brain,
Unmix'd with baser matter: yes, by heaven!
O most pernicious woman!   105
O villain, villain, smiling, damned villain!
My tables, — meet it is I set it down,
That one may smile, and smile, and be a villain;
At least I'm sure it may be so in Denmark: *[Writing]*
So, uncle, there you are. Now to my word;   110
It is 'Adieu, adieu! remember me.'
I have sworn 't.

Horatio *[Within]* My lord, my lord!

Marcellus *[Within]*   Lord Hamlet!

Horatio *[Within]*   Heaven secure him!

Marcellus *[Within]* So be it!

Horatio *[Within]* Hillo, ho, ho, my lord!   115

Hamlet Hillo, ho, ho, boy! come, bird, come.

[Enter HORATIO and MARCELLUS]

Marcellus How is 't, my noble lord?

Horatio   What news, my lord?

Hamlet O wonderful.

Horatio   Good my lord, tell it.

Hamlet No; you will reveal it.

Horatio Not I, my lord, by heaven!

Marcellus   Nor I, my lord.   120

Hamlet How say you then, would heart of man once
    think it?
But you'll be secret?

Horatio and Marcellus   Ay, by heaven, my lord.

Hamlet There's ne'er a villain dwelling in all Denmark
But he's an arrant knave.

---

99.   *fond:* foolish, trifling.

100.   *saws:* sayings, maxims, proverbs.

      forms: sketches.

      pressures: impressions.

107.   *My tables:* Young men of education were in the habit of carrying ivory tablets for the purpose of recording good and worthwhile observations.

      meet: fitting, proper.

110.   *word:* either watchword or motto.

113.   *secure him:* keep him from harm.

116.   *Hillo, ho, ho:* the falconer's cry to recall his hawk.

124.   *arrant:* out-and-out.

      knave: scoundrel; another word for villain.

Horatio There needs no ghost, my lord, come from
    the grave,   125
To tell us this.

Hamlet   Why, right; you are i' the right;
And so without more circumstance at all,
I hold it fit that we shake hands and part;
You, as your business and desire shall point you, —
For every man hath business and desire,   130
Such as it is, — and, for mine own poor part,
Look you, I'll go pray.

Horatio These are but wild and whirling words, my lord.

Hamlet I am sorry they offend you, heartily;
Yes, faith, heartily.

Horatio   There's no offence, my lord.   135

Hamlet Yes, by Saint Patrick, but there is, Horatio,
And much offence, too. Touching this vision here,
It is an honest ghost, that let me tell you;
For your desire to know what is between us,
O'ermaster't as you may. And now, good friends,   140
As you are friends, scholars, and soldiers,
Give me one poor request.

Horatio What is 't, my lord? we will.

Hamlet Never make known what you have seen to-night.

Horatio and Marcellus My lord, we will not.

Hamlet   Nay, but swear 't.

Horatio   In faith,   145
My lord, not I.

Marcellus   Nor I, my lord, in faith.

Hamlet Upon my sword.

Marcellus   We have sworn, my lord, already.

Hamlet Indeed, upon my sword, indeed.

Ghost *[Beneath]* Swear.

Hamlet Ha, ha, boy! sayst thou so? art thou there,
    true-penny?   150
Come on, — you hear this fellow in the cellarage, —
Consent to swear.

127.   *circumstance:* ceremony.

136–137. *Yes . . . too:* These words may have been spoken
in an aside to Horatio, to whom Hamlet will later
confide the truth.

137.   *Touching:* concerning.

140.   *O'ermaster . . . may:* Overcome it as best you can.
In other words, Hamlet says he has no intention
of enlightening them.

145–146. *In faith . . . not I:* I will not reveal it.

150.   *true-penny:* a familiar phrase of affection to a
trustworthy person.

151.   *in the cellarage:* The ghost's voice came from
under the stage.

Horatio　　　　　　　　　Propose the oath, my lord.

Hamlet Never to speak of this that you have seen,
Swear by my sword.

Ghost *[Beneath]* Swear.　　　　　　　　　　　　　　　　　　　　155

Hamlet *Hic et ubique?* then we'll shift our ground.
Come hither, gentlemen,
And lay your hands again upon my sword:
Never to speak of this that you have heard,
Swear by my sword.　　　　　　　　　　　　　　　　　　　160

Ghost *[Beneath]* Swear.

Hamlet Well said, old mole! canst work i' the earth so fast?
A worthy pioner! once more remove, good friends.

Horatio O day and night, but this is wondrous strange!

Hamlet And therefore as a stranger give it welcome.　　　165
There are more things in heaven and earth, Horatio,
Than are dreamt of in your philosophy.
But come;
Here, as before, never, so help you mercy,
How strange or odd soe'er I bear myself,　　　　　　170
As I perchance hereafter shall think meet
To put an antic disposition on,
That you, at such times seeing me, never shall,
With arms encumber'd thus, or this head-shake,
Or by pronouncing of some doubtful phrase,　　　　175
As, 'Well, well, we know,' or, 'We could, an if we would;'
Or, 'If we list to speak,' or, 'There be, an if they might;'
Or such ambiguous giving out, to note
That you know aught of me: this not to do,
So grace and mercy at your most need help you,　　180
Swear.

Ghost *[Beneath]* Swear. *[They swear]*

Hamlet Rest, rest, perturbed spirit! So, gentlemen,
With all my love I do commend me to you:
And what so poor a man as Hamlet is　　　　　　　185
May do, to express his love and friending to you
God willing, shall not lack. Let us go in together;

---

156. *Hic et ubique:* here and everywhere.

163. *pioner:* a person who digs trenches.

remove: move.

165. *And . . welcome:* Welcome it in your mind without understanding it, as you would a stranger into your house.

167. *philosophy:* The word philosophy was commonly used to mean natural philosophy or science.

172. *antic disposition:* mad behavior.

174. *encumber'd:* folded.

177. *'There . . . might':* There are those who could tell a story if only they were permitted.

178. *giving out:* suggestion.

180. *grace and mercy:* God's grace and mercy.

184. *me:* myself. Hamlet requests the sympathy, understanding, and forebearance of his friends, suggesting that they will do this in return for the love he bears them.

186. *friending:* friendship.

And still your fingers on your lips, I pray.
The time is out of joint; O cursed spite,
That ever I was born to set it right!   190
Nay, come, let's go together.

[Exeunt]

COMMENTARY

This scene follows with little break from the last. We see no dramatic change of scenery or tone because Hamlet and the ghost are still on the castle battlements in the middle of the night. The entire play so far has been leading up to this pivotal scene.

Staging the spirit

Staging this part of the drama in the Early Modern theatre required some kind of theatrical device out of which the ghost could emerge and into which he could disappear, which may have been the trapdoor in the stage floor of theatres such as the Globe. Otherwise, the actors would have to move from one part of the stage to another so that the audience could accept the scene change.

Early Modern theatres used devices such as trapdoors to stage the ghost scenes.

The simple fact of placing a ghost onstage was somewhat daring during Shakespeare's day. A newly Protestant audience would expect a Protestant viewpoint to be presented onstage. Shakespeare accommodated that expectation by having Hamlet and Horatio study in Wittenberg, a sixteenth-century center of Protestant thought and education with a scholarly respect for reason and a disregard for superstition and myth. But the older Catholic view of hauntings and spirits and the belief in purgatory are integral parts of this scene as well. Keep in mind that this play was written during the Reformation in England when Catholic and Protestant ideologies were vying for dominance in people's minds. Horatio brings the voice of scholarly reason from Wittenberg; the ghost echoes the voice of the past.

The king seeks revenge

Displaying dignity, authority, gentleness, and sadness, the ghost identifies himself to Hamlet by saying, "I am thy father's spirit" (9). The apparition tells Hamlet that it is condemned to walk the night — it cannot rest until the sins on its soul are burned away. The ghost cannot tell Hamlet what purgatory is like or how the spirit suffers in fire. Mortals could not understand or bear to hear the horrors that wait beyond death for those who die with the stain of sin on their souls.

A virtually speechless Hamlet wants to hear what the ghost has come to tell him. He focuses all his attention on the spirit's words. The words "murder" and "[r]evenge" are stressed, and they resound against Hamlet's ears like physical blows (25). Hamlet finally understands what the ghost is saying, but that understanding comes at a terrible price.

The spirit tells the story of his death. He was not stung by a serpent as everyone had been led to believe; instead he was poisoned by Claudius. The ghost's long narrative describes the extent of Claudius's villainy and deceptiveness. The ghost dwells on the effect of the poison poured in his ear and on the various rewards his brother gained from his death. Claudius killed Hamlet's father and married his mother, and Hamlet must now seek revenge for his father's shame and murder.

Hamlet has no trouble promising the ghost that he will carry out his wishes; remember, Hamlet is passionate and impulsive. But he is also thoughtful, and in the light of day, revenge will not come easily to him.

Absolution denied

Finally, the ghost reveals the most horrifying aspect of his death. In another lapse into Catholic tradition, the ghost cries that he was sent to his afterlife without a chance to confess and do penance for his sins, "With all my imperfections on my head"(79). According to Catholic belief, without absolution (called the Last Rites), the soul of a person is marked with sin and must stay in purgatory until the sins are removed.

With the coming of dawn once again, the spirit must depart. His last words — "remember me" — tear at Hamlet's already wounded soul (91). Up to this point, Hamlet has been criticized for remembering his father and being overly depressed because of his father's death. Hamlet believes that he is the only one who does remember. He cries at the empty air, "Remember thee! / Ay, thou poor ghost, while memory holds a seat / In this distracted globe" (95–97). Does his father think Hamlet could forget him? Does he not realize the extent of Hamlet's love and loyalty? (Note that Hamlet calls his head a "distracted globe," punning on the name of the theatre in which the play was performed.)

Hamlet's second soliloquy is filled with anger, excitement, and resolution. Hamlet now knows that the hatred he has felt towards his uncle has not been unfair or misplaced. Hamlet has no trouble promising his father that this one thing — revenge — will now occupy him solely. He calls on the entire universe to bear witness to his vow and struggles to maintain composure. He condemns Claudius for having placed the burden of revenge upon him. He refers to his mother as that "pernicious woman" and Claudius as that "smiling, damned villain" (105, 106). He bids farewell to his father's ghost and swears that his murder will not go unpunished.

Sworn to silence

Horatio and Marcellus find Hamlet. Their voices are filled with concern, and they sound relieved when Hamlet responds playfully with the old falconer's cry, "Hillo, ho, ho" (115). Their relief is short-lived, however, when they immediately notice a change in Hamlet. He is a little *too* cheerful, a little *too* playful, and most importantly, he will not reveal what has happened.

When the men press him, he dismisses their questions and cuts them off abruptly. He even keeps Horatio at arm's length. Horatio is hurt, but he tries to calm Hamlet, bring some reason back to the prince, and make him stop his "wild and whirling words" (132). Hamlet responds to Horatio's entreaties and apologizes sincerely for offending him. Still, he will not confide in his friend. He will only tell Horatio that the ghost was "honest" (138).

As for the ghost's appearance, Hamlet tells the men that the event must remain a secret. He insists that they never reveal what they have seen no matter what happens. If Hamlet should "put an antic disposition on" (in other words, act crazy), the soldiers are to say nothing (172). Clearly, Hamlet has decided that it will be best for him to assume a false madness. In fact, Hamlet is already pretending a kind of madness in front of the men. He acts silly, answering the concerned questions of Horatio and Marcellus with witty puns and joking replies. He brings the men together to swear their silence. They hesitate. The ghost is watching and its voice rises ominously, demanding that the men do as Hamlet has asked. (In the Early Modern theatre, the ghost's voice probably originated in the *cellarage*, a space underneath the stage.) The voice commands the men to swear themselves to silence not once but three times. The men quickly comply and swear to silence on Hamlet's sword.

Hesitating vengeance

Although Hamlet has promised his father's ghost, the mission of revenge is something he takes no pleasure in. At first he seemed almost anxious to kill his uncle, but by the end of the scene he considers his task in more serious terms. He knows that his job is immense. His father was the king, and the death of a king upsets the balance of the state. (See the discussion of hierarchy in the "Introduction to Early Modern England.") The unnatural demise of King Hamlet bodes evil for an entire society. Hamlet reminds himself that the world — the cosmos itself — must be set right.

This scene forever alters Hamlet's future. From now on, his life must be dedicated to avenging the murder of his father. "Cursed spite" has left him with nothing else, which Hamlet understands (89). Reminding the men of their vow of silence, Hamlet departs with Horatio and Marcellus.

Notes

HAMLET
ACT II

Polonius *Therefore, since brevity is the soul of wit,*
And tediousness the limbs and outward flourishes,
I will be brief. Your noble son is mad:
Mad call I it; for, to define true madness,
What is 't but to be nothing else but mad?

Act II, Scene 1

Polonius sends Reynaldo to Paris to spy on Laertes. A distraught Ophelia tells her father of a strange encounter with Hamlet. She reveals that she has ceased all contact with Hamlet, as her father had ordered. Polonius decides that Hamlet has lost his mind because of his love for Ophelia. Polonius rushes to tell the king and queen.

ACT II, SCENE 1
A room in Polonius's house.

[Enter POLONIUS and REYNALDO]

Polonius Give him this money and these notes, Reynaldo.

Reynaldo I will, my lord.

Polonius You shall do marvellous wisely, good Reynaldo,
Before you visit him, to make inquiry
Of his behaviour.

Reynaldo   My lord, I did intend it.   5

Polonius Marry, well said, very well said. Look you sir,
Inquire me first what Danskers are in Paris;
And how, and who, what means, and where they keep,
What company, at what expense; and finding
By this encompassment and drift of question   10
That they do know my son, come you more nearer
Than your particular demands will touch it:
Take you, as 'twere, some distant knowledge of him;
As thus, 'I know his father, and his friends,
And, in part, him'; do you mark this, Reynaldo?   15

Reynaldo Ay, very well, my lord.

Polonius 'And, in part, him; but,' you may say, 'not well:
But if 't be he I mean, he's very wild,
Addicted so and so;' and there put on him
What forgeries you please; marry, none so rank   20
As may dishonour him; take heed of that;
But, sir, such wanton, wild, and usual slips
As are companions noted and most known
To youth and liberty.

Reynaldo   As gaming, my lord?

Polonius Ay, or drinking, fencing, swearing, quarreling,   25
Drabbing; you may go so far.

NOTES

1.   *him:* Laertes.

     notes: letters.

7.   *Danskers:* Danes.

8.   *what means:* what their income is.

     keep: lodge.

10. *By this . . . question:* by this roundabout mode of inquiry.

11–12. *come you . . . touch it:* without asking any direct questions, find out more about him.

13. *Take:* assume.

19. *put on him:* charge him with.

20. *forgeries:* inventions, that is, of misconduct.

     rank: gross.

23. *companions noted:* frequently observed as accompanying youth.

26. *Drabbing:* associating with prostitutes.

Reynaldo My lord, that would dishonour him.

Polonius Faith, no; as you may season it in the charge.
You must not put another scandal on him,
That he is open to incontinency;   30
That's not my meaning; but breathe his faults so quaintly
That they may seem the taints of liberty,
The flash and outbreak of a fiery mind,
A savageness in unreclaimed blood,
Of general assault.

Reynaldo   But, my good lord, —   35

Polonius Wherefore should you do this?

Reynaldo   Ay, my lord,
I would know that.

Polonius   Marry, sir, here's my drift;
And I believe it is a fetch of warrant:
You laying these slight sullies on my son,
As 'twere a thing a little soil'd i' the working,   40
Mark you,
Your party in converse, him you would sound,
Having ever seen in the prenominate crimes
The youth you breathe of guilty, be assur'd,
He closes with you in this consequence;   45
'Good sir,' or so; 'friend,' or 'gentleman,'
According to the phrase or the addition
Of man and country.

Reynaldo   Very good, my lord.

Polonius And then, sir, does he this, — he does, —
What was I about to say? By the mass I was about   50
To say something: where did I leave?

Reynaldo At 'closes in the consequence.'
At 'friend or so,' and 'gentleman.'

Polonius At 'closes in the consequence,' ay, marry;
He closes with you thus: 'I know the gentleman;   55
I saw him yesterday, or t' other day,
Or then, or then; with such, or such; and, as you say,
There was a' gaming; there o'ertook in 's rouse;
There falling out at tennis;' or perchance,

28. *Faith:* a colloquial interjection meaning "truly."

     season: qualify.

30. *incontinency:* debauchery, sexual indulgence. The explanation of the apparent contradiction between this and line 28 is that Polonius does not mind Laertes drabbing, providing he does not do it too openly.

31. *quaintly:* skillfully, cleverly.

34. *unreclaimed:* untamed.

35. *Of general assault:* common to all men.

37. *drift:* intention.

38. *And I believe . . . warrant:* I believe it is a trick guaranteed to bring results.

39. *sullies:* blemishes.

40. *i' the working:* by use.

42–45. *Your party . . . this consequence:* If the person you are questioning has ever seen Laertes guilty of the aforementioned (prenominate) crimes, be sure he will respond as follows.

47. *addition:* title.

58. *a':* a colloquial expression for "he."

     o'ertook . . . rouse: drunk.

59. *falling out:* quarreling.

'I saw him enter such a house of sale,'　　　　　　60
Videlicet, a brothel, or so forth.
See you now;
Your bait of falsehood takes this carp of truth;
And thus do we of wisdom and of reach,
With windlasses, and with assays of bias,　　　65
By indirections find directions out:
So by my former lecture and advice
Shall you my son. You have me, have you not?

Reynaldo My lord, I have.

Polonius　　　　　　　　God be wi' you; fare you well.

Reynaldo Good my lord!　　　　　　　　　　70

Polonius Observe his inclination in yourself.

Reynaldo I shall, my lord.

Polonius And let him ply his music.

Reynaldo　　　　　　　　　　Well, my lord.

Polonius Farewell!
[Exit REYNALDO. Enter OPHELIA]
　　　　　　　How now, Ophelia! what's the matter?

Ophelia O! my lord, my lord, I have been so affrighted!　75

Polonius With what, in the name of God?

Ophelia My lord, as I was sewing in my closet,
Lord Hamlet, with his doublet all unbrac'd;
No hat upon his head; his stockings foul'd,
Ungarter'd, and down gyved to his ankle;　　　80
Pale as his shirt; his knees knocking each other;
And with a look so piteous in purport
As if he had been loosed out of hell
To speak of horrors, he comes before me.

Polonius Mad for thy love?

Ophelia　　　　　　　　My lord, I do not know;　85
But truly I do fear it.

61.	*Videlicet:* (Latin) that is to say.
63.	*carp:* a fish, known for its subtlety in avoiding capture.
64.	*we . . . reach:* we men of wisdom and breadth of understanding.
65.	*windlasses:* roundabout means.
	assays of bias: This is a metaphor from the game of lawn bowling; the weight in the ball, which causes it to follow a curved line, is called the bias. Hence the meaning of the phrase is "indirect attempts."
66.	*By indirections . . . directions out:* By indirect means, we find out how to proceed.
68.	*You have me:* You understand me.
70.	*Good my lord:* A common form of courtesy and respect, this inversion of "my good lord" is frequent throughout the play.
71.	*in:* for.
73.	*let . . . music:* Let him go his own way and enjoy himself; allow him to give his own pretty story.

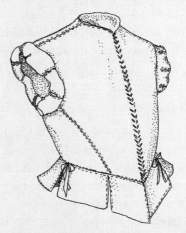

Hamlet's doublet is "unbrac'd" when he encounters Ophelia.

77.	*closet:* private room.
78.	*doublet:* a short, close-fitting coat that was fastened (braced) to the hose (short breeches) by laces. When a man was relaxing or careless of appearance, he "unbrac'd," much like a man today loosens his tie or takes off his suit jacket.
80.	*down gyved:* fallen, like fetters, about his ankles.
85.	*Mad for thy love?:* Polonius's assumption is natural, because Hamlet's appearance was the conventional one of a disappointed lover.

Polonius   What said he?

Ophelia He took me by the wrist and held me hard,
Then goes he to the length of all his arm,
And with his other hand thus o'er his brow,
He falls to such perusal of my face   90
As he would draw it. Long stay'd he so;
At last, a little shaking of mine arm,
And thrice his head thus waving up and down,
He rais'd a sigh so piteous and profound
That it did seem to shatter all his bulk   95
And end his being. That done, he lets me go,
And with his head over his shoulder turn'd,
He seem'd to find his way without his eyes;
For out o' doors he went without their help,
And to the last bended their light on me.   100

Polonius Come, go with me; I will go seek the king.
This is the very ecstasy of love,
Whose violent property fordoes itself
And leads the will to desperate undertakings
As oft as any passion under heaven   105
That does afflict our natures. I am sorry.
What! have you given him any hard words of late?

Ophelia No, my good lord; but, as you did command,
I did repel his letters and denied
His access to me.

Polonius   That hath made him mad.   110
I am sorry that with better heed and judgment
I had not quoted him; I fear'd he did but trifle,
And meant to wrack thee; but, beshrew my jealousy!
By heaven, it is as proper to our age
To cast beyond ourselves in our opinions   115
As it is common for the younger sort
To lack discretion. Come, go we to the king:
This must be known; which, being kept close, might
    move
More grief to hide than hate to utter love.   120
Come. *[Exeunt]*

91. *As:* as if.

102. *ecstasy:* madness

103. *property:* nature.

     fordoes: destroys.

110. *access:* admittance.

112. *quoted:* noted.

113. *beshrew:* a plague upon.

     jealousy: suspicion.

114. *proper:* natural.

115. *cast beyond ourselves:* look beyond what we
     know or understand.

COMMENTARY

The mood in this scene stands in stark contrast to the one we have just witnessed between Hamlet and his father's ghost. Whereas Hamlet and his father have a loving and loyal relationship, capable of spanning the gulf between the living and the dead, Polonius and Laertes have a relationship based on lies and mistrust.

We earlier heard Ophelia hint that Laertes went to Paris for "dalliance" — a word that implies frivolous playing, especially with women. For that reason, perhaps Polonius is somewhat justified in wanting to know how the money he sends Laertes is being spent. Still, to spy on one's own child certainly implies a relationship not founded on trust.

Polonius sends his servant Reynaldo to Paris, ostensibly to bring money to Laertes. In reality, he sends Reynaldo to find out what Laertes is doing and to report back to Polonius. Control, or the illusion of it, is of paramount importance to Polonius.

Polonius's sense of control is based on his ability to eavesdrop, gossip, and spy, all the while acting like an absentminded, forgetful old man. He seems unaware that this kind of intrusion into other people's lives can have disastrous results. His meddling will eventually have deadly consequences for his entire family.

Hamlet's bizarre behavior

As soon as Reynaldo leaves, Ophelia rushes in, obviously frightened and distressed. She has just encountered Hamlet, and she describes the incident to her father. She was alone, sewing, when Hamlet entered, disheveled and distracted, pale and shaken. He looked at her sadly, grabbed her wrist, stared at her face, and sighed deeply. Then, without ever having said a word, still looking at her, Hamlet left.

From this description, Hamlet appears to be a caricature of the Elizabethan melancholy lover. He is disheveled and pale, unable to make a sound beyond a sigh. Hamlet's bizarre behavior in this scene can be interpreted in at least two ways. On one hand, this behavior may be part of Hamlet's feigned "antic disposition." On the other hand, his actions may be the genuine result of his keenly felt disappointment in Ophelia. Hamlet never speaks to Ophelia in this scene, which limits our ability to interpret its meaning precisely.

Mel Gibson and Helena Bonham Carter star in the 1990 film version of *Hamlet. Everett Collection*

If interpreted the first way, Hamlet may be using Ophelia as a pawn in his game of cat-and-mouse. If he feigns madness, surely she will report it to Polonius, who will then tell the king and queen. As Hamlet indicated at the end of Act I, he wants to create the impression that he is not stable.

But the second interpretation seems plausible as well. Hamlet may have spent the day trying to come to terms with the horrifying news he received from the ghost. He may have wanted to talk to someone, and, naturally, Ophelia would be the one he would choose as confidante. But Ophelia has been avoiding him and sending his letters back unopened. Ophelia's rejection could not have come at a worse time for Hamlet. Perhaps his behavior in her room was meant to convey his disappointment.

A dangerous assumption

When Polonius asks Ophelia if she has been talking to Hamlet, she explains that she ceased contact with Hamlet, just as her father ordered. Polonius impetuously declares Hamlet "mad" because of his now rebuffed love for Ophelia (110). He regrets that he was so hasty in his judgment of Hamlet's intentions and admits that he was jealous. Polonius has realized that he was wrong about Hamlet; the prince was not merely toying with Ophelia's affections but did in fact love her. To his credit, Polonius sounds genuinely sorry for his interference, and lines 114–117 reveal a Polonius that we will not see again — one who makes logical sense. Still, in his need to feel important, he decides to bring this news immediately to the king.

Act II, Scene 2

This is the longest scene in the play, and the action involves five distinct movements: 1) The king has summoned Hamlet's childhood friends Rosencrantz and Guildenstern to find out why Hamlet has changed so drastically. 2) Danish ambassadors inform Claudius that Fortinbras, nephew of the king of Norway, will not invade Denmark. 3) Polonius tells the king and queen that Ophelia's rejection has caused Hamlet's madness. Polonius suggests that he and the king eavesdrop on Hamlet and Ophelia. 4) Rosencrantz and Guildenstern begin their efforts on behalf of Claudius. 5). Hamlet temporarily forgets his melancholy when a traveling troupe of actors arrives in Elsinore. Hamlet plans to use a play to prove Claudius's guilt.

ACT II, SCENE 2
A room in the castle.

[Enter KING, QUEEN, ROSENCRANTZ, GUILDEN-
   STERN, and Attendants]

King Welcome, dear Rosencrantz and Guildenstern!
  Moreover that we much did long to see you,
  The need we have to use you did provoke
  Our hasty sending. Something have you heard
  Of Hamlet's transformation; so call it,   5
  Sith nor the exterior nor the inward man
  Resembles that it was. What it should be
  More than his father's death, that thus hath put him
  So much from the understanding of himself,
  I cannot dream of: I entreat you both,   10
  That, being of so young days brought up with him,
  And sith so neighbour'd to his youth and humour,
  That you vouchsafe your rest here in our court
  Some little time; so by your companies
  To draw him on to pleasures, and to gather,   15
  So much as from occasion you may glean,
  Whe'r aught to us unknown afflicts him thus,
  That open'd lies within our remedy.

Queen Good gentlemen, he hath much talk'd of you;
  And sure I am two men there are not living   20
  To whom he more adheres. If it will please you
  To show us so much gentry and good will

NOTES

2.   *Moreover:* besides.

6.   *Sith:* since.

11.   *of . . . days:* since youth.
12.   *neighbour'd:* close to.
     humour: behavior.
13.   *vouchsafe . . . rest:* agree to stay.

16.   *from occasion:* by chance.

18.   *open'd:* revealed.

21.   *To . . . adheres:* whom he regards more highly.
22.   *gentry:* courtesy.

As to expend your time with us awhile,
For the supply and profit of our hope,
Your visitation shall receive such thanks   25
As fits a king's remembrance.

Rosencrantz   Both your majesties
Might, by the sovereign power you have of us,
Put your dread pleasures more into command
Than to entreaty.

Guildenstern   But we both obey,
And here give up ourselves in the full bent,   30
To lay our service freely at your feet,
To be commanded.

King Thanks, Rosencrantz and gentle Guildenstern.

Queen Thanks, Guildenstern and gentle Rosencrantz;
And I beseech you instantly to visit   35
My too much changed son. Go, some of you,
And bring these gentlemen where Hamlet is.

Guildenstern Heavens make our presence and our practices
Pleasant and helpful to him!

Queen   Ay, amen!
[*Exeunt ROSENCRANTZ, GUILDENSTERN, and some
Attendants. Enter POLONIUS*]

Polonius The ambassadors from Norway, my good lord,   40
Are joyfully return'd.

King Thou still hast been the father of good news.

Polonius Have I, my Lord? Assure you, my good liege,
I hold my duty, as I hold my soul,
Both to my God and to my gracious king;   45
And I do think — or else this brain of mine
Hunts not the trail of policy so sure
As it hath us'd to do — that I have found
The very cause of Hamlet's lunacy.

King O! speak of that; that do I long to hear.   50

Polonius Give first admittance to the ambassadors;
My news shall be the fruit to that great feast.

King Thyself do grace to them, and bring them in.
[*Exit POLONIUS*]

24. *supply and profit:* fulfillment and profitable conclusion.

30. *in the full bent:* completely. Like a bow that is bent as far as it can be bent.

38. *practices:* proceedings.

42. *still:* always.

52. *fruit:* dessert.

53. *grace:* honor, with a pun on the prayer before meals.

He tells me, my dear Gertrude, he hath found
The head and source of all your son's distemper.   55

Queen I doubt it is no other but the main;
His father's death, and our o'erhasty marriage.

King Well, we shall sift him.
*[Re-enter POLONIUS, with VOLTIMAND and
    CORNELIUS]*
                                    Welcome, my good friends!
Say, Voltimand, what from our brother Norway?

Voltimand Most fair return of greetings and desires.   60
Upon our first, he sent out to suppress
His nephew's levies, which to him appear'd
To be a preparation 'gainst the Polack;
But, better look'd into, he truly found
It was against your highness: whereat griev'd,   65
That so his sickness, age, and impotence
Was falsely borne in hand, sends out arrests
On Fortinbras; which he, in brief, obeys,
Receives rebuke from Norway, and, in fine,
Makes vow before his uncle never more   70
To give the assay of arms against your majesty.
Whereon old Norway, overcome with joy,
Gives him three thousand crowns in annual fee,
And his commission to employ those soldiers,
So levied as before, against the Polack;   75
With an entreaty, herein further shown, *[Giving a paper]*
That it might please you to give quiet pass
Through your dominions for this enterprise,
On such regards of safety and allowance
As therein are set down.

King   It likes us well;   80
And at our more consider'd time we'll read,
Answer, and think upon this business:
Meantime we thank you for your well-took labour.
Go to your rest; at night we'll feast together:
Most welcome home.

[Exeunt VOLTIMAND and CORNELIUS]

Polonius   This business is well ended.   85
My liege, and madam, to expostulate
What majesty should be, what duty is,

55. *distemper:* mental disorder.

56. *the main:* primary cause.

58. *sift him:* like sifting flour or grain.

61. *first:* when we first spoke.

67. *borne in hand:* deceived.

arrests: orders to stop.

69. *in fine:* in the end.

71. *assay of arms:* try to raise.

77. *quiet pass:* unmolested passage.

79. *regards . . . allowance:* safeguards and permission.

80. *likes:* pleases.

81. *more consider'd:* when we have time for more consideration.

83. *well-took:* well-handled.

86. *expostulate:* debate.

Why day is day, night night, and time is time,
Were nothing but to waste night, day, and time.
Therefore, since brevity is the soul of wit,   90
And tediousness the limbs and outward flourishes,
I will be brief. Your noble son is mad:
Mad call I it; for, to define true madness,
What is 't but to be nothing else but mad?
But let that go.

Queen   More matter, with less art.   95

Polonius Madam, I swear I use no art at all.
That he is mad, 'tis true; 'tis true 'tis pity;
And pity 'tis 'tis true; a foolish figure;
But farewell it, for I will use no art.
Mad let us grant him, then; and now remains   100
That we find out the cause of this effect,
Or rather say, the cause of this defect,
For this effect defective comes by cause;
Thus it remains, and the remainder thus.
Perpend.   105
I have a daughter, have while she is mine;
Who, in her duty and obedience, mark,
Hath given me this: now, gather, and surmise.
To the celestial, and my soul's idol, the most
    beautified Ophelia —
That's an ill phrase, a vile phrase; 'beautified' is a   110
vile phrase; but you shall hear. Thus:
In her excellent white bosom, these, &c.

Queen Came this from Hamlet to her?

Polonius Good madam, stay awhile; I will be faithful.
Doubt thou the stars are fire;   115
Doubt that the sun doth move;
Doubt truth to be a liar;
But never doubt I love.
O dear Ophelia! I am ill at these numbers: I have not art
to reckon my groans; but that I love thee best, O most   120
best! believe it. Adieu.
Thine evermore, most dear lady, whilst this
machine is to him,
Hamlet
This in obedience hath my daughter shown me;   125

90.   *wit:* wisdom.

91.   *flourishes:* ornaments.

95.   *More matter, with less art:* Get down to specifics and never mind the rhetoric.

96.   *Madam, I swear I use no art at all:* Polonius is secretly pleased by what he considers to be the queen's flattering reference to his rhetorical powers.

101.   *effect:* result.

102.   *defect:* Hamlet's madness.

103.   *Effect defective . . . cause:* His madness must have a cause.

105.   *Perpend:* ponder; a stodgy, affected word.

108.   *surmise:* guess the meaning.

109.   *celestial:* heavenly.

       beautified: beautiful.

119.   *numbers:* verses.

123.   *machine:* the human body.

And more above, hath his solicitings,
As they fell out by time, by means, and place,
All given to mine ear.

King   But how hath she
Receiv'd his love?

Polonius   What do you think of me?

King As of a man faithful and honourable.   130

Polonius I would fain prove so. But what might you think,
When I had seen this hot love on the wing —
As I perceiv'd it (I must tell you that)
Before my daughter told me, — what might you,
Or my dear majesty, your queen here, think,   135
If I had play'd the desk or table-book,
Or given my heart a winking, mute and dumb,
Or look'd upon this love with idle sight;
What might you think? No, I went round to work,
And my young mistress thus I did bespeak: 140
'Lord Hamlet is a prince, out of thy star;
This must not be:' and then I prescripts gave her,
That she should lock herself from his resort,
Admit no messengers, receive no tokens.
Which done, she took the fruits of my advice;   145
And he, repulsed, — a short tale to make, —
Fell into a sadness, then into a fast,
Thence to a watch, thence into a weakness,
Thence to a lightness; and by this declension
Into the madness wherein now he raves,   150
And all we mourn for.

King   Do you think 'tis this?

Queen It may be, very like.

Polonius Hath there been such a time, — I'd fain know
    that, —
That I have positively said, ''Tis so,'
When it prov'd otherwise?

King   Not that I know.   155

Polonius Take this from this, if this be otherwise:
    [Pointing to his head and shoulder]

126.	*more above:* moreover.
127.	*fell out:* occurred.
131.	*fain:* wish.
133.	*(I . . . that):* Polonius is trying to prove how extremely perceptive he is.
136.	*If . . . table-book:* if I had kept this secret in my mind like a thing shut up in a desk or book.
137.	*given my heart . . . dumb:* had connived at the affair by saying nothing.
138.	*with sight:* with an indifferent eye.
139.	*round:* Polonius really means straight, but it is his nature to speak indirectly.
140.	*bespeak:* address.
141.	*out of thy star:* beyond your station in life. Stars were believed to govern men's lives.
142.	*prescripts:* instructions, commands.
145.	*took the fruits of:* followed.
148.	*watch:* sleeplessness.
149.	*lightness:* light-headedness.
	this declension: these stages in decline.
151.	*And . . . for:* for which we all mourn.
152.	*like:* likely.

If circumstances lead me, I will find
Where truth is hid, though it were hid indeed
Within the centre.

King   How may we try it further?

Polonius. You know sometimes he walks four hours
    together   160
Here in the lobby.

Queen   So he does indeed.

Polonius. At such a time I'll loose my daughter to him;
Be you and I behind an arras then;
Mark the encounter; if he love her not,
And be not from his reason fallen thereon,   165
Let me be no assistant for a state,
But keep a farm, and carters.

King   We will try it.

Queen But look, where sadly the poor wretch comes reading.

Polonius Away! I do beseech you, both away.
I'll board him presently.
[Exeunt KING, QUEEN, and Attendants. Enter HAMLET,
    reading]
                 O! give me leave.   170
How does my good Lord Hamlet?

Hamlet Well, God a-mercy.

Polonius Do you know me, my lord?

Hamlet Excellent well; you are a fishmonger.

Polonius Not I, my lord.   175

Hamlet Then I would you were so honest a man.

Polonius Honest, my lord!

Hamlet Ay, sir; to be honest, as this world goes, is to
be one man picked out of ten thousand.

Polonius That's very true, my lord.   180

Hamlet For if the sun breed maggots in a dead dog,
being a good kissing carrion, — Have you a daughter?

Polonius I have, my lord.

---

159.   *centre:* center of the earth.

      try it: test it.

163.   *arras:* a tapestry commonly hung in Medieval castles from ceiling to floor to prevent drafts.

167.   *keep . . . carters:* become a farmer.

170.   *board:* accost.

      presently: immediately.

172.   *God-a-mercy:* by God's mercy, or as we would say, "Thank God."

174.   *fishmonger:* someone who sells fish, or someone who sells women.

182.   *carrion:* dead flesh.

Hamlet Let her not walk i' the sun: conception is a
blessing; but as your daughter may conceive, friend,   185
look to 't.

Polonius *[Aside]* How say you by that? Still harping on
my daughter: yet he knew me not at first; he
said I was a fishmonger: he is far gone, far gone:
and truly in my youth I suffered much extremity for   190
love; very near this. I'll speak to him again. What
do you read, my lord?

Hamlet Words, words, words.

Polonius What is the matter, my lord?

Hamlet Between who?   195

Polonius I mean the matter that you read, my lord.

Hamlet Slanders, sir: for the satirical rogue says here
that old men have grey beards, that their faces are
wrinkled, their eyes purging thick amber and
plumtree gum, and that they have a plentiful lack of   200
wit, together with most weak hams: all which, sir,
though I most powerfully and potently believe, yet I
hold it not honesty to have it thus set down; for
yourself, sir, shall grow old as I am, if, like a crab, you
could go backward.   205

Polonius *[Aside]* Though this be madness, yet there is
method in 't. Will you walk out of the air, my
lord?

Hamlet Into my grave?

Polonius Indeed, that is out o' the air. *[Aside]*   210
How pregnant sometimes his replies are! a happiness
that often madness hits on, which reason and
sanity could not so prosperously be delivered of. I
will leave him, and suddenly contrive the means of
meeting between him and my daughter. My honourable   215
lord, I will most humbly take my leave of you.

Hamlet You cannot, sir, take from me anything that
I will more willingly part withal; except my life,
except my life, except my life.

Polonius. Fare you well, my lord. *[Going]*   220

186. *look to 't:* take care.

187. *How . . . that?:* What do you know about that?

199. *purging:* discharging.

amber: resin, hence any yellowish, gummy fluid.

203. *not honesty:* not decent, proper.

207. *method:* order, sense.

211. *pregnant:* full of suggested meaning.

happiness: fortuitous elegance.

213. *prosperously . . . of:* successfully express (give birth to).

214. *suddenly:* very soon, immediately.

218. *withal:* with.

Hamlet These tedious old fools!

[Enter ROSENCRANTZ and GUILDENSTERN]

Polonius You go to seek the Lord Hamlet; there he is.

Rosencrantz *[To POLONIUS]* God save you, sir!

[Exit POLONIUS]

Guildenstern Mine honoured lord!

Rosencrantz My most dear lord!　　　　　　　　　　225

Hamlet My excellent good friends! How dost thou,
Guildenstern? Ah, Rosencrantz! Good lads, how do
ye both?

Rosencrantz As the indifferent children of the earth.

Guildenstern Happy in that we are not over-happy;　　230
On Fortune's cap we are not the very button.

Hamlet Nor the soles of her shoe?

Rosencrantz Neither, my lord.

Hamlet Then you live about her waist, or in the
middle of her favours?　　　　　　　　　　235

Guildenstern Faith, her privates we.

Hamlet In the secret parts of Fortune? O! most true;
she is a strumpet. What news?

Rosencrantz None, my lord, but that the world's
grown honest.　　　　　　　　　　240

Hamlet Then is doomsday near; but your news is
not true. Let me question more in particular: what
have you, my good friends, deserved at the hands of
Fortune, that she sends you to prison hither?

Guildenstern Prison, my lord!　　　　　　　　　　245

Hamlet Denmark's a prison.

Rosencrantz Then is the world one.

Hamlet A goodly one; in which there are many
confines, wards, and dungeons, Denmark being one
o' the worst.　　　　　　　　　　250

Rosencrantz We think not so, my lord.

229.　*indifferent children of the earth:* so-so, middling
well.

231.　*button:* ornamental button at the top of a cap.

235.　*favours:* attractions, charms.

236.　*privates:* intimates, friends.

241.　*doomsday:* the day of judgment.

249.　*confines, wards:* cells.

Hamlet Why then, 'tis none to you; for there is nothing either good or bad, but thinking makes it so: to me it is a prison.

Rosencrantz Why, then your ambition makes it one; 'tis too narrow for your mind.   255

Hamlet O God! I could be bounded in a nutshell, and count myself a king of infinite space, were it not that I have bad dreams.

Guildenstern Which dreams, indeed, are ambition, for the very substance of the ambitious is merely the shadow of a dream.   260

Hamlet A dream itself is but a shadow.

Rosencrantz Truly, and I hold ambition of so airy and light a quality that it is but a shadow's shadow.   265

Hamlet Then are our beggars bodies, and our monarchs and outstretched heroes the beggars' shadows. Shall we to the court? for, by my fay, I cannot reason.

Rosencrantz and Guildenstern We'll wait upon you.

Hamlet No such matter; I will not sort you with the   270
rest of my servants, for, to speak to you like an honest man, I am most dreadfully attended. But, in beaten way of friendship, what make you at Elsinore?

Rosencrantz To visit you, my lord; no other occasion.

Hamlet Beggar that I am, I am even poor in thanks;   275
but I thank you: and sure, dear friends, my thanks are too dear a halfpenny. Were you not sent for? Is it your own inclining? Is it a free visitation? Come, come, deal justly with me: come, come; nay, speak.

Guildenstern What should we say, my lord?   280

Hamlet Why anything, but to the purpose. You were sent for; and there is a kind of confession in your looks which your modesties have not craft enough to colour: I know the good king and queen have sent for you.

Rosencrantz To what end, my lord?   285

---

255. *ambition:* Rosencrantz thinks that thwarted ambition may be the cause of Hamlet's distemper.

259. *bad dreams:* possibly a reference to the haunting thoughts of his father's death.

261. *substance . . . ambitious:* successes of the ambitious man.

262. *shadow . . . dream:* imperfect realization of his desires.

266–267 *Then . . . shadows:* If ambition is a "shadow's shadow," then kings (who are ambitious) are the shadows of beggars (who have no ambition).

267. *outstretched:* aspiring.

268. *fay:* faith, with a pun on fairy.

reason: argue.

269. *We'll wait upon you:* We will be your attendants at court. Hamlet purposely takes the more literal meaning.

270. *No such matter:* not at all.

sort: class.

273. *beaten way of friendship:* speaking as friend to friend.

what . . . Elsinore?: What are you doing at Elsinore?

277. *too . . . halfpenny:* not worth a halfpenny.

278. *free visitation:* voluntary visit.

283. *modesties:* senses of fitness.

colour: conceal.

Hamlet That you must teach me. But let me conjure you, by the rights of our fellowship, by the consonancy of our youth, by the obligation of our ever-preserved love, and by what more dear a better proposer could charge you withal, be even and direct with me, whether you were sent for or no!   290

Rosencrantz *[Aside to GUILDENSTERN]* What say you?

Hamlet *[Aside]* Nay, then, I have an eye of you. If you love me, hold not off.   295

Guildenstern My lord, we were sent for.

Hamlet I will tell you why; so shall my anticipation prevent your discovery, and your secrecy to the king and queen moult no feather. I have of late, — but wherefore I know not, — lost all my mirth, forgone   300 all custom of exercises; and indeed it goes so heavily with my disposition that this goodly frame, the earth, seems to me a sterile promontory; this most excellent canopy, the air, look you, this brave o'erhanging firmament, this majestical roof fretted with golden   305 fire, why, it appears no other thing to me but a foul and pestilent congregation of vapours. What a piece of work is a man! How noble in reason! how infinite in faculty! in form, in moving, how express and admirable! in action how like an angel! in apprehension how   310 like a god! the beauty of the world! the paragon of animals! And yet, to me, what is this quintessence of dust? man delights not me; no, nor woman neither, though, by your smiling, you seem to say so.

Rosencrantz My lord, there was no such stuff in my   315 thoughts.

Hamlet Why did you laugh then, when I said, 'man delights not me?'

Rosencrantz To think, my lord, if you delight not in man, what lenten entertainment the players shall   320 receive from you: we coted them on the way; and hither are they coming, to offer you service.

Hamlet He that plays the King shall be welcome; his majesty shall have tribute of me; the adventurous

286.   *That . . . me:* You will have to tell me that.

287.   *conjure:* require of you.

287.   *fellowship:* comradeship.

288.   *consonancy:* concord, harmoniousness.

289–290.   *better proposer:* more skillful asker. (He may have Claudius in mind.)

290.   *even:* fair

294.   *I have an eye of you:* If that is the way things are, I will keep my eye on you.

297–299.   *so . . . feather:* You do not have to tell me, so you need not betray the confidence of the king and queen.

304.   *canopy:* covering.

305.   *firmament:* sky.

       fretted: ornamented, decorated like the painted ceiling over the stage at the Globe.

309.   *faculty:* active quality or virtue.

       moving: movement.

       express: perfectly modeled for its purpose.

310.   *apprehension:* understanding.

311.   *paragon:* flower of perfection.

312.   *quintessence:* perfection.

320.   *lenten:* meager, as in Lent.

       entertainment: welcome.

321.   *coted:* overtook.

Knight shall use his foil and target; the Lover shall   325
not sigh gratis; the Humorous Man shall end his part
in peace; the Clown shall make those laugh whose
lungs are tickle o' the sere; and the Lady shall say her
mind freely, or the blank verse shall halt for't. What
players are they?   330

Rosencrantz Even those you were wont to take
delight in, the tragedians of the city.

Hamlet How chances it they travel? their residence,
both in reputation and profit, was better both ways.

Rosencrantz I think their inhibition comes by the   335
means of the late innovation.

Hamlet Do they hold the same estimation they did
when I was in the city? Are they so followed?

Rosencrantz No, indeed they are not.

Hamlet How comes it? Do they grow rusty?   340

Rosencrantz Nay, their endeavour keeps in the
wonted pace: but there is, sir, an aery of children,
little eyases, that cry out on the top of question, and
are most tyrannically clapped for 't: these are now the
fashion, and so berattle the common stages, — so they   345
call them, — that many wearing rapiers are afraid of
goose-quills, and dare scarce come thither.

Hamlet What! are they children? who maintains 'em?
how are they escoted? Will they pursue the
quality no longer than they can sing? will they not say   350
afterwards, if they should grow themselves to common
players, — as it is most like, if their means are not
better, — their writers do them wrong, to make them
exclaim against their own succession?

Rosencrantz Faith, there has been much to-do on   355
both sides: and the nation holds it no sin to tarre them
to controversy: there was, for a while, no money bid for
argument, unless the Poet and the Player went to cuffs
in the question.

Hamlet Is it possible?   360

Guildenstern O! there has been much throwing about
of brains.

---

325. *foil and target:* fencing rapier and small shield.

326. *gratis:* for nothing.

      Humorous Man: the player of character parts.

328. *tickle o' the sere:* made to laugh easily.

329. *halt:* limp.

333–354. This dialogue refers to the stage war between the children's companies and the companies of adult actors, a conflict that was raging at the time the play was written. (See commentary.)

333. *travel:* go on tour.

      residence: acting in the city.

335. *inhibition:* curtailment.

336. *late innovation:* recent change in the established order of things.

341–342. *endeavour . . . pace:* They try as hard as ever.

342. *aery:* nest.

343. *eyases:* young hawks.

      cry . . . question: are heard above all others.

344. *tyrannically:* outrageously. ·

345. *berattle:* abuse.

      common stages: ordinary theatres (where the adult professional players performed).

346–347. *many wearing . . . goose-quills:* Many adults are afraid of being ridiculed by the satirists who write for the boy actors.

349. *escoted:* paid.

350. *quality:* acting profession.

352. *means:* financial resources.

354. *exclaim . . . succession:* ridicule the profession they will later work in.

356. *tarre:* urge.

358. *argument:* plot of play.

      cuffs: battle.

Hamlet Do the boys carry it away?

Rosencrantz Ay, that they do, my lord; Hercules and his load too.   365

Hamlet It is not very strange; for my uncle is King of Denmark, and those that would make mows at him while my father lived, give twenty, forty, fifty, a hundred ducats a-piece for his picture in little. 'Sblood, there is something in this more than   370 natural, if philosophy could find it out.

[Flourish of trumpets within]

Guildenstern There are the players.

Hamlet Gentlemen, you are welcome to Elsinore. Your hands, come then; the appurtenance of welcome is fashion and ceremony: let me comply with you in this   375 garb, lest my extent to the players — which, I tell you, must show fairly outward — should more appear like entertainment than yours. You are welcome; but my uncle-father and aunt-mother are deceived.

Guildenstern In what, my dear lord?   380

Hamlet I am but mad north-north-west: when the wind is southerly I know a hawk from a handsaw.

[Enter POLONIUS]

Polonius Well be with you, gentlemen!

Hamlet Hark you, Guildenstern; and you too; at each ear a hearer: that great baby you see there is   385 not yet out of his swaddling-clouts.

Rosencrantz Happily he's the second time come to them; for they say an old man is twice a child.

Hamlet I will prophesy he comes to tell me of the players; mark it. You say right, sir; o' Monday   390 morning; 'twas so indeed.

Polonius My lord, I have news to tell you.

Hamlet My lord, I have news to tell you. When Roscius was an actor in Rome, —

Polonius The actors are come hither, my lord.   395

Hamlet Buz, buz!

---

363.   *carry it away:* win the day.

364–365.   *Hercules and his load:* a reference to the Globe, whose identifying sign featured Hercules carrying the globe on his shoulders.

367.   *mows:* grimaces. Hamlet is not surprised at the sudden revolution of popular favor.

369.   *picture in little:* miniature.

370.   *'Sblood:* by God's blood, a common oath.

371.   *philosophy:* science.

374.   *appurtenance:* proper accompaniment.

375.   *fashion and ceremony:* formal ceremony.

375–376.   *comply . . . garb:* put it into practice in this way, such as by shaking hands.

376.   *extent:* extending of formal ceremony.

378.   *entertainment:* welcome.

381.   *north-north-west:* on one point of the compass only.

382.   *I know . . . handsaw:* I am not as mad as you think.

    hawk: may refer to hack, a tool of the ax family.

386.   *clouts:* clothes.

394.   *Roscius:* the most famous of ancient Roman actors.

396.   *Buz, buz:* a slang expression for "tell me something I don't know."

Polonius Upon my honour, —

Hamlet Then came each actor on his ass, —

Polonius The best actors in the world, either for
tragedy, comedy, history, pastoral, pastoral-comical,   400
historical-pastoral, tragical-historical, tragical-comical-
historical-pastoral, scene individable, or poem unlimited: Seneca cannot be too heavy, nor Plautus too
light. For the law of writ and the liberty, these are
the only men.   405

Hamlet O Jephthah, judge of Israel, what a treasure
hadst thou!

Polonius What a treasure had he, my lord?

Hamlet Why
One fair daughter and no more,   410
The which he loved passing well.

Polonius *[Aside]* Still on my daughter.

Hamlet Am I not i' the right, old Jephthah?

Polonius If you call me Jephthah, my lord, I have a
daughter that I love passing well.   415

Hamlet Nay, that follows not.

Polonius What follows, then, my lord?

Hamlet Why,
As by lot, God wot.
And then, you know,   420
It came to pass, as most like it was. —
The first row of the pious chanson will show you
more; for look where my abridgment comes.
[Enter four or five Players]
You are welcome, masters; welcome, all. I am glad to
see thee well: welcome, good friends. O, my old friend!   425
Why, thy face is valanced since I saw thee last: comest
thou to beard me in Denmark? What! my young
lady and mistress! By 'r lady, your ladyship is nearer
heaven than when I saw you last, by the altitude of a
chopine. Pray God, your voice, like a piece of uncurrent   430
gold, be not cracked within the ring. Masters,
you are all welcome. We'll e'en to 't like French
falconers, fly at anything we see: we'll have a speech

399–405. *The best actors . . . the only men:* Polonius may be reading from the players' official license, offered on arrival.

402. *scene individable:* preserving the unities.

402–403. *poem unlimited:* a play that observed none of the ancient rules.

403. *Seneca, Plautus:* Roman writers of tragedy and comedy.

404. *law of writ:* classical plays.

liberty: modern plays.

406. *Jephthah:* Scriptural character from Judges 11.

410–411. *One . . . well:* Hamlet quotes from a ballad about Jephthah.

419. *wot:* knows.

422. *row:* line.

pious chanson: holy song.

423. *abridgment:* cutting short, such as an interruption.

425. *old friend:* the leading player.

426. *valanced:* bearded.

427–428. *young lady:* Female roles on the Elizabethan stage were taken by trained boy actors, and this is a reference to one of them.

430. *chopine:* a high-heeled shoe. In other words, the boy had grown.

430–431. *uncurrent gold:* bad gold coin.

431. *cracked . . . ring:* Seeing how much the boy has grown, Hamlet is afraid his voice may be changing.

straight. Come, give us a taste of your quality; come,
a passionate speech.　　　　　　　　　　　　　　　　　　　　435

First Player What speech, my good lord?

Hamlet I heard thee speak me a speech once, but it
was never acted; or, if it was, not above once; for
the play, I remember, pleased not the million; 'twas
caviare to the general: but it was — as I received it,　　　440
and others, whose judgments in such matters cried in
the top of mine — an excellent play, well digested in
the scenes, set down with as much modesty as cunning.
I remember one said there were no sallets in the
lines to make the matter savoury, nor no matter in the　　445
phrase that might indict the author of affectation; but
called it an honest method, as wholesome as sweet,
and by very much more handsome than fine. One
speech in it I chiefly loved; 'twas Aeneas' tale to Dido
and thereabout of it especially, where he speaks of　　　450
Priam's slaughter. If it live in your memory, begin
at this line: let me see, let me see: —
The rugged Pyrrhus, like the Hyrcanian beast, —
'tis not so, it begins with Pyrrhus: —
The rugged Pyrrhus, he, whose sable arm,　　　　　　455
Black as his purpose, did the night resemble
When he lay couched in the ominous horse,
Hath now this dread and black complexion smear'd
With heraldry more dismal; head to foot
Now is he total gules, horridly trick'd　　　　　　　　460
With blood of fathers, mothers, daughters, sons,
Bak'd and impasted with the parching streets,
That lend a tyrannous and damned light
To their vile murders: roasted in wrath and fire,
And thus o'er-sized with coagulated gore,　　　　　　465
With eyes like carbuncles, the hellish Pyrrhus
Old grandsire Priam seeks.
So proceed you.

Polonius 'Fore God, my lord, well spoken; with
good accent and good discretion.

First Player　　　　　　　　　　　Anon, he finds him　　470
Striking too short at Greeks; his antique sword,
Rebellious to his arm, lies where it falls,

434.　　*quality:* skill as an actor.

440.　　*caviare . . . general:* too great a delicacy for the common herd.

441–442.　*cried . . . mine:* surpassed mine.

442.　　*digested:* organized.

443.　　*modesty:* moderation, hence also good taste.

444.　　*sallets:* tasty bits.

445–446.　*no . . . phrase:* nothing in the language.

448.　　*fine:* subtle.

449.　　*Aeneas' . . . Dido:* the story of the sack of Troy as told to Queen Dido by Aeneas. (Virgil's *Aeneid* contains the story.)

451.　　*Priam:* the King of Troy.

453.　　*Pyrrhus:* the son of Achilles and one of the Greeks concealed in the famous wooden horse.

　　　　Hyrcanian beast: tiger from Hyrcania, mentioned in the *Aeneid.*

455.　　*sable:* black.

457.　　*ominous horse:* fateful, especially for the Trojans.

459.　　*heraldry:* painting or insignia.

460.　　*total gules:* completely red.

　　　　trick'd: painted.

462.　　*impasted:* made into a paste (the slain, not Pyrrhus).

465.　　*o'er-sized . . . gore:* painted over with congealed blood.

466.　　*carbuncles:* precious stones of fiery red color.

470.　　*accent:* enunciation.

　　　　discretion: interpretation and understanding.

　　　　Anon: after a while.

Repugnant to command. Unequal match'd,
Pyrrhus at Priam drives; in rage strikes wide;
But with the whiff and wind of his fell sword   475
The unnerved father falls. Then senseless Ilium,
Seeming to feel this blow, with flaming top
Stoops to his base, and with a hideous crash
Takes prisoner Pyrrhus' ear: for lo! his sword,
Which was declining on the milky head   480
Of reverend Priam, seem'd i' the air to stick:
So, as a painted tyrant, Pyrrhus stood,
And like a neutral to his will and matter,
Did nothing.
But, as we often see, against some storm,   485
A silence in the heavens, the rack stand still,
The bold winds speechless and the orb below
As hush as death, anon the dreadful thunder
Doth rend the region; so, after Pyrrhus' pause,
Aroused vengeance sets him new a-work;   490
And never did the Cyclops' hammer fall
On Mars's armour, forg'd for proof eterne,
With less remorse than Pyrrhus' bleeding sword
Now falls on Priam.
Out, out, thou strumpet, Fortune! All you gods,   495
In general synod, take away her power;
Break all the spokes and fellies from her wheel,
And bowl the round nave down the hill of heaven,
As low as to the fiends!

Polonius This is too long.   500

Hamlet It shall to the barber's with your beard.
Prithee, say on: he's for a jig or a tale of bawdry,
or he sleeps. Say on; come to Hecuba.

First Player But who, O! who had seen the mobled
queen —

Hamlet 'The mobled queen?' —   505

Polonius That's good; 'mobled queen' is good.

First Player Run barefoot up and down, threat'ning the
flames
With bisson rheum; a clout upon that head
Where late the diadem stood; and, for a robe,
About her lank and all o'er-teemed loins,   510

---

473. *Repugnant to command:* refusing to be used, owing to Priam's weakness.

476. *Ilium:* Troy

478. *Stoops . . . base:* collapses.

479. *Takes . . . ear:* stuns Pyrrhus.

480. *declining:* descending, falling.

482. *painted:* as in a painting, perfectly motionless.

483. *like . . . to:* as if indifferent to.

matter: purpose.

485. *against:* before.

486. *rack:* cloud formations.

487. *orb:* earth.

491. *Cyclops:* the one-eyed giants who assisted Vulcan, the god of fire.

492. *proof eterne:* everlasting protection.

493. *remorse:* pity.

496. *synod:* council.

497. *fellies:* felloes (of a wheel), such as sections of the rim.

498. *nave:* rim.

502. *Prithee:* I pray thee.

jig: a merry dance or tune.

503. *Hecuba:* Priam's queen.

504. *mobled:* wearing ruffled collars popular in Elizabethan England.

508. *bisson rheum:* blinding tears.

clout: rag, cloth.

510. *o'er-teemed:* worn out with childbearing.

A blanket, in the alarm of fear caught up;
Who this had seen, with tongue in venom steep'd,
'Gainst Fortune's state would treason have pronounc'd:
But if the gods themselves did see her then,
When she saw Pyrrhus make malicious sport   515
In mincing with his sword her husband's limbs,
The instant burst of clamour that she made —
Unless things mortal move them not at all —
Would have made milch the burning eyes of heaven,
And passion in the gods.   520

Polonius Look! wh'er he has not turned his colour
and has tears in 's eyes. Prithee, no more.

Hamlet 'Tis well; I'll have thee speak out the rest
soon. Good my lord, will you see the players well
bestowed? Do you hear, let them be well used; for   525
they are the abstracts and brief chronicles of the time:
after your death you were better have a bad epitaph
than their ill report while you live.

Polonius My lord, I will use them according to their
desert.   530

Hamlet God's bodikins, man, much better; use every
man after his desert, and who shall 'scape whipping?
Use them after your own honour and dignity:
the less they deserve, the more merit is in your
bounty. Take them in.   535

Polonius Come, sirs.

Hamlet Follow him, friends: we'll hear a play
to-morrow.
[Exit POLONIUS, with all the Players but the First]
Dost thou hear me, old friend; can you play The
Murder of Gonzago?   540

First Player Ay, my lord.

Hamlet We'll ha't tomorrow night. You could, for a
need, study a speech of some dozen or sixteen lines,
which I would set down and insert in 't, could you
not?   545

First Player Ay, my lord.

512–513. *Who this . . . pronounc'd:* Anyone seeing this would have bitterly pronounced treason against Fortune's tyranny.

519. *milch:* milky, moist.

525. *bestowed:* provided for.

526. *abstracts . . . chronicles:* condensed histories, which are socially useful.

530. *desert:* what they deserve.

531. *God's bodikins:* an oath; literally, by God's little body (the communion wafer).

543. *study:* learn.

Hamlet Very well. Follow that lord; and look you
mock him not. *[Exit First Player. To ROSENCRANTZ
and GUILDENSTERN]* My good friends, I'll
leave you till night; you are welcome to Elsinore.   550

Rosencrantz Good my lord!

[Exeunt ROSENCRANTZ and GUILDENSTERN]

Hamlet Ay, so, God be wi' ye! Now I am alone.
O! what a rogue and peasant slave am I:
Is it not monstrous that this player here,
But in a fiction, in a dream of passion,   555
Could force his soul so to his own conceit
That from her working all his visage wann'd,
Tears in his eyes, distraction in 's aspect,
A broken voice, and his whole function suiting
With forms to his conceit? and all for nothing!   560
For Hecuba!
What's Hecuba to him or he to Hecuba
That he should weep for her? What would he do
Had he the motive and the cue for passion
That I have? He would drown the stage with tears,   565
And cleave the general ear with horrid speech,
Make mad the guilty and appal the free,
Confound the ignorant, and maze indeed
The very faculties of eyes and ears.
Yet I,   570
A dull and muddy-mettled rascal, peak,
Like John-a-dreams, unpregnant of my cause,
And can say nothing; no, not for a king,
Upon whose property and most dear life
A damn'd defeat was made. Am I a coward?   575
Who calls me villain? breaks my pate across?
Plucks off my beard and blows it in my face?
Tweaks me by the nose? gives me the lie i' the throat,
As deep as to the lungs? Who does me this, ha?
'Swounds, I should take it, for it cannot be   580
But I am pigeon-liver'd, and lack gall
To make oppression bitter, or ere this
I should have fatted all the region kites

555.   *dream of passion:* imaginary emotion.

556.   *conceit:* artfulness.

557.   *her working:* "her" refers to conceit, such as the effect of imagination.

       wann'd: paled.

558.   *distraction:* frenzy.

       aspect: countenance.

559.   *function:* behavior.

560.   *With . . . conceit:* to the shape of his imagination.

564.   *cue:* signal that motivates speech or action.

566.   *general ear:* ears of the audience.

567.   *free:* innocent.

568.   *Confound:* confuse or amaze.

571.   *muddy-mettled:* dull-spirited.

       peak: mope.

572.   *unpregnant of my cause:* inactive in my duty.

574.   *property:* personality, life.

575.   *defeat:* destruction.

576.   *pate:* head.

580.   *'Swounds:* by God's wounds, another common oath.

581.   *pigeon-liver'd:* lily-livered, a coward. Pigeons were considered to be timid because they lacked gall, or yellow bile, the humor believed to cause people to be angry.

       gall: yellow bile.

583.   *the region kites:* the kites of the air. The kite is a bird of prey in the falcon family.

With this slave's offal. Bloody, bawdy villian!
Remorseless, treacherous, lecherous, kindless villain!   585
O! vengeance!
Why, what an ass am I! This is most brave
That I, the son of a dear father murder'd,
Prompted to my revenge by heaven and hell,
Must, like a whore, unpack my heart with words,   590
And fall a-cursing, like a very drab,
A scullion! Fie upon 't foh!
About, my brain; hum, I have heard,
That guilty creatures sitting at a play
Have by the very cunning of the scene   595
Been struck so to the soul that presently
They have proclaim'd their malefactions;
For murder, though it have no tongue, will speak
With most miraculous organ. I'll have these players
Play something like the murder of my father   600
Before mine uncle; I'll observe his looks;
I'll tent him to the quick: if he but blench
I know my course. The spirit that I have seen
May be the devil: and the devil hath power
To assume a pleasing shape; yea, and perhaps   605
Out of my weakness and my melancholy —
As he is very potent with such spirits —
Abuses me to damn me. I'll have grounds
More relative than this: the play's the thing
Wherein I'll catch the conscience of the king. *[Exit]*   610

584. *this slave's offal:* the king's guts.

585. *kindless:* unnatural.

591. *drab:* slut.

592. *scullion:* the lowest form of the kitchen servants.

593. *About:* turn around.

596. *presently:* immediately.

597. *malefactions:* crimes.

599. *With . . . organ:* through the most miraculous instruments.

602. *tent . . . quick:* probe him to the very soul.
       blench: flinch.

608. *Abuses . . . me:* deludes me in order that my soul may be damned by committing a sin (murder).

609. *More . . . this:* more conclusive than the word of a ghost.

COMMENTARY

This is the longest scene in the play. The action has shifted back to the court where the tension that began in Act I, Scene 2 continues to build. Hamlet's behavior and attitude have changed dramatically, and this switch has not gone unnoticed by the court. Gertrude has a maternal concern for Hamlet's well-being. Claudius, on the other hand, is worried because he is unsure about the authenticity of Hamlet's madness. The question Claudius must ask himself is, "Why is Hamlet behaving this way? He has never appeared to be an emotionally frail person before. If he is pretending, what is his purpose?"

Keep in mind that the king is Hamlet's uncle and presumably has known the prince since infancy. Claudius is shrewd; he understands and can therefore manipulate human nature. Hamlet is acting out of character, and this alerts Claudius to possible danger.

The king has good reason not to trust his nephew, because Claudius has a terrible secret. Discovery could cost Claudius his hard-earned criminal gains — his crown and his marriage — as well as his life.

The 1997 Royal Shakespeare Company Swan Theatre production of Hamlet.
Clive Barda/PAL

Investigating the source of Hamlet's ills

The king's first avenue of defense against the potential threat Hamlet poses is the summoning of Rosencrantz and Guildenstern, Hamlet's old school friends. The king wants them to draw out the cause of Hamlet's "transformation" (5). Claudius intends to use these two foolish men as pawns. Under the guise of parental concern, he asks them to spy on the prince, hoping that Hamlet may share information with his peers that he would keep from his mother and uncle.

Claudius charms and flatters Rosencrantz and Guildenstern, making them feel invaluable. Gertrude supports his endeavor, even implying that the two will be monetarily rewarded for their efforts: "Your visitation shall receive such thanks / As fits a king's remembrance" (25–26). The insincerity of their friendship with Hamlet is clear from the fact that the two men are willing to spy on the prince and then report back to the king.

The queen seems to display genuine concern for Hamlet and may believe that his friends are sincere as well. At this point, we cannot yet know the extent of her involvement with Claudius's crimes and plans. But her statement to Claudius in lines 56 and 57 indicates that she is innocent of her husband's murder. The queen suspects that Hamlet is hurt and angry because she remarried so quickly; she and Claudius wed without waiting at least one year for the traditional proper mourning time to pass. Later in the scene, she also accepts Polonius's explanation that Hamlet is acting strangely because his love for Ophelia has been rejected. Her conviction that these two sources are creating Hamlet's agitation seems to indicate her ignorance of Claudius's schemes.

Polonius's self-importance

Polonius plays a game of wait-and-see when he enters the court. He tantalizes the royal couple by announcing that he has discovered the "very cause of Hamlet's lunacy" (49). But he postpones delivering his heady news and instead announces that the ambassadors Voltimand and Cornelius have returned from Norway. The ambassadors bring the news that young Fortinbras has accepted his uncle's request — Fortinbras will march his troops through Denmark without attacking it. The young man has promised that he will never raise an army against the Danish crown. Claudius's diplomacy is successful once again.

After the ambassadors leave, Polonius tells the king and queen why Hamlet is mad. Polonius is long-winded, even as he declares that it is best to be brief. The royal couple barely tolerates his rambling explanation. This scene is intentionally comic, but it also divulges a great deal about the characters onstage. Gertrude prefers that Polonius get to the point, without so much rhetoric. Polonius, however, feels excessively self-important, and he will draw out his explanations as long as he can.

Polonius reads Hamlet's love letter, written for Ophelia. The recitation is awkward, and Polonius even seems to stumble over the words. Hamlet's letter is a conventional poem written in the Elizabethan style. The expression sounds amateurish and intense, and it reveals the passion he feels toward Ophelia.

This letter reveals just how far their relationship had progressed. Obviously, they were in love, as Hamlet will later admit at Ophelia's graveside. The letter opens with a compliment to Ophelia, continues with a declaratory verse, and concludes humbly and hopefully. His use of the word "machine" reflects Hamlet's low opinion of the body when compared with the spirit (123).

Polonius tells the king and queen how he handled the situation after he realized that Hamlet and Ophelia were in a serious relationship. Like Laertes, he refers to Hamlet's noble birth and the improbability that he would be free to marry Ophelia (141–142). Polonius explains that with this fact in mind, he told Ophelia to break off her relationship with Hamlet (142–145). She obeyed him and, Polonius claims, Hamlet became depressed immediately thereafter.

Gertrude responds to Polonius sympathetically and wants to believe that this is, indeed, the cause of

Hamlet's deterioration. Claudius is skeptical of the expla-nation. He cannot believe that Hamlet (or anyone) could lose his mind for love. No matter what Gertrude wants to believe and no matter how determined Polonius is to maintain his standing with the court, Claudius is too alert and suspicious to be mollified by this explanation.

While trying to appear more important to the court, Polonius becomes less the counselor and more the fool. He talks too much, relies heavily on outdated cliches and parables, and has a tendency towards forgetfulness (see II.i.49–51). Claudius is beginning to think that he will have to discover Hamlet's ruse for himself. Still he agrees to try Polonius's plan to eavesdrop on the prince and Ophe-lia. This scheme shows Polonius's thoughtless cruelty toward his daughter as he concerns himself only with the king's favor. He wagers his office on the gamble that this trick will reveal the source of Hamlet's ills. He vows that he will be a farmer and drive a cart if he is wrong.

Feigning madness

After Claudius and Gertrude exit, Hamlet enters reading a book. Polonius takes the opportunity to speak to him. The result is an interaction that moves from satire to suspicion, with Hamlet carefully keeping Polonius off balance. Hamlet's intention is to frustrate Polonius and make him question Hamlet's madness while at the same time verifying that he is, indeed, mad.

Polonius plays easily into Hamlet's hands. The old man does not even understand when Hamlet insults him by calling him a "fishmonger" (174). As if being referred to as a man who sells fish isn't insult-ing enough for a man in Polonius's position, in Shakespeare's time the term also meant a pimp. A fishmonger's daughter was a harlot. Hamlet's speech is filled with bitter irony and vicious puns, which Polonius fails to detect.

Hamlet makes several references to physical decay and death. A commonly held Early Modern belief asserted that the heat of the sun caused maggots to spontaneously appear in carrion (dead flesh). Hamlet moves from the subject of rotting flesh to Polonius's daughter, advising him to "[l]et her not walk i' the sun" (184). Hamlet may be referring to Psalm 121 in this pas-sage. The scripture reads, "So that the sun shall not burn thee by day, nor the moon by night." The passage implies that the sun is to blame for causing maidens to experience lust. By extension, Hamlet seems to be call-ing Ophelia a whore. Hamlet's digression is so confus-ing to Polonius that, instead of angering him, the dialogue convinces him more than ever that he was right to suspect that Ophelia was the cause of Hamlet's madness.

Hamlet then mocks Polonius to his face, saying that old men "have a plentiful lack of wit" (200–201). Look-ing right at Polonius, Hamlet insults him again and again; he tells Polonius that old men are ugly and weak — that if they could they would be young again. Polonius feels uneasy with Hamlet's message. He is convinced that Hamlet is mad, but at the same time, because he cannot figure out Hamlet's riddles, Polonius detects some kind of strange wisdom in Hamlet's words.

Hamlet and Polonius in a scene from the 1996 film directed by Kenneth Branagh.
Everett Collection

Exposing insincerity

Rosencrantz and Guildenstern enter as Polonius departs. Hamlet greets them as he had greeted Horatio earlier, happily and exuberantly: "My excellent good friends!" (226). But the conversation that follows is superficial compared with the conversations between Hamlet and Horatio. Hamlet engages the two men politely, but his initial enthusiasm at seeing his old friends dissipates steadily until, by the end of the encounter, he is darkly depressed and disappointed. The hypocrisy of Rosencrantz and Guildenstern is so transparent that Hamlet begins to question their motives for coming to see him. He knows they are not genuinely concerned about him, and he deduces that they were sent for. They self-consciously evade Hamlet's questions as to why they have come.

Alex Jennings in a 1997 production.
Clive Barda/PAL

Hamlet turns the tables on the two men. Although Claudius sent them to sound out Hamlet, Hamlet sounds them out instead in a brilliant turnabout. Hamlet asks them directly, "Were you not sent for?" (277). When they avoid the question, Hamlet states it as a fact: "You were sent for. . . I know the good king and queen have sent for you" (281–284).

Guildenstern gives up and admits the truth. In return, Hamlet tells them earnestly in calm, direct prose what has happened since his mother's remarriage. Hamlet explains that he is no longer happy and that he has lost faith in his fellow man and in himself. (Horatio is the only person thus far in the play who has not disappointed him.) Hamlet declares pessimistically that man has everything going for him, but somehow he manages to disappoint himself and everyone around him. His words refer back to his first soliloquy (I.2.129–159).

Theatrical relief

Rosencrantz tells Hamlet that a traveling troupe of players is on its way to the court. We learn here that Hamlet enjoys theatre and is a devotee of drama. As Hamlet discusses the players' arrival, he begins to lose his melancholy and show interest in something other than his own problems. He shows genuine pleasure in seeing the players, and he obviously knows them per-

sonally. This is new information about Hamlet's personality, and the insight tells us something about the man he used to be. From other references in the play, we can deduce that Hamlet is a lover, a scholar, a quick wit, and a loyal son and friend. Now we see that he is also a patron of the theatre.

The anticipation of the players brings relief from the strained conversation between Hamlet and Rosencrantz and Guildenstern. Now they exchange dialogue on neutral ground — conversation that's easy and distantly friendly. Hamlet asks Rosencrantz why the players are traveling. Rosencrantz's answer reflects a real problem occurring at the time Shakespeare wrote *Hamlet:* the establishment and popularity of children's acting companies. These acting troupes created significant competition for adult companies. The popularity of children's companies undermined the security of the adult players, who often took their performances on the road in order to make money.

The players enter and Hamlet welcomes them warmly. Polonius hears their arrival and comes to join the group. Hamlet resumes his antic disposition, which he had forgotten about for a short time with the entrance of the players. He points Polonius out to Rosencrantz and Guildenstern as a doddering old man in his second childhood, an insult that escapes Polonius entirely. "Buz, buz" is Hamlet's way of saying "Why don't you tell us something we don't know" — the phrase was part of an old Oxford tradition (396).

The reference to Roscius the Roman actor in line 394 is another jab at Polonius's tendency to over-define all of his points. The story of Roscius was old news; by referring to it, Hamlet calls attention to Polonius's stale message. Hamlet then refers to Jephthah, a character from scripture who sacrificed his daughter because she wept for her virginity (see Judges 9, lines 30–40). Jephthah was the opposite of a "fishmonger." In lines 410–411 Hamlet quotes from *Jephthah, Judge of Israel*, a popular ballad of the times. The connection to Polonius is inescapable.

At ease with the players

The exchange with Polonius mercifully ends with the reentry of the players. Hamlet's interest in the troupe is clear. The players know Hamlet, and their dialogue with him is easy and familiar. Hamlet greets a boy actor with the hope that his voice has not changed. The phrase "cracked within the ring" in line 431 refers to coins. Before milled coins were common, coins were often cut (cracked) for their metal, rendering them worthless. Here, Hamlet puns on the phrase to indicate that if the boy's voice is cracked, it will lose its value, too. (Young boys played female roles onstage at that time because women were barred from performing as a matter of legal and moral principle. Actresses did not appear on the public stage until after the Restoration of Charles II to the English throne in 1660. When a boy's voice changed, his career usually ended. Only a few went on to perform the adult male roles.)

Hamlet tells the players that he has heard a reading of a play and judged it suitable for this company. He remembers and recites 13 lines, to the admiration of his audience. The Pyrrhus speech starting at line 453 is reminiscent of the writings of Christopher Marlowe, whose plays were staged at the Rose Theatre, the Globe's chief competition. Marlowe's *Dido, Queen of Carthage*, though not containing a passage exactly like this one, nevertheless resonates with the speech Hamlet makes here. The language here is not unlike early Shakespeare, but it is very unlike the Shakespeare of 1600 when this revision was staged. The speech is bombastic and the rhythm stiff, making it sound staged and unnatural. Shakespeare may mean for the players in this scene to collectively represent a caricature of Marlowe's company, The Lord Admiral's Men.

Obviously, the story of Pyrrhus parallels Hamlet's dilemma to some extent. A state has collapsed after the death of its king, but unlike Gertrude, the queen is faithful to the memory of her husband. Even Polonius cannot help but notice the emotional impact of the speech.

A self-reproaching soliloquy

The players exit and Hamlet, after reminding Polonius to treat the players well, dismisses the old man and his two old friends (531–535). Alone, he reveals his thoughts once more. This well-known soliloquy, the third one we have heard from Hamlet, is full of reproach for his failure to act on the revenge he promised his father. He accuses himself of cowardice. He speaks of his silence and villainy, and he is filled with self-hate. "[W]hat an ass am I!" he cries (586). He tells himself that he had a good father who deserves a just revenge. He says that only a whore would waste time with talk, and only the meanest maid would waste time cursing fate.

The time for action is now, and Hamlet has an idea. The player's recent speech moved him deeply. Hamlet knows that plays can often reach into the soul of the audience and draw out a response where none was expected. He marvels at the force of imagination that can produce real emotion from a make-believe grief.

Hamlet recognizes that the theatre can help him to expose the king's conscience and, in doing so, verify what the ghost has told him. Hamlet believes that with proof of Claudius's guilty conscience, he will be able to act. Even after all that has happened, Hamlet is still not completely convinced that the spirit was his father, that it spoke the truth, and that the revenge it seeks is valid. Hamlet fears he may be a victim of Satan's handiwork.

Hamlet knows he must make Claudius reveal his guilt. Accusing the current king of murder is grave business, and enacting revenge against him may have dire consequences for the state. These factors have caused Hamlet's hesitation up to this moment. Now, he believes that he has found a way to justify his mission of revenge.

Hamlet has good reason to reproach himself for his hesitation. The ghost appeared to him some time ago, and he has done nothing in the way of formulating a plan of action against Claudius. Until the arrival of the players, he could not think past what he had heard on the castle battlements. Now Hamlet has found a way to ease his own conscience by trapping "the conscience of the king" (610).

Notes

CLIFFSCOMPLETE

HAMLET
ACT III

King *O! my offence is rank, it smells to heaven;*
It hath the primal eldest curse upon 't;
A brother's murder! Pray can I not,
Though inclination be as sharp as will:
My stronger guilt defeats my strong intent;
And like a man to double business bound,
I stand in pause where I shall first begin,
And both neglect.

Act III, Scene 1

Hamlet muses about life and death in his fourth and most famous soliloquy. Polonius and Claudius eavesdrop on Hamlet and Ophelia to try to discover if Ophelia's rejection has caused Hamlet's madness. The scene between the lovers is filled with the pain of lost love. Polonius is convinced that Hamlet's madness has been caused by "neglected love" and suggests that Gertrude talk to her son. Claudius suspects that Hamlet's madness has other origins.

ACT III, SCENE 1
A room in the castle.

[Enter KING, QUEEN, POLONIUS, OPHELIA, ROSEN-
CRANTZ, and GUILDENSTERN]

King And can you, by no drift of conference,
  Get from him why he puts on this confusion,
  Grating so harshly all his days of quiet
  With turbulent and dangerous lunacy?

Rosencrantz He does confess he feels himself distracted;   5
  But from what cause he will by no means speak.

Guildenstern Nor do we find him forward to be sounded,
  But, with a crafty madness, keeps aloof,
  When we would bring him on to some confession
  Of his true state.

Queen   Did he receive you well?   10

Rosencrantz Most like a gentleman.

Guildenstern But with much forcing of his disposition.

Rosencrantz Niggard of question, but of our demands
  Most free in his reply.

Queen   Did you assay him
  To any pastime?   15

Rosencrantz Madam, it so fell out that certain players
  We o'er-raught on the way; of these we told him,
  And there did seem in him a kind of joy
  To hear of it: they are here about the court,
  And, as I think, they have already order   20
  This night to play before him.

NOTES

1.   *drift of conference*: roundabout methods.

3.   *Grating*: disturbing.

7.   *forward to be sounded*: willing to be questioned.

12. *much forcing . . . disposition*: It took some effort on his part to be civil to us.

13–14. *Niggard . . . reply*: not asking many questions but freely replying to ours.

14. *assay*: attempt to induce.

17. *o'er-raught*: overtook.

Polonius　　　　　　　　　'Tis most true;
And he beseech'd me to entreat your majesties
To hear and see the matter.

King With all my heart; and it doth much content me
To hear him so inclin'd.　　　　　　　　　　　25
Good gentlemen, give him a further edge,
And drive his purpose on to these delights.

Rosencrantz We shall, my lord.

[Exeunt ROSENCRANTZ and GUILDENSTERN]

King　　　　　　　　　Sweet Gertrude, leave us too;
For we have closely sent for Hamlet hither,
That he, as 'twere by accident, may here　　　30
Affront Ophelia.
Her father and myself, lawful espials,
Will so bestow ourselves, that, seeing, unseen,
We may of their encounter frankly judge,
And gather by him, as he is behav'd,　　　　35
If 't be the affliction of his love or no
That thus he suffers for.

Queen　　　　　　　　I shall obey you.
And for your part, Ophelia, I do wish
That your good beauties be the happy cause
Of Hamlet's wildness; so shall I hope your virtues　40
Will bring him to his wonted way again,
To both your honours.

Ophelia　　　　　　　　Madam, I wish it may.

[Exit QUEEN]

Polonius Ophelia, walk you here. Gracious, so please you,
We will bestow ourselves. *[To OPHELIA]* Read on
　　this book;
That show of such an exercise may colour　　45
Your loneliness. We are oft to blame in this,
'Tis too much prov'd, that with devotion's visage
And pious action we do sugar o'er
The devil himself.

King *[Aside]*　　　O! 'tis too true;
How smart a lash that speech doth give my conscience!　50
The harlot's cheek, beautied with plastering art,
Is not more ugly to the thing that helps it

26.	*edge:* sharpness, keenness.
29.	*closely:* secretly.
31.	*Affront:* confront, encounter.
32.	*lawful espials:* spies who are justified in their action.
35.	*by . . . behav'd:* by observing his behavior.
41.	*wonted way:* normal or customary state.
43.	*Gracious:* your grace.
44.	*book:* of devotions.
45.	*exercise:* religious exercise.
	colour: give an excuse for.
47.	*devotion's visage:* the appearance of religious devotion.
52.	*to . . . it::* compared to the paint on her cheek.

Than is my deed to my most painted word:
O heavy burden!

Polonius I hear him coming; let's withdraw my lord.   55

[Exeunt KING and POLONIUS. Enter HAMLET]

Hamlet. To be, or not to be: that is the question:
Whether 'tis nobler in the mind to suffer
The slings and arrows of outrageous fortune,
Or to take arms against a sea of troubles,
And by opposing end them? To die: to sleep;   60
No more; and, by a sleep to say we end
The heart-ache and the thousand natural shocks
That flesh is heir to, 'tis a consummation
Devoutly to be wish'd. To die, to sleep;
To sleep: perchance to dream: ay, there's the rub;   65
For in that sleep of death what dreams may come
When we have shuffled off this mortal coil,
Must give us pause. There's the respect
That makes calamity of so long life;
For who would bear the whips and scorns of time,   70
The oppressor's wrong, the proud man's contumely,
The pangs of dispriz'd love, the law's delay,
The insolence of office, and the spurns
That patient merit of the unworthy takes,
When he himself might his quietus make   75
With a bare bodkin? who would fardels bear,
To grunt and sweat under a weary life,
But that the dread of something after death,
The undiscover'd country from whose bourn
No traveller returns, puzzles the will,   80
And makes us rather bear those ills we have
Than fly to others that we know not of?
Thus conscience does make cowards of us all;
And thus the native hue of resolution
Is sicklied o'er with the pale cast of thought,   85
And enterprises of great pitch and moment
With this regard their currents turn awry,
And lose the name of action. Soft you now!
The fair Ophelia! Nymph, in thy orisons
Be all my sins remember'd.

53. *painted:* fair-seeming, hence, by implication, false.

s.d.: *Enter Hamlet:* Hamlet is again reading and is too absorbed to notice Ophelia.

56. *the question:* the proposition put forward for argument.

58. *outrageous:* cruel.

59. *sea:* an endless turmoil.

65. *rub:* impediment. This is a lawn bowling term; a rub is a roughness in the lawn causing a diversion in the course of the ball.

67. *shuffled . . . coil:* cast off this mortal body which, like a coil of rope, binds us to this earthly existence.

68. *respect:* reason.

71. *contumely:* insults.

73. *insolence of office:* insolent behavior of officials.

73–74. *spurns . . . takes:* the contemptuous treatment that men of merit must patiently endure from the less worthy.

75. *quietus:* release (from life), a legal term.

76. *bodkin:* dagger.

fardels: burdens.

79. *bourn:* boundary.

80. *puzzles the will:* obstructs the resolution or ability to act.

83. *conscience:* reflection, speculation as to what the afterlife may hold for us.

84. *native hue:* natural color.

85. *cast:* tinge.

86. *pitch and moment:* height and importance.

87. *With this regard:* on account of this.

awry: aside.

88. *Soft you now!:* Hold on, now. (Hamlet has just noticed Ophelia.)

89. *Nymph:* lovely maid.

orisons: prayers.

Ophelia   Good my lord,   90
How does your honour for this many a day?

Hamlet. I humbly thank you; well, well, well.

Ophelia My lord, I have remembrances of yours,
That I have longed long to re-deliver;
pray you, now receive them.

Hamlet.   No, not I;   95
I never gave you aught.

Ophelia My honour'd lord, you know right well you did;
And, with them, words of so sweet breath compos'd
As made the things more rich: their perfume lost,
Take these again; for to the noble mind   100
Rich gifts wax poor when givers prove unkind.
There, my lord.

Hamlet. Ha, ha! are you honest?

Ophelia My lord!

Hamlet. Are you fair?   105

Ophelia What means your lordship?

Hamlet. That if you be honest and fair, your honesty
should admit no discourse to your beauty.

Ophelia Could beauty, my lord, have better commerce
than with honesty?   110

Hamlet. Ay, truly; for the power of beauty will
sooner transform honesty from what it is to a bawd
than the force of honesty can translate beauty into
his likeness: this was sometime a paradox, but the
time gives it proof. I did love you once.   115

Ophelia Indeed, my lord, you made me believe so.

Hamlet. You should not have believed me; for virtue
cannot so inoculate our old stock but we shall relish of
it: I loved you not.

Ophelia I was the more deceived.   120

Hamlet. Get thee to a nunnery: why wouldst thou
be a breeder of sinners? I am myself indifferent
honest; but yet I could accuse me of such things that
it were better my mother had not borne me. I am

93.   *remembrances:* love tokens.

101.   *wax:* grow, become.

103.   *honest:* chaste, a regular meaning.

107–108. *That if . . . your beauty:* Your chastity should have nothing to do with your beauty. Hamlet is implying, in his bitterness, that beautiful women are seldom chaste.

109.   *commerce:* association.

112.   *bawd:* brothel-keeper.

113.   *translate:* transform.

114.   *sometime a paradox:* at one time an apparent contradiction.

115.   *gives it proof:* Hamlet may be thinking of his mother, or Ophelia, or both.

117–119. *virtue . . . it:* No matter how we may try to bond virtue to our "old stock" — our human nature — we still are tainted by original sin.

122–123. *indifferent honest:* fairly virtuous.

very proud, revengeful, ambitious; with more 125
offences at my beck than I have thoughts to put them
in, imagination to give them shape, or time to act
them in. What should such fellows as I do crawling
between heaven and earth? We are arrant knaves,
all; believe none of us. Go thy ways to a nunnery. 130
Where's your father?

Ophelia At home, my lord.

Hamlet. Let the doors be shut upon him, that he may
play the fool nowhere but in's own house. Farewell.

Ophelia O! help him, you sweet heavens! 135

Hamlet. If thou dost marry, I'll give thee this plague
for thy dowry: be thou as chaste as ice, as pure as
snow, thou shalt not escape calumny. Get thee to a
nunnery, go; farewell. Or, if thou wilt needs marry,
marry a fool; for wise men know well enough what 140
monsters you make of them. To a nunnery, go; and
quickly too. Farewell.

Ophelia O heavenly powers, restore him!

Hamlet. I have heard of your paintings too, well
enough; God hath given you one face, and you make 145
yourselves another: you jig, you amble, and you lisp,
and nickname God's creatures, and make your wantonness
your ignorance. Go to, I'll no more on 't: it
hath made me mad. I say, we will have no more
marriages; those that are married already, all but one, 150
shall live; the rest shall keep as they are. To a
nunnery, go. *[Exit]*

Ophelia O! what a noble mind is here o'erthrown:
The courtier's, soldier's, scholar's, eye, tongue, sword;
The expectancy and rose of the fair state, 155
The glass of fashion and the mould of form,
The observ'd of all observers, quite, quite down!
And I, of ladies most deject and wretched,
That suck'd the honey of his music vows,
Now see that noble and most sovereign reason, 160
Like sweet bells jangled, out of tune and harsh;
That unmatch'd form and feature of blown youth

---

129. *arrant knaves:* out-and-out rascals.

137. *dowry:* marriage portion.

138. *calumny:* slander.

141. *monsters:* beasts with horns, hence cuckolds. (A cuckold was a man with an unfaithful wife or lover and was said to wear invisible horns.)

144. *paintings:* women's makeup.

146. *jig:* dance lecherously.

amble: walk with exaggerated swing of hips.

lisp: talk affectedly, coquettishly.

147. *nickname:* give indecent names to.

147–148. *make . . . ignorance:* pretend that you are too naive to understand the meaning of your lewd nicknames and actions.

155. *expectancy and rose:* bright hope (as future king).

156. *glass:* mirror.

mould of form: pattern of manly beauty and behavior.

162. *unmatch'd:* unmatchable.

blown: in full blossom.

Blasted with ecstasy: O! woe is me,
To have seen what I have seen, see what I see!

[Re-enter KING and POLONIUS]

King Love! his affections do not that way tend;   165
Nor what he spake, though it lack'd form a little,
Was not like madness. There's something in his soul
O'er which his melancholy sits on brood;
And, I do doubt, the hatch and the disclose
Will be some danger; which for to prevent,   170
I have in quick determination
Thus set it down: he shall with speed to England,
For the demand of our neglected tribute:
Haply the seas and countries different
With variable objects shall expel   175
This something-settled matter in his heart,
Whereon his brains still beating puts him thus
From fashion of himself. What think you on 't?

Polonius It shall do well: but yet do I believe
The origin and commencement of his grief   180
Sprung from neglected love. How now, Ophelia!
You need not tell us what Lord Hamlet said;
We heard it all. My lord, do as you please;
But, if you hold it fit, after the play,
Let his queen mother all alone entreat him   185
To show his grief: let her be round with him;
And I'll be plac'd, so please you, in the ear
Of all their conference. If she find him not,
To England send him, or confine him where
Your wisdom best shall think.   190

King   It shall be so:
Madness in great ones must not unwatch'd go.

[Exeunt]

163. *Blasted with ecstasy:* ruined by madness.

165. *affections:* emotions.

168. *on brood:* hatching; Hamlet broods on his troubles like a bird sits on her nest.

169–170. *doubt . . . danger:* suspect the result of his brooding will be dangerous.

173. *neglected tribute:* money owed as a result of war with Denmark.

174. *Haply:* perhaps.

175. *variable objects:* various sights.

176. *something-settled:* partly established; not yet incurable.

178. *fashion of himself:* his normal self.

186. *grief:* grievance.
round: direct.

187–188. *in . . . conference:* within hearing of all that is said.

188. *find him not:* does not discover his secret.

COMMENTARY

Again we are in the presence of the king, the queen, Polonius, Ophelia, and the infamous Rosencrantz and Guildenstern. Polonius, Rosencrantz, and Guildenstern are still trying to discover the cause of Hamlet's madness. Claudius is beginning to break down. He can no longer pretend that he cares for Hamlet or wants to help him. Up to this point, Claudius has been guarded in his attitude towards Hamlet; now he asks pointed questions, and his previous deception becomes apparent. He does not think that Hamlet is truly mad. Claudius believes that Hamlet's behavior is designed with a specific purpose in mind, and he implies that Hamlet may pose a danger to the state. Claudius hopes to discover this supposed purpose.

The queen asks about Hamlet's "pastime" — the official reason for calling Rozencrantz and Guildenstern to Elsinore in the first place (15). She wants to know if the two men have been able to raise Hamlet's spirits. Gertrude demonstrates again that she is a caring mother. She does not ask whether Rosencrantz and Guildenstern have been able to sound Hamlet out and discover the true reason for his behavior. She asks instead how Hamlet "received" them (10). Although she may feel responsible for Hamlet's depression, Gertrude does not seem to know anything about the murder of her first husband. She tentatively believes that Hamlet's madness may have been triggered by Ophelia's rejection of him, suggesting that Ophelia's charms may bring Hamlet back to his senses.

In this scene, Claudius first reveals his sense of guilt. In an aside, he calls his "deed" a "heavy burden" (53–54). Claudius has an active conscience, and his conscience is now bothering him. Without realizing it, he is primed for Hamlet's plan.

The prince enters as Claudius and Polonius hide themselves in preparation to spy on Ophelia and Hamlet. Polonius has put Ophelia in a compromising position. She knows that he is watching her; she has no choice but to obey her father. She must wonder what this compliance will mean both for herself and for Hamlet.

"To be"

Hamlet, seemingly unaware that anyone is listening, now delivers his fourth and best-known soliloquy. His solitary moodiness and his self-reproach have occupied his thoughts since the night he witnessed the apparition. Hamlet has given up love and any hope for a future and is now resigned to his fate.

This soliloquy is more meditative than angry, more weary than passionate, and its subject is not just Hamlet's plight but his view of the common plight of all people. In one way, contemplating suicide at this point is inconsistent with the preparations that Hamlet has made to prick Claudius's conscience and the results he

hopes to achieve. Rather than speaking earnestly about his own desire to die, Hamlet may be speaking of the choice that all men must make between suffering the demands and hurts of the world or taking action against those insults. Perhaps the crux of his debate is whether personal revenge can be justified.

But perhaps, despite the plans he has set in place, Hamlet does seriously consider ending his struggle. He searches for some kind of dignity in life, some kind of meaning in death. He longs to take action, but, until now, he has not had direction. The more he has sought direction, the more confused and aimless he has became. Hamlet wonders if life is worth living at all in a world filled with anguish and despair. Perhaps suicide is preferable; but it occurs to him that death is not a way out, because we cannot know what lies beyond life. The passage to death may lead us to eternal sleep, but it may not; the next life may be worse than the life we know. It is the unknown that deters people from ending their lives.

Hamlet wonders if it is morally better to endure evil passively or if our moral duty requires us to right wrongs, even if we have to use violence to effect that justice. The question is difficult because church, state, and society teach us that killing is a mortal sin. To kill is to condemn oneself to hell. "Thus," Hamlet says resignedly, "conscience does make cowards of us all" (83).

"I never gave you aught"

Hamlet's reverie is broken by the appearance of Ophelia. Hamlet greets her almost reverentially and seems hesitantly happy to see her. Ophelia is happy to see him; we can assume that she would prefer to talk to him in private. But she knows that they are being observed, and her nature doesn't allow her to disobey her father. She asks Hamlet how he has been, and for a moment they are as they were — in love. But Ophelia must perform her duty, and she breaks the spell by returning gifts that Hamlet has given her. His hurt is apparent in the sarcastic answer he flings at her: "I never gave you aught" (97). He may mean that Ophelia is not the woman he had thought her to be. Likewise, he is not the person he once was.

Hamlet has lost his faith in humanity, and this final slight from Ophelia is all he can bear. He begins subtly, but his words are filled with self-loathing. He is bitter about the loss of any chance for a normal life, and he feels robbed of happiness. He is filled with mistrust, and in that state of mind, he asks Ophelia where her father is. Her obvious lie turns Hamlet from her, and his next words are filled with anger. He accuses her of infidelity, and he implies that she is like all other women, false and like a chameleon.

Hamlet's words gain force and become more emotional, hysterical, and cruel. He moves from the individual to the general, from Ophelia to every woman. Hamlet's warning about marriage obviously condemns his mother's marriage to his uncle as well.

This scene is usually handled in such a way that Hamlet understands that he is being spied on by Claudius and Polonius. No specific stage directions explain this revelation to the reader or the actor, but the change in Hamlet's manner, from an almost tender sadness to a bitter rage, can tell us something of Hamlet's awareness. His most dramatic change is a result of Ophelia's single lie. He has been betrayed again by someone whom he has trusted with his love.

Kenneth Branagh and Kate Winslet in the 1996 film version of Hamlet. *Everett Collection*

Ophelia, unprepared for the force of Hamlet's anger but surely understanding it, can only pray. When Hamlet storms out, Ophelia delivers a beautifully tragic soliloquy. She reveals her true nature; she is unselfish and loyal to the memory of the prince she has loved. Her words also give us a better idea of what Hamlet must have been like before the murder of his father. He used to be the ideal Renaissance prince, displaying social graces, military prowess, and artistic gifts. Ophelia's language is filled with the imagery of flowers. This imagery will remain with her even after she has left the world.

Convinced of Hamlet's sanity

The focus now shifts to Polonius and Claudius, who have watched the entire encounter between Hamlet and Ophelia. Claudius is suspicious. Hamlet has not lost his mind for love; in fact, Hamlet has not lost his mind at all. Something else is wrong, and Claudius thinks he may know what.

The king needs to rid himself of the threat of the prince. He wants to send Hamlet away to England so he can be rid of the threat for good. Polonius, still convinced that Hamlet has gone mad from thwarted love, comforts Ophelia and suggests that Hamlet may open up to Gertrude about his problems. Polonius suggests that they delay any further action until the queen has a chance to speak to the prince; if Gertrude cannot reach Hamlet, then Claudius should send Hamlet to England. Claudius agrees but vows to watch Hamlet carefully.

Hamlet and Ophelia, *artist unknown.*
Stock Montage/SuperStock

Act III, Scene 2

Hamlet puts his plan to reveal Claudius's guilt into action. The king and queen attend the players' performance, and Claudius flees when the story portrayed reflects his own actions. Rosencrantz and Guildenstern summon Hamlet to Gertrude's chamber. Hamlet reveals his new determination to carry out the command expressed by his father's spirit.

Act III, Scene 2
A hall in the castle.

[Enter HAMLET and certain Players]

Hamlet Speak the speech, I pray you, as I pronounced
it to you, trippingly on the tongue; but if you
mouth it, as many of your players do, I had as lief the
town-crier spoke my lines. Nor do not saw the air too
much with your hand, thus; but use all gently: for   5
in the very torrent, tempest, and — as I may say
whirlwind of passion, you must acquire and beget
a temperance, that may give it smoothness. O! it
offends me to the soul to hear a robustious periwig-
pated fellow tear a passion to tatters, to very rags, to   10
split the ears of the groundlings, who for the most part
are capable of nothing but inexplicable dumb-shows
and noise: I would have such a fellow whipped for
o'er-doing Termagant; it out-herods Herod: pray you,
avoid it.   15

First Player I warrant your honour.

Hamlet Be not too tame neither, but let your own
discretion be your tutor: suit the action to the word,
the word to the action; with this special observance,
that you o'erstep not the modesty of nature; for any-   20
thing so overdone is from the purpose of playing, whose
end, both at the first and now, was and is, to hold, as
'twere, the mirror up to nature; to show virtue her
own feature, scorn her own image, and the very age and
body of the time his form and pressure. Now, this   25
overdone, or come tardy off, though it make the
unskilful laugh, cannot but make the judicious grieve;
the censure of which one must in your allowance o'er-
weigh a whole theatre of others. O! there be players
that I have seen play, and heard others praise, and   30

NOTES

1.   *the speech:* the words Hamlet has written for his players' performance.

2.   *trippingly:* smoothly, easily.

3.   *mouth:* shout, or exaggerate enunciation.

     lief: soon.

8.   *temperance:* control.

9.   *robustious:* ranting.

9–10. *periwig-pated:* bewigged.

11. *groundlings:* the poorer and less critical section of the audience who stood in the pit.

12. *capable of:* understanding.

     inexplicable dumb-shows: the unintelligible pantomime preceding the play proper.

14. *Termagant Herod:* favorite characters in the old miracle plays, who were always portrayed as blustering tyrants.

20. *modesty:* moderation.

21. *from:* away from, contrary to.

24–25. *very . . . pressure:* an exact reproduction of the age.

25. *form:* shape.

     pressure: imprint.

26. *come tardy off:* slackly performed.

28. *which one:* the judicious spectator.

     allowance: estimation.

that highly, not to speak it profanely, that, neither
having the accent of Christians nor the gait of Christian,
pagan, nor man, have so strutted and bellowed
that I have thought some of nature's journeymen
had made men and not made them well, they   35
imitated humanity so abominably.

First Player I hope we have reformed that indifferently
with us.

Hamlet O! reform it altogether. And let those that
play your clowns speak no more than is set down   40
for them; for there be of them that will themselves
laugh, to set on some quantity of barren spectators to
laugh too, though in the mean time some necessary
question of the play be then to be considered; that's
villainous, and shows a most pitiful ambition in the   45
fool that uses it. Go, make you ready. *[Exit Players]*
[Enter POLONIUS, ROSENCRANTZ, and
GUILDENSTERN]
How now, my lord! will the king hear this piece of
work?

Polonius And the queen too, and that presently.

Hamlet Bid the players make haste.   50
[Exit POLONIUS]
Will you two help to hasten them?

Guildenstern and Rosencrantz We will, my lord.

[Exeunt ROSENCRANTZ and GUILDENSTERN]

Hamlet What, ho! Horatio!

[Enter HORATIO]

Horatio Here, sweet lord, at your service.

Hamlet Horatio, thou art e'en as just a man   55
As e'er my conversation cop'd withal.

Horatio O! my dear lord, —

Hamlet   Nay, do not think I flatter;
For what advancement may I hope from thee,
That no revenue hast but thy good spirits
To feed and clothe thee? Why should the poor be flattered? 60
No; let the candied tongue lick absurd pomp,

34.	*journeymen:* not masters of their trade.
38.	*indifferently:* fairly well.
42.	*barren:* barren-witted.
45.	*pitiful:* contemptible.
49.	*presently:* immediately.
56.	*As e'er . . . cop'd withal:* as ever I met.
58.	*advancement::* promotion.
61.	*candied:* sugared with hypocrisy.

And crook the pregnant hinges of the knee
Where thrift may follow fawning. Dost thou hear?
Since my dear soul was mistress of her choice
And could of men distinguish, her election   65
Hath seal'd thee for herself; for thou hast been
As one, in suffering all, that suffers nothing,
A man that fortune's buffets and rewards
Hast ta'en with equal thanks; and bless'd are those
Whose blood and judgment are so well co-mingled   70
That they are not a pipe for fortune's finger
To sound what stop she please. Give me that man
That is not passion's slave, and I will wear him
In my heart's core, ay, in my heart of heart,
As I do thee. Something too much of this.   75
There is a play to-night before the king;
One scene of it comes near the circumstance
Which I have told thee of my father's death:
I prithee, when thou seest that act afoot,
Even with the very comment of thy soul   80
Observe mine uncle; if his occulted guilt
Do not itself unkennel in one speech,
It is a damned ghost that we have seen
And my imaginations are as foul
As Vulcan's stithy. Give him heedful note;   85
For I mine eyes will rivet to his face,
And after we will both our judgments join
In censure of his seeming.

Horatio   Well, my lord:
If he steal aught the whilst this play is playing,
And 'scape detecting, I will pay the theft.   90

Hamlet They are coming to the play; I must be idle:
Get you a place.

[Danish march. A Flourish. Enter KING, QUEEN,
POLONIUS, OPHELIA, ROSENCRANTZ,
GUILDENSTERN, and Others]

King How fares our cousin Hamlet?

Hamlet Excellent, i' faith; of the chameleon's dish:
I eat the air, promise-crammed; you cannot feed   95
capons so.

---

62.   *pregnant:* ready at the least opportunity to bend.

63.   *Where . . . fawning:* where gain will follow flattery.

65.   *of:* among.

66.   *seal'd:* fixed upon.

67.   *suffering:* putting up with.

70.   *blood and judgment:* passion and reason.

71.   *pipe:* a recorder or flute. The stops are the fingerholes.

Hamlet says fortune does not play Horatio like a pipe.

80.   *comment:* close observation.

81.   *occulted:* hidden.

82.   *Do not itself . . . one speech:* is not brought to light by one of the speeches in the play.

83.   *damned ghost:* a devil.

85.   *Vulcan's stithy:* the workshop of the Roman god of fire and metalworking.

      heedful note: careful observation.

88.   *censure of his seeming:* judgment of his reaction.

89.   *steal:* conceal.

91.   *be idle:* seem crazy.

94.   *chameleon's dish:* The chameleon was supposed to feed on air.

95.   *promise-crammed:* stuffed with empty promises.

King I have nothing with this answer, Hamlet; these words are not mine.

Hamlet No, nor mine now. *[To POLONIUS]* My lord, you played once i' the university, you say? 100

Polonius That did I, my lord, and was accounted a good actor.

Hamlet And what did you enact?

Polonius I did enact Julius Caesar: I was killed i' the Capitol; Brutus killed me. 105

Hamlet It was a brute part of him to kill so capital a calf there. Be the players ready?

Rosencrantz Ay, my lord; they stay upon your patience.

Queen Come hither, my good Hamlet, sit by me. 110

Hamlet No, good mother, here's metal more attractive.

Polonius *[To the KING]* O ho! do you mark that?

Hamlet Lady, shall I lie in your lap?

[Lying down at OPHELIA'S feet]

Ophelia No, my lord. 115

Hamlet I mean, my head upon your lap?

Ophelia Ay, my lord.

Hamlet Do you think I meant country matters?

Ophelia I think nothing, my lord.

Hamlet That's a fair thought to lie between maid's legs. 120

Ophelia What is, my lord?

Hamlet Nothing.

Ophelia You are merry, my lord.

Hamlet Who, I? 125

Ophelia Ay, my lord.

Hamlet O God, your only jig-maker. What should a man do but be merry? for, look you, how cheerfully

97. *I have nothing with this answer:* I can make nothing of this answer.

108. *stay . . . patience:* They await your convenience.

111-112. *metal more attractive:* Hamlet has a magnetic attraction to Ophelia.

127. *your only jig-maker:* I am the funniest man alive (ironic).

my mother looks, and my father died within's two
hours.   130

Ophelia Nay, 'tis twice two months, my lord.

Hamlet So long? Nay, then, let the devil wear black, for
I'll have a suit of sables. O heavens! die two months
ago, and not forgotten yet? Then there's hope a
great man's memory may outlive his life half a year;   135
but, by'r lady, he must build churches then, or else
shall he suffer not thinking on, with the hobby-horse,
whose epitaph is, 'For, O! for, O! the hobby-horse
is forgot.'

[Hautboys play. The dumb-show enters]

*[Enter a King and a Queen, very lovingly; the Queen
embracing him, and he her. She kneels, and makes
show of protestation unto him. He takes her up,
and declines his head upon her neck; lays him
down upon a bank of flowers: she, seeing him
asleep, leaves him. Anon comes in a fellow, takes
off his crown, kisses it, and pours poison in the
King's ears, and exits. The Queen returns, finds
the King dead, and makes passionate action. The
Poisoner, with some two or three Mutes, comes in
again, seeming to lament with her. The dead body
is carried away. The Poisoner wooes the Queen
with gifts; she seems loath and unwilling awhile
but in the end accepts his love. Exeunt]*

Ophelia What means this, my lord?   140

Hamlet Marry, this is miching mallecho; it means
mischief.

Ophelia Belike this show imports the argument of
the play.

[Enter Prologue]

Hamlet We shall know by this fellow: the players   145
cannot keep counsel; they'll tell all.

Ophelia Will he tell us what this show meant?

Hamlet Ay, or any show that you'll show him; be not
you ashamed to show, he'll not shame to tell you what
it means.   150

133.   *suit of sables:* suit trimmed with fur.

137.   *not thinking on:* not being thought of.

hobby-horse: a familiar object in a May Day cele-
bration. (See commentary.)

s.d.   *Hautboys:* oboes.

141.   *miching mallecho:* slinking mischief.

143.   *argument:* plot.

Ophelia You are naught, you are naught. I'll mark the
   play.

Prologue *For us and for our tragedy,*
   Here stooping to your clemency,
   We beg your hearing patiently.   155

Hamlet Is this a prologue, or the posy of a ring?

Ophelia 'Tis brief, my lord.

Hamlet As woman's love.

[Enter two Players, King and Queen]

Player King Full thirty times hath Phoebus' cart gone
   round Neptune's salt wash and Tellus' orbed ground,   160
   And thirty dozen moons with borrow'd sheen
   About the world have times twelve thirties been,
   Since love our hearts and Hymen did our hands
   Unite commutual in most sacred bands.

Player Queen So many journeys may the sun and moon   165
   Makes us again count o'er ere love be done!
   But, woe is me! you are so sick of late,
   So far from cheer and from your former state,
   That I distrust you. Yet, though I distrust,
   Discomfort you, my lord, it nothing must;   170
   For women's fear and love holds quantity,
   In neither aught, or in extremity.
   Now, what my love is, proof hath made you know;
   And as my love is siz'd, my fear is so.
   Where love is great, the littlest doubts are fear;   175
   Where little fears grow great, great love grows there.

Player King Faith, I must leave thee, love, and shortly too;
   My operant powers their functions leave to do:
   And thou shalt live in this fair world behind,
   Honour'd, belov'd; and haply one as kind   180
   For husband shalt thou —

Player Queen   O! confound the rest;
   Such love must needs be treason in my breast:
   In second husband let me be accurst;
   None wed the second but who kill'd the first.

Neptune, god of the sea.

151.   *naught:* of no consequence, unimportant.

156.   *posy of a ring:* as brief and silly as the inscription inside a ring.

159.   *Phoebus' cart:* the chariot of the sun.

160.   *Neptune's:* god of the seas.

      Tellus': goddess of earth.

      orbed: spherical.

161.   *borrow'd sheen:* light borrowed from the sun.

163.   *Hymen:* god of marriage.

164.   *commutal:* mutually.

169.   *distrust:* fear, uneasiness.

171.   *quantity:* equal proportion.

172.   *In neither . . . extremity:* either nothing or too much.

178.   *operant powers:* bodily strength.

      leave: cease.

Hamlet *[Aside]* Wormwood, wormwood.   185

Player Queen The instances that second marriage move,
Are base respects of thrift, but none of love;
A second time I kill my husband dead,
When second husband kisses me in bed.

Player King I do believe you think what now you speak; 190
But what we do determine oft we break.
Purpose is but the slave to memory,
Of violent birth, but poor validity;
Which now, like fruit unripe, sticks on the tree,
But fall unshaken when they mellow be.   195
Most necessary 'tis that we forget
To pay ourselves what to ourselves is debt;
What to ourselves in passion we propose,
The passion ending, doth the purpose lose.
The violence of either grief or joy   200
Their own enactures with themselves destroy;
Where joy most revels grief doth most lament,
Grief joys, joy grieves, on slender accident.
This world is not for aye, nor 'tis not strange,
That even our love should with our fortunes change; 205
For 'tis a question left us yet to prove
Whe'r love lead fortune or else fortune love.
The great man down, you mark his favourite flies;
The poor advanc'd makes friends of enemies.
And hitherto doth love on fortune tend,   210
For who not needs shall never lack a friend;
And who in want a hollow friend doth try
Directly seasons him his enemy.
But, orderly to end where I begun,
Our wills and fates do so contrary run   215
That our devices still are overthrown,
Our thoughts are ours, their ends none of our own:
So think thou wilt no second husband wed;
But die thy thoughts when thy first lord is dead.

Player Queen Nor earth to me give food, heaven light! 220
Sport and repose lock from me day and night!
To desperation turn my trust and hope!
An anchor's cheer in prison be my scope!
Each opposite that blanks the face of joy
Meet what I would have well, and it destroy!   225

185.   *Wormwood:* bitterness. (Wormwood is a plant with bitter qualities.)

186.   *instances:* arguments.

187.   *respects of thrift:* considerations of gain.

192.   *Purpose . . . memory:* Our purpose is soon forgotten.

193.   *validity:* strength.

201.   *enactures:* performances.

204.   *aye:* ever.

210.   *tend:* wait, depend.

213.   *Directly . . . enemy:* immediately makes an enemy of him.

       seasons: brings to maturity.

216.   *devices:* plans.

       still: always.

223.   *anchor's:* hermit's.

       my scope: all that is permitted me.

224.   *blanks:* blanches, makes pale.

But here and hence pursue me lasting strife,
If, once a widow, ever I be wife!

Hamlet If she should break it now!

Player King 'Tis deeply sworn. Sweet, leave me here awhile;
My spirits grow dull, and fain I would beguile   230
The tedious day with sleep. *[Sleeps]*

Player Queen   Sleep rock thy brain;
And never come mischance between us twain! *[Exit]*

Hamlet Madam, how like you this play?

Queen The lady doth protest too much methinks.

Hamlet O! but she'll keep her word.   235

King Have you heard the argument? Is there no
offence in 't?

Hamlet No, no, they do but jest, poison in jest; no
offence i' the world.

King What do you call the play?   240

Hamlet The Mouse-trap. Marry, how? Tropically.
This play is the image of a murder done in Vienna:
Gonzago is the duke's name; his wife, Baptista. You
shall see anon; 'tis a knavish piece of work: but what
of that? your majesty and we that have free souls, it   245
touches us not: let the galled jade wince, our withers
are unwrung.
[Enter Player as Lucianus]
This is one Lucianus, nephew to the king.

Ophelia You are a good chorus, my lord.

Hamlet I could interpret between you and your love, if   250
I could see the puppets dallying.

Ophelia You are keen, my lord, you are keen.

230.   *beguile:* entertain.

236.   *argument:* plot of a play.

241.   *Mouse-trap:* Hamlet is using the play to trap Claudius.

        Tropically: figuratively, a trope being a figure of speech.

244.   *knavish:* villainous — referring to the subject matter, that is, murder.

245.   *free:* innocent.

246–247.   *let . . . unwrung:* Let he who has a guilty conscience wince; it doesn't bother us.

246.   *galled jade:* a nag with saddle sores.

        withers: the juncture of the shoulder bones of a horse.

247.   *unwrung:* uninjured.

249.   *chorus:* used in Greek drama to assist the audience in the interpretation of the play.

250.   *interpret:* The puppet master, like the chorus, explains what is happening as he manipulates the puppets.

251.   *dallying:* fondling one another.

252.   *keen:* severe, sarcastic. Hamlet takes a more literal meaning as point of departure for his cruelly suggestive rejoinder.

Hamlet It would cost you a groaning to take off my edge.

Ophelia Still better, and worse. 255

Hamlet So you mis-take your husbands. Begin, murderer; pox, leave thy damnable faces, and begin. Come; the croaking raven doth bellow for revenge.

Lucianus Thoughts black, hands apt, drugs fit, and time agreeing;
Confederate season, else no creature seeing; 260
Thou mixture rank, of midnight weeds collected,
With Hecate's ban thrice blasted, thrice infected,
Thy natural magic and dire property,
On wholesome life usurp immediately.

[Pours the poison into the Sleeper's ears]

Hamlet He poisons him i' the garden for 's estate. 265
His name's Gonzago; the story is extant, and writ in very choice Italian. You shall see anon how the murderer gets the love of Gonzago's wife.

Ophelia The king rises.

Hamlet What! frighted with false fire? 270

Queen How fares my lord?

Polonius Give o'er the play.

King Give me some light: away!

All Lights, lights, lights!

[Exeunt all except HAMLET and HORATIO]

Hamlet Why, let the striken deer go weep, 275
The hart ungalled play;
For some must watch, while some must sleep:
So runs the world away.
Would not this, sir, and a forest of feathers, if the rest of my fortunes turn Turk with me, with two 280
Provincial roses on my razed shoes, get me a fellowship in a cry of players, sir?

Horatio Half a share.

253. *a groaning:* a good deal of pain, possibly a reference to sex.

256. *So . . . husbands:* a reference to the "for better, for worse" portion of marital vows, as well as to his previous speech.
      mis-take: a suggestion that women are not true to their marriage vows.

260. *Confederate season:* suitable opportunity.
      else no creature: no other creature.

262. *Hecate's ban:* the curse of Hecate, the goddess of witchcraft.

263. *dire property:* dreadful power.

270. *false fire:* a blank cartridge.

279. *forest of feathers:* plumed hat much worn by players.

280. *turn Turk:* turn bad.

281. *Provincial roses:* rosettes for concealing the laces on shoes.
      razed: slashed for ornamentation.
      fellowship: partnership.

282. *cry:* pack.

Hamlet A whole one, I.
For thou dost know, O Damon dear,   285
This realm dismantled was
Of Jove himself; and now reigns here
A very, very — pajock.

Horatio You might have rhymed.

Hamlet O good Horatio! I'll take the ghost's word for   290
a thousand pound. Didst perceive?

Horatio Very well, my lord.

Hamlet Upon the talk of the poisoning?

Horatio I did very well note him.

[Re-enter ROSENCRANTZ and GUILDENSTERN]

Hamlet Ah, ha! Come, some music! come, the   295
recorders!
For if the king like not the comedy,
Why then, belike he likes it not, perdy.
Come, some music!

Guildenstern Good my lord, vouchsafe me a word   300
with you.

Hamlet Sir, a whole history.

Guildenstern The king, sir, —

Hamlet Ay, sir, what of him?

Guildenstern Is in his retirement marvellous   305
distempered.

Hamlet With drink, sir?

Guildenstern No, my lord, rather with choler.

Hamlet Your wisdom should show itself more richer
to signify this to his doctor; for, for me to put him to   310
his purgation would perhaps plunge him into far more
choler.

Guildenstern Good my lord, put your discourse into
some frame, and start not so wildly from my affair.

Hamlet I am tame, sir; pronounce.   315

Guildenstern The queen, your mother, in most great
affliction of spirit, hath sent me to you.

285.   *Damon:* perfect friend.

286.   *dismantled:* robbed.

288.   *pajock:* peacock.

Hamlet compares Claudius to a peacock.

296.   *recorders:* flageolets; the pre-eighteenth century form of flute.

298.   *perdy:* by God.

306.   *distempered:* disordered, upset. Hamlet deliberately interprets this as a physical disorder.

308.   *choler:* anger. Again Hamlet takes the meaning in its physical sense, that is, excess of bile.

311.   *purgation:* Hamlet probably intends a pun — to administer a purgative to get rid of the bile and to purge him of his guilt. The word recalls Hamlet's father, who is in purgatory.

314.   *frame:* shape, order.

Hamlet You are welcome.

Guildenstern Nay, good my lord, this courtesy is not
of the right breed. If it shall please you to make   320
me a wholesome answer, I will do your mother's
commandment; if not, your pardon and my return shall
be the end of my business.

Hamlet Sir, I cannot.

Guildenstern What, my lord?   325

Hamlet Make you a wholesome answer; my wit's
diseased; but, sir, such answer as I can make, you shall
command; or, rather, as you say, my mother:
therefore no more, but to the matter: my mother,
you say, —   330

Rosencrantz Then, thus she says: your behaviour hath
struck her into amazement and admiration.

332. *admiration:* wonder.

Hamlet O wonderful son, that can so astonish a
mother! But is there no sequel at the heels of this
mother's admiration? Impart.   335

Rosencrantz She desires to speak with you in her
closet ere you go to bed.

337. *closet::* private room.

Hamlet We shall obey, were she ten times our mother.
Have you any further trade with us?

Rosencrantz My lord, you once did love me.   340

Hamlet So I do still, by these pickers and stealers.

341. *pickers and stealers:* hands.

Rosencrantz Good my lord, what is your cause of
distemper? you do surely bar the door upon your own
liberty, if you deny your griefs to your friend.

344. *deny your griefs:* refuse to unburden yourself.

Hamlet Sir, I lack advancement.   345

345. *advancement:* promotion.

Rosencrantz How can that be when you have the voice
of the king himself for your succession in Denmark?

346–347. *voice of the king:* a powerful influence toward his election to the throne.

Hamlet. Ay, sir, but 'While the grass grows,' — the
proverb is something musty.
[Enter Players, with recorders]
O! the recorders: let me see one. To withdraw with   350
you: why do you go about to recover the wind of me,
as if you would drive me into a toil?

348. *'While . . . grows':* an old proverb — while the grass grows, the trees are green.

350. *withdraw:* go aside.

351. *recover the wind:* a hunting phrase — to get to windward.

352. *toil:* net.

Guildenstern O! my lord, if my duty be too bold, my
love is too unmannerly.

Hamlet I do not well understand that. Will you play   355
upon this pipe?

Guildenstern My lord, I cannot.

Hamlet I pray you.

Guildenstern Believe me, I cannot.

Hamlet I do beseech you.   360

Guildenstern I know no touch of it, my lord.

Hamlet 'Tis as easy as lying; govern these ventages
with your finger and thumb, give it breath with your
mouth, and it will discourse most eloquent music.
Look you, these are the stops.   365

Guildenstern But these cannot I command to any
utterance of harmony; I have not the skill.

Hamlet Why, look you now, how unworthy a thing
you make of me. You would play upon me; you would
seem to know my stops; you would pluck out the heart   370
of my mystery; you would sound me from my lowest
note to the top of my compass; and there is much
music, excellent voice, in this little organ, yet cannot you
make it speak. 'Sblood, do you think I am easier
to be played on than a pipe? Call me what instrument   375
you will, though you can fret me, you cannot
play upon me.
[Enter POLONIUS]
God bless you, sir!

Polonius My lord, the queen would speak with you,
and presently.   380

Hamlet Do you see yonder cloud that's almost in
shape of a camel?

Polonius By the mass, and 'tis like a camel, indeed.

Hamlet Methinks it is like a weasel.

Polonius It is backed like a weasel.   385

Hamlet Or like a whale?

Polonius Very like a whale.

353–354. *if . . . unmannerly:* If I have been too forward in questioning you, it is only because of the greatness of my affection for you.

362. *ventages:* holes, stops.

372. *compass:* the range of a musical instrument.

373. *this little organ:* the recorder.

376. *fret:* annoy, with a pun on the frets or bars on the fingerboard of a stringed instrument.

380. *presently:* immediately.

Hamlet Then I will come to my mother by and by.
[Aside] They fool me to the top of my bent.
[Aloud] I will come by and by.   390

Polonius I will say so. *[Exit]*

Hamlet 'By and by' is easily said. Leave me, friends.
[Exeunt all but HAMLET]
'Tis now the very witching time of night,
When churchyards yawn and hell itself breathes out
Contagion to this world: now could I drink hot blood,   395
And do such bitter business as the day
Would quake to look on. Soft! now to my mother.
O heart! lose not thy nature; let not ever
The soul of Nero enter this firm bosom;
Let me be cruel, not unnatural;   400
I will speak daggers to her, but use none;
My tongue and soul in this be hyprocrites;
How in my words soever she be shent,
To give them seals never, my soul, consent! *[Exit]*

389. *top of my bent:* the extent to which I am willing to be fooled.

393. *witching time:* the time when witches roam.

395. *Contagion:* infection.

399. *Nero:* Roman Emperor who killed his own mother.

403. *shent:* rebuked.

404. *To give them seals:* to seal my words with action.

COMMENTARY

This scene involves significant changes in character and character motivations. The action also involves some significant onstage adjustments. The play-within-a-play requires specific scenery to accommodate the court and the players. The players need a stage of their own, the court will observe the play from the main stage, and the audience needs to be able to observe both, either at once or alternately.

Hamlet directs the players

The scene is an intricate dance between Claudius's world of pretense and the make-believe world of the players. Barely containing his nervous anticipation, Hamlet puts his plan to trap the king's conscience into motion. When addressing the players, he sounds directorial and somewhat critical, but the course of his life from this time on depends on how Claudius receives and is affected by the play. The actors' lines must be delivered realistically and with conviction. Any performance that sounds too wooden, too artificial, or too bombastic may remove the appearance of reality, and that recognizable artificiality might extinguish any chance of Claudius being able to identify with it. The play must be convincingly real.

Another challenge for Hamlet and the players involves the delicate balance between illusion and reality. Claudius hides his reality and lives behind a mask that he has assumed. The players create an illusion that Hamlet hopes will reveal who Claudius really is and the crimes he has committed. Out of this encounter of two illusions, one hiding what the other imitates, the truth will emerge.

Hamlet's advice to the players may echo the voice of Shakespeare himself. We have had no previous indication that Hamlet is any more than a patron of the arts. He has written the lines that the players will deliver, but his lack of experience as a director/player would preclude the extent of acting knowledge that Hamlet displays here. Again, as in Act II, Scene 2, Shakespeare may be parodying the work of Christopher Marlowe and the players at the Rose Theatre, the Lord Admiral's Men. Edward Alleyn, the leading tragedian for the Lord Admiral's Men, was a player with a reputation for overblown gestures and a somewhat melodramatic style of delivery. These theatrics were appropriate for Marlowe's plays because he used more formal language. But Shakespeare's more flexible verse and prose required a natural and adaptable style of delivery.

The stage is set for the night's performance. Polonius, Rosencrantz, and Guildenstern arrive to watch the preparations. Hamlet asks them to call the king and queen and prepare for the festivities.

One true friend

Horatio, the one person who Hamlet still trusts, enters at Hamlet's exuberant call. Hamlet pauses in his preparations to praise Horatio, but Horatio modestly shrugs off Hamlet's compliment. Hamlet will not let it go. He tells Horatio that he has no reason for insincerity; what can a prince hope to gain by flattering a commoner? As far as Hamlet is concerned, Horatio is the one decent person left in the world, and Hamlet wants to tell him how much his loyalty and honesty mean in a world turned upside down.

"Give me that man / That is not passion's slave," Hamlet says of Horatio, "and I will wear him / In my heart's core, ay, in my heart of heart" (72–74). Horatio's honor and dignity are painted clearly; he stands in contrast to everyone else in the play. He displays the best that is within the human character, while Claudius displays the worst.

Hamlet takes his friend into his confidence once more with his next request. Hamlet tells Horatio of his plan and his intention to watch the king for any signs of guilt. He asks Horatio to join him in watching Claudius during the performance. Horatio agrees to help. Hamlet may not trust himself completely, but with Horatio, he can reach what he knows will be a fair judgment of Claudius's guilt or innocence.

Addressing the court

The court enters. Musicians play a Danish march, kettledrums sound, and much fanfare abounds. The scene is festive and colorful; the entire court has gathered for Hamlet's play. Claudius speaks first, asking

about Hamlet's health. Hamlet assures the king that he is "[e]xcellent" and "of the chameleon's dish" (94). This image has double meaning. On one hand, Claudius is like a chameleon, adapting himself to any situation. But also, according to Early Modern belief, a chameleon feeds on air. Hamlet may indicate here that he feels as if he does not need food because he can feed on the essence of his victory.

Hamlet's answer confuses Claudius, who cannot think of an adequate reply. The two men are wary of each other, the king more so than Hamlet. Claudius still believes that he may have a chance to eliminate Hamlet and maintain control. Hamlet believes that he has conceived a foolproof plan to ensnare Claudius. They are locked in a duel that neither will admit but neither will retreat from.

Hamlet turns to Polonius, always a target for Hamlet's wit. The old man is easy to humiliate, and Hamlet does not hesitate to do exactly that. Watching such harassment is embarrassing and uncomfortable — perhaps that is Hamlet's intention. Even his mother is not safe from Hamlet's barbs; he is openly scornful towards Gertrude. He rebuffs her before turning to Ophelia.

Hamlet's comments to Ophelia are blatantly suggestive and insulting. We know that she does not deserve this treatment, and we know that Hamlet is above acting this way. He impresses us as unnecessarily cruel in this scene. Ophelia seems oddly composed under Hamlet's abusive treatment. She matches him pun for pun. She counters his insolence with grace and dignity. She does not hesitate to answer him and correct him when he is wrong, calmly reminding Hamlet that his father has been dead four months, not "two hours" (129–130).

Hamlet is not swayed by Ophelia's answer; he replies with more sarcasm, including a reference to a ballad sung in Shakespeare's day about the hobby-horse. The hobby-horse was a May Day character — a carnival horse created by two men under a blanket. The hobby-horse was associated with bawdiness and immorality. Note how each one of the ballads, songs, and biblical and classical references Shakespeare uses has a specific parallel to the story of Hamlet. Shakespeare's audiences would generally have been familiar with these allusions, but modern audiences often miss their meanings.

"The Mouse-trap"

The players begin their entertainment at the sound of the *hautboys*, or oboe players, and Hamlet turns his full, too eager attention on them. The initial performance is a dumb show, so called because it is done in mime. The players' movements are greatly exaggerated, just as pantomimes are performed today. Here, the players act out the basic plot of the play in order to prepare the audience for what they are about to see. After the mimes, the players recite the prologue. This brief poem breaks the action between the dumb show and the play.

Finally, Hamlet's play-within the play begins; the speeches of the Player King and the Player Queen immediately captivate the court audience. The characters' lives parallel those of Hamlet's parents and set the stage for a series of similarities between this theatrical creation and the recent events at Elsinore.

Claudius immediately notices the parallels between the play and reality. His guilty conscience has made him suspicious, and he finds the similarities extremely disconcerting — exactly what Hamlet had hoped would happen. The king feels hemmed in by the presence of the court. If he remains silent he looks guilty, but if he objects he sounds guilty. He is temporarily impotent. When Hamlet puts Gertrude on the spot by asking her what she thinks of the play, Claudius makes an ineffectual attempt to intervene. But his intentions are transparent, and Hamlet almost claps his hands in approval. He triumphantly reveals the title of his play-within-the-play, "The Mouse-trap" (241).

Hamlet explains that the play tells the story of a murder committed in Vienna by a Duke named Gonzago. Shakespeare's source for this tale was probably a

A representation of The Mouse-Trap *in the 1997 Hackney Empire production of* Hamlet.
Henrietta Butler/PAL

report of a factual murder that occurred in 1598. The Duke of Urbino was married to a woman from the Gonzaga family. Her brother, Luigi Gonzaga, supposedly killed his sister's husband by dropping poison in the duke's ear. This Italian story differs significantly from the original Danish story of Amlothi or Amleth (see the "Introduction to *Hamlet*"). There, the king was murdered openly and violently. But Claudius does not display typical Viking characteristics. He is more crafty and suave — more Mediterranean than Northern, according to assumptions made in Shakespeare's time. Perhaps that is why Shakespeare based this play-within-a-play on the Urbino account.

Silent duel

The players' performance has put into tight focus the silent duel between Hamlet's provocations and Claudius's resistance. Hamlet's speech to the king in lines 243 through 247 must feel very like the cut of a blade to Claudius. Hamlet coyly dismisses the idea that the play has any real importance. It's just a play, after all. The fantasy cannot touch anyone with a "free soul"; only a person with a heavy conscience could possibly react to something like this performance (245).

Hamlet now feels certain that he has trapped the king's conscience, just as he had hoped. He cannot let go of his moment of victory, and he continues to press his advantage. He taunts Claudius further, to see the extent of the reaction he can coax from the distressed king.

Claudius, primarily a diplomat, has learned the fine art of deceit. He is a master at maintaining his composure and steady demeanor even under the most intense external pressure. But the internal pressure caused by his guilt is now beginning to equal or even outweigh the external pressure. The two forces will soon be too much to bear, even for Claudius. As Hamlet watches the king watching the play, he senses the imminent breakdown of the illusion Claudius has created.

Ophelia's brief exchange with Hamlet beginning with line 249 sounds distant and clipped. She will not open herself up to him again, and his barbs and needlessly cruel retorts are relentless. The dialogue between them is uncomfortable in the extreme, and because of that, it is tragic. Their behavior mirrors the waning and lost love portrayed onstage.

Notice Hamlet's attention to the action swirling around him. His normally reserved manner is now animated, brittle, and hysterical. He saves any warmth or kindness he can muster for Horatio. Everyone else has disappointed him, so everyone else suffers from his chilling detachment and mistrust. His ready and quick wit only serves now to hurt and insult.

For the rest of the scene, Hamlet displays his sense of victory. He dances around the players, the audience, and the king in particular. The focus is on Claudius, but we watch him through Hamlet's filter. Claudius was positive that no one witnessed his crime. He cannot understand how Hamlet came upon his secret, but the play is proof enough that he has.

Exposed

However the secret managed to surface, Claudius now realizes that Hamlet knows. He tries to stop the performance, change the subject, and divert attention from himself. In the end nothing works, and Claudius loses his composure. He cannot sit through one more moment of the play. He calls for light and hurries away, accompanied by the entire court except for Hamlet and Horatio. Horatio confirms what Hamlet has seen; the ghost has not lied, nor was it an illusion. Claudius has a conscience, and Hamlet has trapped it.

Hamlet cannot contain his hysterical triumph. Claudius and his court of illusion is dissolving before Hamlet's eyes. He sings bits of a ballad about Damon and Pythias — legendary friends who changed the course of a tyrannical government by setting an example of constancy and loyalty. In an obvious reference to Claudius, Hamlet uses the word "pajock," an old word for peacock — a bird known for its preening and strutting (288).

Hamlet asks Horatio if he saw Claudius's reaction to the "poisoning" (293). Horatio confirms Hamlet's observations. No doubt remains. The ghost was honest, and now Hamlet can act.

Rosencrantz and Guildenstern enter and Hamlet uses this opportunity to expose their hypocrisy as well. As allies of the king, they are no friends to him. Hamlet keeps them at a distance but toys with them, reviving his "antic disposition" for the purpose of having sport with them. He teases in order to humiliate and reject them.

"Marvellous distempered"

The two men tell Hamlet that the king is "marvellous distempered" (305–306). Hamlet cannot contain his insults, asking if he is distempered "[w]ith drink" (307). Guildenstern's reply that the king is distempered with "choler," or anger, is exactly what Hamlet hoped to hear (308). He tells them to report this to a doctor; any assistance he might give the king would only make Claudius's condition worse.

Guildenstern grows impatient, and he tries to convince Hamlet to calm down. Gertrude has sent Guildenstern to Hamlet to tell the prince that his behavior has been upsetting. She wants to see the prince in her chambers. Hamlet's answers are quick and his wit has an angry edge to it. He feels no peace in this victory. He treats his childhood friends as he has been treating Polonius, with ridicule and barely concealed contempt.

Rosencrantz reminds Hamlet of their old friendship, to which Hamlet responds only briefly (340–341). Rosencrantz also reminds Hamlet that he is next in line for the throne, and he even has the king's "voice" in favor of the succession (346). Again, in an elected monarchy, the former king's voice is of primary importance. Hamlet's response in line 348 refers to an old proverb, which states, "While the grass doth grow oft starves the seely steed." Hamlet means that although he is named to be the next king, the crown is not among his ambitions; his satisfaction will be found elsewhere.

Played like a pipe

Players come in with "recorders," flute-like instruments that are held between the lips and extend outward. Hamlet takes one from the players and holds it out to Guildenstern to play. Guildenstern, unlike Hamlet, is a man of few achievements. He cannot play the pipe nor can he be honest with his supposed friend. He can, however, lie, and this is the point that Hamlet tries to make.

Hamlet's childhood friends have tried to use him; they have tried to play on him as they would on a pipe. They have tried to use friendship as a method of discovering Hamlet's secrets, and those secrets, if discovered, would be reported to the king and used against Hamlet as effectively as a weapon. Hamlet dismisses Rosencrantz and Guildenstern with disgust, telling them that they are not skilled enough to "play upon" him (377).

Gertrude must be growing impatient with Hamlet. He has been summoned to her chambers, and he has still not arrived. She now sends Polonius to bring Hamlet to her. Upon seeing the old man, Hamlet dismisses Rosencrantz and Guildenstern and turns his ridicule once again toward Polonius. He poses riddles that Polonius cannot answer. Polonius decides that agreeing with anything Hamlet says, no matter how ridiculous, is his safest tactic. After a brief banter, Polonius delivers his message from Gertrude and quickly departs.

Hamlet, left alone once more, recites his fifth soliloquy, a brief but telling speech. This time, he sounds full of revenge, unlike the Hamlet we have seen in the previous soliloquies. He has experienced a change in his spirit, and the transformation shows. A new strain of willful cruelty replaces his reflective, gentle side. Now he is hardened and ready to do battle, not with his soul but with the flesh and blood of his stepfather. First Hamlet must face his mother, tell her the truth, and make her face up to her part in this tragedy.

Act III, Scene 3

The king employs Rosencrantz and Guildenstern to accompany Hamlet to England. When he is alone, Claudius falls to his knees and tries to pray. He admits his sin but realizes that he cannot repent without losing his crown and his wife. Hamlet enters and, believing that the king is praying, decides to postpone his revenge.

ACT III, SCENE 3
A room in the castle.

[Enter KING, ROSENCRANTZ, and GUILDENSTERN]

King I like him not, nor stands it safe with us
  To let his madness range. Therefore prepare you;
  I your commission will forthwith dispatch,
  And he to England shall along with you.
  The terms of our estate may not endure   5
  Hazard so dangerous as doth hourly grow
  Out of his lunacies.

Guildenstern   We will ourselves provide.
  Most holy and religious fear it is
  To keep those many many bodies safe
  That live and feed upon your majesty.   10

Rosencrantz The single and peculiar life is bound
  With all the strength and armour of the mind
  To keep itself from noyance; but much more
  That spirit upon whose weal depend and rest
  The lives of many. The cease of majesty   15
  Dies not alone, but, like a gulf doth draw
  What's near it with it; it is a massy wheel,
  Fix'd on the summit of the highest mount,
  To whose huge spokes ten thousand lesser things
  Are mortis'd and adjoin'd; which, when it falls,   20
  Each small annexment, petty consequence,
  Attends the boisterous ruin. Never alone
  Did the king sigh, but with a general groan.

King Arm you, I pray you, to this speedy voyage;
  For we will fetters put upon this fear,   25
  Which now goes too free-footed.

Rosencrantz and Guildenstern We will haste us.

*[Exeunt ROSENCRANTZ and GUILDENSTERN. Enter
  POLONIUS]*

NOTES

2.   *range:* roam freely.

5.   *terms of our estate:* our position as head of the state.

7.   *ourselves provide:* make our preparations.

8.   *fear:* anxiety.

9.   *many bodies:* the king's subjects

11.   *peculiar:* private.

13.   *noyance:* harm.

14.   *weal:* welfare.

15.   *cease of majesty:* death of a king.

16.   *gulf:* whirlpool.

17.   *massy:* massive.

20.   *mortis'd:* firmly joined.

21.   *annexment, petty consequence:* attachment, smallest thing connected with it.

22.   *Attends:* is included in.

23.   *general groan:* the grief of all his people.

Polonius My lord, he's going to his mother's closet:
Behind the arras I'll convey myself
To hear the process; I'll warrant she'll tax him home;   30
And, as you said, and wisely was it said,
'Tis meet that some more audience than a mother,
Since nature makes them partial, should o'erhear
The speech, of vantage. Fare you well, my liege:
I'll call upon you ere you go to bed   35
And tell you what I know.

King   Thanks, dear my lord.
[Exit POLONIUS]
O! my offence is rank, it smells to heaven;
It hath the primal eldest curse upon 't;
A brother's murder! Pray can I not,
Though inclination be as sharp as will: 40
My stronger guilt defeats my strong intent;
And like a man to double business bound,
I stand in pause where I shall first begin,
And both neglect. What if this cursed hand
Were thicker than itself with brother's blood,   45
Is there not rain enough in the sweet heavens
To wash it white as snow? Whereto serves mercy
But to confront the visage of offence?
And what's in prayer but this two-fold force,
To be forestalled, ere we come to fall,   50
Or pardon'd, being down? Then, I'll look up;
My fault is past. But, O! what form of prayer
Can serve my turn? 'Forgive me my foul murder?'
That cannot be since I am still possess'd
Of those effects for which I did the murder,   55
My crown, mine own ambition, and my queen.
May one be pardon'd and retain the offence?
In the corrupted currents of this world
Offence's gilded hand may shove by justice,
And oft 'tis seen the wicked prize itself   60
Buys out the law; but 'tis not so above;
There is no shuffling, there the action lies
In his true nature, and we ourselves compell'd
Even to the teeth and forehead of our faults
To give in evidence. What then? what rests?   65
Try what repentance can: what can it not?

---

29. *arras:* a tapestry wall hanging.

30. *process:* proceedings.

     tax him home: effectually take him to task.

34. *of vantage:* from some place of vantage.

37. *rank:* foul.

38. *primal eldest curse:* that is, the one pronounced upon Cain in Genesis 4 for the murder of his brother. Primal here means original.

40. *will:* desire.

48. *confront . . . offence:* oppose sin face to face, like a champion.

50. *forestalled:* prevented.

55. *effects:* advantages.

57. *offence:* sin.

58. *currents:* courses, ways.

60. *wicked prize:* proceeds of the crime.

62–63. *there . . . nature:* the case is tried on its merits.

64. *teeth and forehead:* in the very face of.

65. *rests:* remains (to be done).

Yet what can it, when one can not repent?
O wretched state! O bosom black as death!
O limed soul, that struggling to be free
Art more engaged! Help, angels! make assay; 70
Bow, stubborn knees; and heart with strings of steel
Be soft as sinews of the new-born babe.
All may be well. *[Retires and kneels. Enter HAMLET]*

Hamlet Now might I do it pat, now he is praying;
And now I'll do 't: and so he goes to heaven; 75
And so am I reveng'd. That would be scann'd:
A villain kills my father; and for that,
I, his sole son, do this same villain send
To heaven.
Why, this is hire and salary, not revenge. 80
He took my father grossly, full of bread,
With all his crimes broad blown, as flush as May;
And how his audit stands who knows save heaven?
But in our circumstance and course of thought
'Tis heavy with him. And am I then reveng'd, 85
To take him in the purging of his soul,
When he is fit and season'd for his passage?
No.
Up, sword, and know thou a more horrid hent;
When he is drunk asleep, or in his rage, 90
Or in the incestuous pleasure of his bed,
At gaming, swearing, or about some act
That has no relish of salvation in 't;
Then trip him, that his heels may kick at heaven,
And that his soul may be as damn'd and black 95
As hell, whereto it goes. My mother stays:
This physic but prolongs thy sickly days.

[Exit. The KING rises and advances]

King My words fly up, my thoughts remain below:
Words without thoughts never to heaven go. *[Exit]*

69.	*limed:* caught in lime, a substance that was used to capture birds.
70.	*engaged:* entangled.
	assay: an attempt.
74.	*pat:* easily.
76.	*That . . . scann'd:* It demands closer examination.
80.	*hire and salary:* action deserving pay, a kind act.
81.	*grossly:* in a state of sin.
82.	*broad blown:* in full blossom.
	flush: fresh.
83.	*audit:* account (with heaven).
84.	*circumstance . . . thought:* the way we on earth look at things.
87.	*season'd:* ripe, ready.
89.	*hent:* literally grasp, hence a time for action.
96.	*stays:* waits for me.
97.	*physic:* medicine, that is, prayer.

COMMENTARY

After leaving Hamlet, Rosencrantz and Guildenstern go immediately to the king to report what they have seen. This scene begins with the two men in conference with the king. This is their third meeting in the play and the one with the darkest purpose, as the king becomes increasingly suspicious and less able to tolerate Hamlet.

By this point, Claudius is convinced that Hamlet is not crazy and that, somehow, Hamlet has discovered the king's secret. The king tells Rosencrantz and Guildenstern that he is ready to send Hamlet away. He uses the excuse that the prince's madness is becoming dangerous to the state. Rosencrantz and Guildenstern are, as usual, only too anxious to serve the king whom they "live and feed upon" (10). The parasite imagery is unmistakable.

Ordered to England

Fearing for himself and unconcerned with Gertrude's feelings on the subject, Claudius orders Rosencrantz and Guildenstern to prepare to depart for England. They are to accompany Hamlet and serve as couriers from Claudius to the King of England. Rosencrantz justifies their betrayal of Hamlet by telling Claudius that because the king deems Hamlet dangerous, as loyal subjects they must defer to his royal judgment. As the mind is to the body, so the monarch is to the state.

Rosencrantz delivers a speech starting in line 11 that expresses an opinion with which Elizabethan audiences, who viewed their queen as the embodiment of England, would heartily agree. If Claudius were the rightful king, Rosencrantz would be correct to follow his orders. But Claudius has killed the rightful king, usurped the throne, and corrupted Denmark with his crime. The audience knows all that has transpired and can appreciate the irony of Rosencrantz's words under the circumstances.

Polonius has scurried from Gertrude to Hamlet and now finds Claudius to report that the queen and her son will soon meet. Polonius will return to Gertrude's chambers and hide "[b]ehind the arras" in order to eavesdrop on their conversation (29). He assures the king that Gertrude will be able to reach Hamlet, find out the cause of his behavior, and set him right once again. "Fare you well, my leige" will be Polonius's last words to Claudius (34).

The appearance of prayer

Claudius thanks Polonius, but he has already made up his mind to kill Hamlet, an act that will allow the king to feel safe again. Hamlet's continued presence in court is unbearable, and exile from Denmark holds the possibility of return — a possibility that Claudius will not entertain. Hamlet must die.

The thought of another murder on his already overburdened conscience weighs Claudius down, and he falls to his knees. He experiences a moment of weary

defeat. He clearly understands the gravity of his sins, and he admits his guilt. Claudius regrets having been discovered, but repentance would require confession and penance, followed by the surrender of his throne and his queen — the two treasures for which he committed the murder in the first place. Prayer has not served him, so evil must. His is the reasoning of a hardened sinner: If I am damned, then all I have is this life, and nothing I do can lighten my punishment. Claudius decides that he cannot do what would be required of him for salvation, so he will finish what he started and accept his ultimate damnation.

When Hamlet enters the scene, Claudius is on his knees. Hamlet is still excited and expectant, because the king's response to the play has vindicated Hamlet. This is exactly the kind of opportunity Hamlet has been waiting for: Claudius has confirmed his guilt to Hamlet, and now Hamlet finds him alone and easy prey for revenge.

Without knowing what is happening in Claudius's mind, Hamlet assumes that he is repenting his sins. Hamlet stops himself from approaching Claudius when he remembers that Claudius killed old Hamlet without giving the king an opportunity to confess his sins. For that reason, the ghost of the king is "doomed for a certain time" to "fast in fires" (I.5.10–11). In other words, the king is in purgatory, having died without last rites or confession.

In the old Catholic tradition, inherited by the Church of England, a person who died without confessing his or her sins to a priest and receiving penance and absolution (forgiveness) did not go to heaven, at least not immediately. If the person died with unconfessed venial sins (less serious, unpremeditated sins such as lying, cheating, stealing), his soul would be required to spend some time in purgatory as punishment for those sins. If a person died with even one mortal sin (a very serious premeditated sin like murder and adultery), she would be condemned to hell for eternity.

Hamlet believes that the king is praying. If Hamlet kills Claudius while he is repenting, Claudius's soul will go to heaven. To assure revenge, Hamlet decides to wait until he can catch his uncle in sin and unprepared for death. He loses this opportunity for revenge, and Claudius loses his opportunity to repent. They are each now fully committed to a specific course of action.

Act III, Scene 4

In Gertrude's chamber, the queen reprimands her son for being disrespectful while Polonius listens from a hiding place. Hamlet, thinking that the voice he hears belongs to the king, mistakenly kills Polonius. Then Hamlet berates his mother angrily for her recent behavior. The spirit reappears and reminds Hamlet not to hurt his mother. Hamlet advises Gertrude to reform her life. He then drags the body of Polonius out of the room.

ACT III, SCENE 4
The queen's apartment.

[Enter QUEEN and POLONIUS]

Polonius He will come straight. Look you lay home to him;
Tell him his pranks have been too broad to bear with,
And that your Grace hath screen'd and stood between
Much heat and him. I'll silence me e'en here.
Pray you, be round with him.   5

Hamlet *[Within]* Mother, mother, mother!

Queen   I'll warrant you;
Fear me not. Withdraw, I hear him coming.

[POLONIUS hides behind the arras. Enter HAMLET]

Hamlet Now, mother, what's the matter?

Queen Hamlet, thou hast thy father much offended.

Hamlet Mother, you have my father much offended.   10

Queen Come, come, you answer with an idle tongue.

Hamlet Go, go, you question with a wicked tongue.

Queen Why, how now, Hamlet!

Hamlet   What's the matter now?

Queen Have you forgot me?

Hamlet   No, by the rood, not so:
You are the queen, your husband's brother's wife;   15
And, — would it were not so! — you are my mother.

Queen Nay then, I'll set those to you that can speak.

Hamlet Come, come, and sit you down; you shall not budge;
You go not, till I set up a glass
Where you may see the inmost part of you.   20

NOTES

1.   *lay home to him:* tell him what's what.

2.   *broad:* open and unrestrained.

4.   *heat:* anger.
     silence me: hide myself.

11. *idle:* foolish.

14. *rood:* cross, crucifix.

17. *I'll . . . speak:* an understated threat.

19. *glass:* mirror.

Queen What wilt thou do? thou wilt not murder me?
  Help, help, ho!

Polonius *[Behind]*   What, ho! help! help! help!

Hamlet *[Draws]* How now! a rat? Dead, for a ducat, dead!

[Makes a pass through the arras]

Polonius *[Behind]* O! I am slain.

Queen O me! what hast thou done?   25

Hamlet Nay, I know not: is it the king?

Queen O! what a rash and bloody deed is this!

Hamlet A bloody deed! almost as bad, good mother,
  As kill a king, and marry with his brother.

Queen As kill a king!

Hamlet   Ay, lady, 'twas my word.   30
  [Lifts up the arras and discovers POLONIUS]
  [To POLONIUS] Thou wretched, rash, intruding fool,
      farewell!
  I took thee for thy better; take thy fortune;
  Thou find'st to be too busy in some danger.
  Leave wringing of your hands: peace! sit you down,
  And let me wring your heart; for so I shall   35
  If it be made of penetrable stuff,
  If damned custom have not brass'd it so
  That it is proof and bulwark against sense.

Queen What have I done that thou dar'st wag thy tongue
  In noise so rude against me?

Hamlet   Such an act   40
  That blurs the grace and blush of modesty,
  Calls virtue hypocrite, takes off the rose
  From the fair forehead of an innocent love
  And sets a blister there, make marriage vows
  As false as dicers' oaths; O! such a deed   45
  As from the body of contraction plucks
  The very soul, and sweet religion makes
  A rhapsody of words; heaven's face doth glow,
  Yea, this solidity and compound mass,
  With tristful visage, as against the doom,   50
  Is thought-sick at the act.

---

23. *for a ducat:* would stake a coin on it.

32. *thy better:* that is, the king.

37. *If . . . so:* if habitual vice hasn't made your heart impenetrable.

38. *sense:* feeling.

44. *sets a blister:* In Elizabethan England, prostitutes were sometimes branded with a hot iron.

46. *contraction:* the marriage contract.

48. *rhapsody of words:* a mere string of meaningless words.

49. *solidity and compound mass:* the earth.

50. *tristful:* sorrowful.

as against the doom: as before the Day of Judgment.

Queen   Ay me! what act,
That roars so loud and thunders in the index?

Hamlet Look here, upon this picture, and on this;
The counterfeit presentment of two brothers.
See, what a grace was seated on this brow;   55
Hyperion's curls, the front of Jove himself,
An eye like Mars to threaten and command,
A station like the herald Mercury
New-lighted on a heaven-kissing hill,
A combination and a form indeed,   60
Where every god did seem to set his seal,
To give the world assurance of a man.
This was your husband: look you now, what follows.
Here is your husband; like a mildew'd ear,
Blasting his wholesome brother. Have you eyes?   65
Could you on this fair mountain leave to feed,
And batten on this moor? Ha! have you eyes?
You cannot call it love, for at your age
The hey-day in the blood is tame, it's humble,
And waits upon the judgment; and what judgment   70
Would step from this to this? Sense, sure, you have,
Else could you not have motion; but sure, that sense
Is apoplex'd; for madness would not err.
Nor sense to ecstasy was ne'er so thrall'd
But it reserv'd some quantity of choice,   75
To serve in such a difference. What devil was't
That thus hath cozen'd you at hoodman-blind?
Eyes without feeling, feeling without sight,
Ears without hands or eyes, smelling sans all,
Or but a sickly part of one true sense   80
Could not so mope.
O shame! where is thy blush? Rebellious hell,
If thou canst mutine in a matron's bones,
To flaming youth let virtue be as wax,
And melt in her own fire: proclaim no shame   85
When the compulsive ardour gives the charge,
Since frost itself as actively doth burn,
And reason panders will.

Queen   O Hamlet! speak no more;
Thou turn'st mine eyes into my very soul;

52.	*index:* prologue.
54.	*counterfeit presentment:* portrait.
56.	*front:* forehead.
58.	*station:* stature, posture.
	Mercury: the graceful messenger of the gods.
59.	*New-lighted:* newly alighted.
60.	*combination:* of physical attributes.
61.	*set his seal:* place his stamp of approval.
64–65.	*like . . . brother:* as a mildewed ear of corn infects the one next to it.
66.	*leave to feed:* leave off feeding.
67.	*batten:* glut yourself.
69.	*hey-day:* excitement.
71.	*Sense:* feeling.
72.	*motion:* impulses.
73.	*apoplex'd:* paralyzed.
74.	*ecstasy:* passion.
	thrall'd: enslaved.
77.	*cozen'd:* cheated.
	hoodman-blind: blindman's bluff.
79.	*sans:* without.
81.	*so mope:* be so stupid.
83.	*mutine:* mutiny.
86.	*compulsive ardour:* compelling passions of youth.
87.	*frost:* aging causes the hair to turn gray or frosty white.
88.	*panders:* serves.
	will: desire.

And there I see such black and grained spots   90
As will not leave their tinct.

Hamlet   Nay, but to live
In the rank sweat of an enseam'd bed,
Stew'd in corruption, honeying and making love
Over the nasty sty, —

Queen   O! speak to me no more;
These words like daggers enter in mine ears;   95
No more, sweet Hamlet!

Hamlet   A murderer, and a villain;
A slave that is not twentieth part the tithe
Of your precedent lord; a vice of kings;
A cut-purse of the empire and the rule,
That from a shelf the precious diadem stole,   100
And put it in his pocket!

Queen   No more!

Hamlet A king of shreds and patches, —
[Enter Ghost]
Save me and hover o'er me with your wings,
You heavenly guards! What would your gracious figure?

Queen Alas! he's mad!   105

Hamlet Do you not come your tardy son to chide,
That, laps'd in time and passion, lets go by
The important acting of your dread command?
O! say.

Ghost   Do not forget: this visitation
Is but to whet thy almost blunted purpose.   110
But, look! amazement on thy mother sits;
O! step between her and her fighting soul;
Conceit in weakest bodies strongest works:
Speak to her, Hamlet.

Hamlet   How is it with you, lady?

Queen Alas! how is't with you,   115
That you do bend your eye on vacancy
And with the incorporal air do hold discourse?
Forth at your eyes your spirits wildly peep;
And, as the sleeping soldiers in the alarm,
Your bedded hair, like life in excrements,   120

90. *grained:* dyed in the grain.

91. *leave their tinct:* give up their color.

92. *enseam'd:* greasy, with a pun on semen.

97. *tithe:* tenth part of one's income, usually the share that goes to the church.

98. *precedent:* former.

    vice of kings: caricature of a king. Vice, who represented sin, was a stock character in morality plays.

99. *cut-purse:* thief.

102. *king . . . patches:* a king in fool's dress, a clown.

110. *whet:* sharpen.

113. *Conceit:* imagination.

117. *incorporal:* bodiless.

118. *at:* from.

120. *bedded:* lying flat.

    excrements: outgrowths of the body, such as hair and nails.

Starts up and stands an end. O gentle son!
Upon the heat and flame of thy distemper
Sprinkle cool patience. Whereon do you look?

Hamlet On him, on him! Look you, how pale he glares!
His form and cause conjoin'd, preaching to stones,   125
Would make them capable. Do not look upon me;
Lest with this piteous action you convert
My stern effects: then what I have to do
Will want true colour; tears perchance for blood.

Queen To whom do you speak this?

Hamlet   Do you see nothing there?   130

Queen Nothing at all; yet all that is I see.

Hamlet Nor did you nothing hear?

Queen   No, nothing but ourselves.

Hamlet. Why, look you there! look, how it steals away;
My father, in his habit as he liv'd;
Look! where he goes, even now, out at the portal.   135

[Exit Ghost]

Queen This is the very coinage of your brain:
This bodiless creation ecstasy
Is very cunning in.

Hamlet Ecstasy!
My pulse, as yours, doth temperately keep time,   140
And makes as healthful music. It is not madness
That I have utter'd: bring me to the test,
And I the matter will re-word, which madness
Would gambol from. Mother, for love of grace,
Lay not that flattering unction to your soul,   145
That not your trespass but my madness speaks;
It will but skin and film the ulcerous place,
Whiles rank corruption, mining all within,
Infects unseen. Confess yourself to heaven;
Repent what's past; avoid what is to come;   150
And do not spread the compost on the weeds
To make them ranker. Forgive me this my virtue:
For in the fatness of these pursy times

121. *an:* on.
122. *distemper:* mental disturbance.

125. *His . . . conjoin'd:* his ghostly appearance combined with the reason for it (that is, his murder).
126. *capable:* of feeling and action.
128. *My stern effects:* the results that Hamlet intends to bring about.
129. *colour:* character or kind.
    for: instead of.

134. *in . . . liv'd:* in his ordinary dress.

137. *ecstasy:* madness.

144. *gambol:* wander.
145. *unction:* ointment, salve; used for medical and/or religious purposes.
147. *It:* refers back to "that flattering unction."
148. *mining:* undermining.

151. *compost:* manure.
152. *my virtue:* my virtuous pleading.
153. *fatness:* grossness.
    pursy: sensual.

Virtue itself of vice must pardon beg,
Yea, curb and woo for leave to do him good.   155

Queen O Hamlet! thou hast cleft my heart in twain.

Hamlet O! throw away the worser part of it,
And live the purer with the other half.
Good night; but go not to mine uncle's bed;
Assume a virtue, if you have it not.   160
That monster, custom, who all sense doth eat,
Of habits devil, is angel yet in this,
That to the use of actions fair and good
He likewise gives a frock or livery,
That aptly is put on. Refrain to-night;   165
And that shall lend a kind of easiness
To the next abstinence: the next more easy;
For use almost can change the stamp of nature,
And exorcise the devil or throw him out
With wondrous potency. Once more, good-night: 170
And when you are desirous to be bless'd,
I'll blessing beg of you. For this same lord,
[Pointing to POLONIUS]
I do repent: but heaven hath pleas'd it so,
To punish me with this, and this with me,
That I must be their scourge and minister.   175
I will bestow him, and will answer well
The death I gave him. So, again, good-night.
I must be cruel only to be kind:
Thus bad begins and worse remains behind.
One word more, good lady.

Queen   What shall I do?   180

Hamlet Not this, by no means, that I bid you do:
Let the bloat king tempt you again to bed;
Pinch wanton on your cheek; call you his mouse;
And let him, for a pair of reechy kisses,
Or paddling in your neck with his damn'd fingers,   185
Make you to ravel all this matter out,
That I essentially am not in madness,
But mad in craft. 'Twere good you let him know;
For who that's but a queen, fair, sober, wise,
Would from a paddock, from a bat, a gib,   190
Such dear concernings hide? who would do so?

---

155. *curb:* bend, bow low.

leave: permission.

161–165. *That monster . . . put on:* Though evil can become ingrained through custom, virtue also can become just as much a habit.

162. *devil:* evil spirit presiding over habits.

163. *use:* practice.

165. *aptly:* readily.

168. *stamp:* one's natural proclivities.

171. *desirous to be bless'd:* penitent.

175. *their:* powers of heaven.

176. *bestow:* get rid of.

179. *worse remains behind:* Hamlet still has the king to deal with.

182. *bloat:* bloated.

183. *wanton:* lewdly.

mouse: a common term of endearment.

184. *reechy:* literally smoky, foul.

186. *ravel:* unravel, reveal.

187. *essentially:* truly.

190. *paddock:* toad.

gib: tomcat.

191. *dear concernings:* matters of such close concern (to the king).

No, in despite of sense and secrecy,
Unpeg the basket on the house's top,
Let the birds fly, and, like the famous ape,
To try conclusions, in the basket creep,   195
And break your own neck down.

Queen Be thou assur'd, if words be made of breath,
And breath of life, I have no life to breathe
What thou hast said to me.

Hamlet I must to England; you know that?

Queen   Alack!   200
I had forgot: 'tis so concluded on.

Hamlet There's letters seal'd; and my two schoolfellows,
Whom I will trust as I will adders fang'd,
They bear the mandate; they must sweep my way,
And marshal me to knavery. Let it work;   205
For 'tis the sport to have the enginer
Hoist with his own petard: and 't shall go hard
But I will delve one yard below their mines,
And blow them at the moon. O! 'tis most sweet,
When in one line two crafts directly meet.   210
This man shall set me packing;
I'll lug the guts into the neighbour room.
Mother, good-night. Indeed this counsellor
Is now most still, most secret, and most grave,
Who was in life a foolish prating knave.   215
Come, sir, to draw toward an end with you.
Good-night, mother.

[Exeunt severally; HAMLET tugging in POLONIUS]

192. *despite:* spite.

195. *To try conclusions:* to see what will happen.

204. *mandate:* command.

205. *marshal me to knavery:* Conduct me to the place where the villainy will take place. (Hamlet suspects that an attempt will be made on his life.)

206. *enginer:* engineer.

207. *Hoist . . . petard:* blown up by his own landmine (petard).

210. *crafts:* designs, schemes.

211. *packing:* on my way.

212. *neighbour:* neighboring.

COMMENTARY

This intense domestic scene is the pivotal moment between Hamlet and Gertrude, and neither of them will ever be the same from this time on. Hamlet must confront his mother before he can move forward with his plans for revenge. He will speak to Gertrude and make her understand what she has done. Gertrude, too, has been waiting to speak to Hamlet. She cannot know what is in her son's heart or that this night will change their lives forever.

Moved to murder

Polonius, who had hidden behind the *arras* (a hanging tapestry) in order to eavesdrop on the queen and Hamlet, hears more than he bargained for — Hamlet's rage and Gertrude's cry, "[T]hou wilt not murder me?" (21). The old man calls out for help and Hamlet, thinking the voice belongs to Claudius, stabs Polonius.

The murder of Polonius is completely impulsive. Hamlet has moved from contemplating murder to committing it. Barely pausing to acknowledge his action, he turns back to Gertrude, accusing her of being an accomplice to murder and an adulterer. His passion and anger rise steadily towards hysteria as he verbally attacks his mother. She backs away from her defiance, and she is soon reduced to anguish and guilt.

Hamlet shows his mother portraits of Claudius and his father. The display drives Hamlet's point home; Gertrude quickly understands the contrast, and her guilt over her marriage to Claudius is evident. However, her shock at the mention of murder seems a clear indication of her innocence in that matter.

The force of Hamlet's momentum cannot be slowed, even after Gertrude understands what he is telling her. He "roars" and "thunders" at her; his language becomes increasingly more vulgar, with more sexual references (52). When Gertrude begs Hamlet to stop, her pleas only drive him to more intense anger.

Hamlet (Laurence Olivier) stabs Polonius in the 1948 film version of Hamlet.
Everett Collection

The apparition reappears

The appearance of the ghost stops Hamlet instantly. He turns his attention towards the spirit, protecting himself, once again, with a prayer. Gertrude cannot see the ghost; she can only see Hamlet's wide-eyed stare and silenced mouth. The ghost speaks, reminding Hamlet not to harm his mother. As if conscious of the difference between the castle battlements and his former wife's bedchamber, the spirit appears not in armor but "in his habit as he liv'd" (134).

Hamlet begins to calm down, and Gertrude, still in shock, is convinced now more than ever that her son is mad. Hamlet assures Gertrude that this vision is "not madness" (141).

Now that his anger is spent, Hamlet speaks directly to his mother. He tells her that she can repent by giving up her life with Claudius. Gertrude still has time to restore her soul to purity. Gertrude is emotionally drained and now leans upon Hamlet. She does not know what to do or where else to turn, because she no longer trusts herself.

Hamlet's advice to his mother recalls the Player King's notion of fortune leading love, but now both mother and son can see some hope for the future. If time can kill a virtuous love, it can do the same for an immoral one. Gertrude asks Hamlet what she should do; their roles are now reversed. Hamlet tells her that she must never sleep with Claudius, "the bloat king," again (182). She must reestablish her virtue and her soul.

Hamlet tells Gertrude that he knows Claudius will send him to England in the company of Rosencrantz and Guildenstern, and he is aware of the existence of letters meant for England's king. He does not trust his old childhood friends; he knows about their allegience to Claudius.

Hamlet indicates that he may be aware of Claudius's plan to use Rosencrantz and Guildenstern to kill him. He tells Gertrude that they will not succeed — he will "blow them at the moon" (209). Hamlet finally addresses the dead councilor, Polonius, and, in a rhymed couplet, eulogizes the old man briefly (214–215). Trusting that Gertrude will not tell Claudius what she knows, Hamlet drags the body of Polonius out of the room.

Notes

CLIFFSCOMPLETE

HAMLET
ACT IV

Hamlet *How all occasions do inform against me,*
And spur my dull revenge! What is a man,
If his chief good and market of his time
Be but to sleep and feed? a beast, no more.
Sure he that made us with such large discourse,
Looking before and after, gave us not
That capability and god-like reason
To fust in us unus'd.

Act IV, Scene 1

Gertrude tells Claudius that Hamlet has killed Polonius. The king sends Rosencrantz and Guildenstern to find Hamlet.

ACT IV, SCENE 1
A room in the castle.

[Enter KING, QUEEN, ROSENCRANTZ, and
   GUILDENSTERN]

King There's matter in these sighs, these profound heaves:
  You must translate; 'tis fit we understand them.
  Where is your son?

Queen *[To ROSENCRANTZ and GUILDENSTERN]*
  Bestow this place on us a little while.
  [Exeunt ROSENCRANTZ and GUILDENSTERN]
  Ah! my good lord, what have I seen to-night.   5

King What, Gertrude? How does Hamlet?

Queen Mad as the sea and wind, when both contend
  Which is the mightier. In his lawless fit,
  Behind the arras hearing something stir,
  Whips out his rapier, cries, 'A rat! a rat!'   10
  And, in his brainish apprehension, kills
  The unseen good old man.

King   O heavy deed!
  It had been so with us had we been there.
  His liberty is full of threats to all;
  To you yourself, to us, to every one.   15
  Alas! how shall this bloody deed be answer'd?
  It will be laid to us, whose providence
  Should have kept short, restrain'd, and out of haunt,
  This mad young man: but so much was our love,
  We would not understand what was most fit,   20
  But, like the owner of a foul disease,
  To keep it from divulging, let it feed
  Even on the pith of life. Where is he gone?

Queen To draw apart the body he hath kill'd;
  O'er whom his very madness, like some ore   25

NOTES

1.   *matter:* something serious.

4.   *Bestow this place on us:* Leave this place to us.

11.   *brainish apprehension:* mad notion (that he heard a rat).

17.   *providence:* foresight.

18.   *out of haunt:* away from others.

22.   *divulging:* becoming known.

23.   *pith:* marrow.

25.   *ore:* gold.

Among a mineral of metals base,
Shows itself pure: he weeps for what is done.

King O Gertrude! come away.
The sun no sooner shall the mountains touch
But we will ship him hence; and this vile deed   30
We must, with all our majesty and skill,
Both countenance and excuse. Ho! Guildenstern!
[Re-enter ROSENCRANTZ and GUILDENSTERN]
Friends both, go join you with some further aid:
Hamlet in madness hath Polonius slain,
And from his mother's closet hath he dragg'd him: 35
Go seek him out; speak fair, and bring the body
Into the chapel. I pray you, haste in this.
[Exeunt ROSENCRANTZ and GUILDENSTERN]
Come, Gertrude, we'll call up our wisest friends;
And let them know both what we mean to do,
And what's untimely done: so, haply, slander,   40
Whose whisper o'er the world's diameter,
As level as the cannon to his blank
Transports his poison'd shot, may miss our name,
And hit the woundless air. O! come away;
My soul is full of discord and dismay. *[Exeunt]*   45

26.   *mineral:* rock sample.

32.   *countenance:* recognize.

42.   *level:* straight to the mark.
      blank: bull's-eye.
44.   *woundless:* invulnerable.

COMMENTARY

Immediately after Hamlet drags Polonius's body out of the room, the king enters and the queen tells him about Hamlet's madness and rage. Gertrude describes the murder of Polonius. Claudius sounds genuinely distressed. He realizes that if he had been in Gertrude's chamber, Hamlet would surely have killed him, too: "It had been so with us had we been there" (14).

Claudius informs Gertrude that they are to blame for this murder. If they had addressed Hamlet's madness in a more definitive way instead of indulging him, Polonius would still be alive. In any case, the court and the country will view the situation that way. Claudius must get Hamlet out of the country as soon as possible.

Rosencrantz and Guildenstern seem to hover near the king now. They enter the scene with Claudius and then depart when the queen asks them for privacy. After the conversation between Gertrude and Claudius, the king summons Guidenstern back and both men return. Unknown to Gertrude, Claudius has already made arrangements for Hamlet's departure, and now he sends Rosencrantz and Guildenstern to find the prince and leave as quickly as possible.

Polonius's death at Hamlet's hands foreshadows the ultimate fate of Claudius. Still, the king cannot yet know that the death of the old man occurred simultaneously with the end of his marital relationship with Gertrude. This sad moment marks a point of no turning back for Claudius. Hamlet has succeeded in exposing the hypocrisy and evil of the court. Hamlet is now a threat to Claudius's throne, plus he has ruined the taste of victory. The king still has the crown, but his conscience haunts him and his wife is turning away from him. Claudius's world of illusion is being replaced by a hideous reality.

Act IV, Scene 2

Hamlet is discovered by Rosencrantz and Guildenstern and accompanies them to where Claudius waits.

ACT IV, SCENE 2
Another room in the same.

[Enter HAMLET]

Hamlet Safely stowed.

Rosencrantz and Guildenstern *[Within]* Hamlet! Lord
    Hamlet!

Hamlet What noise? who calls on Hamlet?
    O! here they come.

[Enter ROSENCRANTZ and GUILDENSTERN]

Rosencrantz What have you done, my lord, with the   5
    dead body?

Hamlet Compounded it with dust, whereto 'tis kin.

Rosencrantz Tell us where 'tis, that we may take it thence
    And bear it to the chapel.

Hamlet Do not believe it.

Rosencrantz Believe what?   10

Hamlet That I can keep your counsel and not mine
    own. Besides, to be demanded of a sponge! what
    replication should be made by the son of a king?

Rosencrantz Take you me for a sponge, my lord?

Hamlet Ay, sir, that soaks up the king's countenance,   15
    his rewards, his authorities. But such officers
    do the king best service in the end: he keeps them,
    like an ape, in the corner of his jaw; first mouthed,
    to be last swallowed: when he needs what you have
    gleaned, it is but squeezing you, and, sponge, you   20
    shall be dry again.

Rosencrantz I understand you not, my lord.

Hamlet I am glad of it: a knavish speech sleeps in a
    foolish ear.

NOTES

6.   *Compounded:* restored, mingled.

11.   *counsel:* secrets.

12.   *demanded of:* questioned by.

      sponge: soaking up royal favor.

13.   *replication:* answer, reply.

15.   *countenance:* looks.

18.   *first mouthed:* put into the mouth first in order that all the goodness may be extracted before swallowing.

23–24.   *a knavish . . . foolish ear:* a roguish speech is never understood by a fool.

Rosencrantz My lord, you must tell us where the   25
body is, and go with us to the king.

Hamlet The body is with the king, but the king is
not with the body. The king is a thing —

Guildenstern A thing, my lord!

Hamlet Of nothing: bring me to him. Hide fox,   30
and all after.

[Exeunt]

30–31. *Hide . . . after:* a game like hide-and-seek.

COMMENTARY

This scene opens with Hamlet's grisly comment on the mock-burial of Polonius; Hamlet has put the old man's body somewhere, but that location is not disclosed. Rosencrantz and Guildenstern have been looking for the prince, and they call out to him. Hamlet stops his grim work. He answers their questions about Polonius's body with riddles and puns.

The comedy of the scene provides slight relief in the midst of intensity. The humor reminds us of Hamlet's wit, but it is now somewhat tarnished by his crime. Rosencrantz and Guildenstern are no match for Hamlet's quick wit, as we have already seen.

Rosencrantz and Guildenstern are rather pathetic in their inability to understand that Hamlet's madness is no more than a maddening escapade. He calls them "sponge[s]," benefiting from their friendship with him by soaking up "the king's countenance, his rewards, his authorities" (12, 15–16). But in reality, he tells them, they are nothing but nuts in the mouth of an ape. Their usefulness will be sucked out, and then they will be spit out and discarded. They will be nothing and have nothing, because they have already surrendered their honor. They press Hamlet about the whereabouts of the body, but he continues to act as if all this is just a prank. Hamlet is now making the rules.

Act IV, Scene 3

The king declares that Hamlet must leave Denmark for his own safety. Rosencrantz and Guildenstern enter with Hamlet. Claudius orders Hamlet to England in the company of Rosencrantz and Guildenstern, who carry a letter for England's king.

ACT IV, SCENE 3
Another room in the same.

[Enter KING, attended]

King I have sent to seek him, and to find the body.
How dangerous is it that this man goes loose!
Yet must not we put the strong law on him:
He's lov'd of the distracted multitude,
Who like not in their judgment, but their eyes;   5
And where 'tis so, the offender's scourge is weigh'd,
But never the offence. To bear all smooth and even,
This sudden sending him away must seem
Deliberate pause: diseases desperate grown
By desperate appliance are reliev'd,   10
Or not at all.
[Enter ROSENCRANTZ]
⠀⠀⠀⠀⠀⠀⠀How now! what hath befall'n?

Rosencrantz Where the dead body is bestow'd, my lord,
We cannot get from him.

King⠀⠀⠀⠀⠀⠀⠀⠀⠀But where is he?

Rosencrantz Without, my lord; guarded, to know your
pleasure.

King Bring him before us.   15

Rosencrantz Ho, Guildenstern! bring in my lord.

[Enter HAMLET and GUILDENSTERN]

King Now, Hamlet, where's Polonius?

Hamlet At supper.

King At supper! Where?

Hamlet Not where he eats, but where he is eaten: a   20
certain convocation of politic worms are e'en at him.
Your worm is your only emperor for diet: we fat all

NOTES

4.⠀⠀*of:* by.

⠀⠀⠀*distracted:* dim-witted, foolish.

5.⠀⠀*Who like . . . their eyes:* who judge not by reason but by outward appearance.

6.⠀⠀*scourge:* punishment.

7.⠀⠀*bear all smooth:* pass everything off smoothly.

9.⠀⠀*Deliberate pause:* a deliberate step, taken after due consideration.

21.⠀⠀*convocation of politic worms:* a political assembly of worms; an allusion to the Diet of Worms (1521), a convocation held by the Catholic Church to allow Martin Luther to explain his reform doctrine. He had first set his beliefs forth in Wittenberg, where Hamlet and Horatio have studied.

creatures else to fat us, and we fat ourselves for
maggots: your fat king and your lean beggar is but
variable service; two dishes, but to one table: that's the   25
end.

King Alas, alas!

Hamlet A man may fish with the worm that hath eat of
a king, and eat of the fish that hath fed of that
worm.   30

King What dost thou mean by this?

Hamlet Nothing, but to show you how a king may go
a progress through the guts of a beggar.

King Where is Polonius?

Hamlet In heaven; send thither to see: if your   35
messenger find him not there, seek him i' the other place
yourself. But, indeed, if you find him not within this
month, you shall nose him as you go up the stairs
into the lobby.

King *[To some Attendants]* Go seek him there.   40

Hamlet He will stay till you come.

[Exeunt Attendants]

King Hamlet, this deed, for thine especial safety,
Which we do tender, as we dearly grieve
For that which thou hast done, must send thee hence
With fiery quickness: therefore prepare thyself;   45
The bark is ready, and the wind at help.
The associates tend, and every thing is bent
For England.

Hamlet   For England!

King   Ay, Hamlet

Hamlet   Good.

King So is it, if thou knew'st our purposes.

Hamlet I see a cherub that sees them. But, come; for   50
England! Farewell, dear mother.

King Thy loving father, Hamlet.

Hamlet My mother: father and mother is man and

25.   *variable service:* different courses.

33.   *a progress:* the term used for a royal journey of
state.

43.   *tender:* have regard for.

46.   *at help:* favorable.

47.   *The associates tend:* your companions await you.

bent: ready.

wife, man and wife is one flesh, and so, my mother.
Come, for England! *[Exit]*   55

King Follow him at foot; tempt him with speed aboard:
Delay it not, I'll have him hence to-night.
Away! for every thing is seal'd and done
That else leans on the affair: pray you, make haste.
[Exeunt ROSENCRANTZ and GUILDENSTERN]
And, England, if my love thou hold'st at aught, —   60
As my great power thereof may give these sense,
Since yet thy cicatrice looks raw and red
After the Danish sword, and thy free awe
Pays homage to us, — thou mayst not coldly set
Our sovereign process, which imports at full,   65
By letters congruing to that effect
The present death of Hamlet. Do it, England;
For like the hectic in my blood he rages,
And thou must cure me. Till I know 'tis done,
Howe'er my haps, my joys were ne'er begun. *[Exit]*   70

56.	*at foot:* at his heels.	
	tempt: entice.	
58–59.	*for every thing . . . the affair:* Everything necessary to ensure the success of this affair has been done.	
60.	*England:* the King of England.	
62.	*cicatrice:* scar or wound.	
63.	*thy free awe:* your submission even after our armies have been withdrawn.	
64.	*set:* set aside, disregard.	
65.	*sovereign process:* royal mandate or command.	
66.	*congruing:* agreeing.	
67.	*present:* immediate.	
68.	*hectic:* fever.	
70.	*Howe'er my haps:* whatever happens to me (probably reference to his afterlife.)	

COMMENTARY

As the scene opens, Claudius explains to his attendants that Hamlet has killed Polonius, hidden the body, and hidden himself somewhere in the castle. Although the stage directions are not explicit, the attendants in this scene are probably Claudius's councilors, men such as Polonius who serve as the king's advisors.

Claudius realizes that because Hamlet is popular with the people of Denmark, he has to move quickly without seeming to threaten Hamlet (4). He wants everything done smoothly and without a great deal of negative publicity. Claudius wants to give the impression that sending Hamlet away will give everyone time to cool off and think the problem through. Of course, no one knows what Claudius has in store for Hamlet at the hands of the English king.

Matching wits

Rosencrantz and Guildenstern escort Hamlet in. They have not found the body of Polonius. Hamlet continues the antics that he began in the previous scene, but with Claudius he is playing a very dangerous game. Unlike Polonius, Rosencrantz, and Guildenstern, Claudius *is* a match for Hamlet's wit, and the king grows increasingly angry and impatient with Hamlet's riddles and nonsensical answers. Given the obvious intelligence of both men, the loss of their leadership later in the play seems all the more tragic for Denmark.

The conversation between Hamlet and Claudius is an exercise in futility. Claudius cannot get a straight or sane answer out of Hamlet. The angrier the king grows, the more frustrating Hamlet's riddles become. Claudius, the ultimate diplomat, finds it more and more difficult to keep up appearances.

Beloved by the people

Claudius does keep Hamlet's popularity in mind, which is to the king's credit. Hamlet is a prince beloved by the people. He converses easily with people of every social strata, as demonstrated by his ease in conversation with everyone he encounters outside of court: soldiers, players, and gravediggers (who we meet in Act V). Ophelia's recollection of the Hamlet she knew — "The observ'd of all observers" — tells us how the court as well as the people followed his movements and his career (III.1.157).

Claudius enjoys no such popularity. His election was based on deal-making with the court nobles. The election was not democratic, and people will not hesitate to think the worst if rumors suggest that the king had a hand in any harm done to the prince. Claudius would suffer, not Hamlet. The need to maintain appearances and prevent trouble are pressuring Claudius to eliminate Hamlet quickly.

To England

Claudius gives up asking Hamlet about Polonius's whereabouts. With difficulty, the king regains his almost lost composure and tells Hamlet that for his own safety, he must leave Denmark and go to England. He sends Rosencrantz and Guildenstern with their orders to see Hamlet safely out of the country. Hamlet's jaunty farewell does nothing to assuage Claudius's fears.

After everyone has gone, Claudius delivers a chilling soliloquy. Hamlet will go to England, but not for safety's sake. The King of England owes favors to Denmark. Claudius has sent letters directing the king to see to it that Hamlet dies. But, Claudius admits, whatever happens, his fate is sealed — this king will never find joy.

Act IV, Scene 4

Before leaving Denmark, Hamlet encounters Fortinbras's army bound for Poland. Hamlet questions the validity of war and certain death. Still, he thinks, if men can accept the risks involved with battle, he can accept the risks involved with revenge.

ACT IV, SCENE 4
A plain in Denmark.

[Enter FORTINBRAS, a Captain, and Soldiers, marching]

Fortinbras Go, captain, from me greet the Danish king;
  Tell him that, by his licence, Fortinbras
  Claims the conveyance of a promis'd march
  Over his kingdom. You know the rendezvous.
  If that his majesty would aught with us,   5
  We shall express our duty in his eye,
  And let him know so.

Captain I will do't, my lord.

Fortinbras Go softly on.

[Exeunt FORTINBRAS and Soldiers]

[Enter HAMLET, ROSENCRANTZ, GUILDENSTERN, & C]

Hamlet Good sir, whose powers are these?

Captain They are of Norway, sir.   10

Hamlet How purpos'd, sir, I pray you?

Captain Against some part of Poland.

Hamlet Who commands them, sir?

Captain The nephew to old Norway, Fortinbras.

Hamlet Goes it against the main of Poland, sir,   15
  Or for some frontier?

Captain Truly to speak, and with no addition,
  We go to gain a little patch of ground
  That hath in it no profit but the name.
  To pay five ducats, five, I would not farm it;   20
  Nor will it yield to Norway or the Pole
  A ranker rate, should it be sold in fee.

Hamlet Why, then the Polack never will defend it.

NOTES

3.   *conveyance:* convoy, conduct.

6.   *We . . . eye:* We will pay him our respects in person.

8.   *softly:* slowly, carefully.

9.   *powers:* forces.

15.   *main:* main body, the country as a whole.

17.   *addition:* exaggeration.

20.   *To pay:* in rent.

22.   *ranker:* greater.
      in fee: outright.

Captain Yes, 'tis already garrison'd.

Hamlet Two thousand souls and twenty thousand ducats   25
Will not debate the question of this straw:
This is the imposthume of much wealth and peace,
That inward breaks, and shows no cause without
Why the man dies. I humbly thank you, sir.

Captain God be wi' you, sir. *[Exit]*   30

Rosencrantz Will't please you go, my lord?

Hamlet I'll be with you straight. Go a little before.
[Exeunt all except HAMLET]
How all occasions do inform against me,
And spur my dull revenge! What is a man,
If his chief good and market of his time
Be but to sleep and feed? a beast, no more.   35
Sure he that made us with such large discourse,
Looking before and after, gave us not
That capability and god-like reason
To fust in us unus'd. Now, whe'r it be
Bestial oblivion, or some craven scruple   40
Of thinking too precisely on the event,
A thought, which, quarter'd, hath but one part wisdom,
And ever three parts coward, I do not know
Why yet I live to say 'This thing's to do;'
Sith I have cause and will and strength and means   45
To do 't. Examples gross as earth exhort me:
Witness this army of such mass and charge
Led by a delicate and tender prince,
Whose spirit with divine ambition puff'd
Makes mouths at the invisible event,   50
Exposing what is mortal and unsure
To all that fortune, death and danger dare,
Even for an egg-shell. Rightly to be great
Is not to stir without great argument,
But greatly to find quarrel in a straw   55
When honour's at the stake. How stand I then,
That have a father kill'd, a mother stain'd,
Excitements of my reason and my blood,
And let all sleep, while, to my shame, I see
The imminent death of twenty thousand men,   60
That, for a fantasy and trick of fame,

26.   *debate the question:* settle the dispute.

27.   *imposthume:* abscess or festering sore.

31.   *straight:* immediately.

32.   *inform against:* accuse.

34.   *market:* employment.

36.   *discourse:* power of reasoning.

37.   *Looking before and after:* considering the future and the past.

39.   *fust:* grow moldy.

40.   *Bestial oblivion:* the forgetfulness of a mere beast.

40–41.   *some . . . event:* thinking too precisely about how the deed should be carried out — a cowardly hesitation.

46.   *gross:* large and obvious.

47.   *charge:* cost.

50.   *Makes mouths . . . event:* mocks at the uncertain outcome.

53–56.   *Rightly . . . stake:* True greatness consists not in waiting on a great cause for which to fight, but rather in fighting over a trifle where honor is at stake.

58.   *blood:* passion.

60.   *twenty thousand:* Note the inconsistency with line 25, where the number was "[t]wo thousand souls."

61.   *fantasy:* mere whim.

    trick: something trifling.

Go to their graves like beds, fight for a plot
Whereon the numbers cannot try the cause,
Which is not tomb enough and continent
To hide the slain? O! from this time forth,   65
My thoughts be bloody, or be nothing worth! *[Exit]*

63.   *Whereon the numbers . . . cause:* not big enough to hold the armies fighting for it.

64.   *continent:* containing enough ground.

COMMENTARY

Fortinbras is in Denmark, outside of Elsinore. This very brief scene reminds us that the Norwegian prince and his army are ominously marching through Denmark on the way to invade Poland. Fortinbras's captain will be the last person with whom Hamlet speaks before leaving Elsinore.

Fortinbras was identified early in the play as a threat to Denmark, and his desire for revenge was prevented by Claudius's shrewd and careful diplomacy. The king sent Danish ambassadors to the Norwegian king, who is Fortinbras's uncle. As a result of successful negotiations, Old Norway used his influence with Young Fortinbras and convinced him not to invade Denmark. By bringing Fortinbras back at this point, Shakespeare sets the stage for his reentry at the end of the play.

In this scene, we see Hamlet's potential as a king as he deals with Fortinbras's captain. The captain has been sent by Norway's prince to pay his respects to Claudius and to request permission for Norway's army to cross through Denmark peacefully. Hamlet encounters the captain first and asks the officer why this army is nearby. The captain tells Hamlet that the army is on its way to invade Poland for "a little patch of ground" (18). Hamlet is sure that the Polish army will not bother to defend it, but the captain disagrees, telling the prince that the land under discussion is already manned with Polish troops.

This exchange serves as an introduction to Hamlet's sixth and final soliloquy. He sounds more mature, more calmly accepting of his destiny than he ever has before when he says, "How all occasions do inform against me" (32). The tone and form of this speech are very different from the earlier ones. Here, Hamlet is self-assured and certain of his mission because he no longer harbors any doubts about the ghost's honesty or the extent of Claudius's treachery.

In the previous soliloquy, Hamlet sounded hard and his words had a violent edge. After the second appearance of his father's ghost, and after Hamlet's cathartic encounter with Gertrude, he remembered who he was and rediscovered his place in the cosmos. He is now able to do what is expected of him. He is ready to act; he has rid himself of melancholy and uncertainty by staging the play and confronting Gertrude. He can speak of evil without the fury of frustration. His newfound confidence is reflected in the orderly progression of these lines.

Hamlet admires Fortinbras's resolution, even as he abhors war and the imminent loss of lives over "a plot" — a piece of ground (62). Hamlet concludes that if Fortinbras can lead these men into battle and death, he can revenge his father's murder and his mother's ruin. He vows to keep his thoughts on the act that he is now determined to carry out.

Act IV, Scene 5

Ophelia has gone mad because of the death of her father and the loss of Hamlet's love. Gertrude and Claudius are deeply affected by the change in Ophelia. Laertes arrives from Paris to revenge the death of his father, only to discover that his sister is lost to him as well.

ACT IV, SCENE 5
Elsinore. A room in the castle.

[Enter QUEEN, HORATIO, and a Gentleman]

Queen I will not speak with her.

Gentleman She is importunate, indeed distract:
Her mood will needs be pitied.

Queen   What would she have?

Gentleman She speaks much of her father; says she hears
There's tricks i' the world; and hems, and beats her heart;   5
Spurns enviously at straws; speaks things in doubt,
That carry but half sense: her speech is nothing,
Yet the unshaped use of it doth move
The hearers to collection; they aim at it,
And botch the words up fit to their own thoughts;   10
Which, as her winks, and nods, and gestures yield them,
Indeed would make one think there might be thought,
Though nothing sure, yet much unhappily.

Horatio 'Twere good she were spoken with, for she may strew
Dangerous conjectures in ill-breeding minds.   15

Queen Let her come in. *[Exit Gentleman]*
To my sick soul, as sin's true nature is,
Each toy seems prologue to some great amiss:
So full of artless jealousy is guilt,
It spills itself in fearing to be spilt.   20

[Re-enter Gentleman, with OPHELIA]

Ophelia Where is the beauteous majesty of Denmark?

Queen How now, Ophelia!

Ophelia *How should I your true love know*
From another one?
By his cockle hat and staff,   25
And his sandal shoon.

NOTES

2.   *importunate:* insistent.

     distract: distracted, extremely moved.

5.   *tricks:* trickery.

6.   *Spurns . . . straws:* stamps (in anger) over unimportant matters.

8.   *unshaped:* incoherent.

9.   *collection:* inference.

     aim: guess.

10.   *botch:* patch

17.   *as sin's true nature is:* Sin is truly a sickness; the main symptom is anxiety and suspicion.

18.   *toy:* trifle.

     amiss: calamity.

19.   *artless jealousy:* uncontrolled suspicion.

20.   *It spills . . . spilt:* It is revealed by its very efforts to conceal itself.

25.   *cockle hat:* adorned with cockle shells and worn by pilgrims.

26.   *shoon:* shoes. Cockle hats and sandals were worn by pilgrims. Lovers were called pilgrims.

Queen Alas! sweet lady, what imports this song?

Ophelia Say you? nay, pray you, mark.
He is dead and gone, lady,
He is dead and gone;   30
At his head a grass-green turf;
At his heels a stone.
O, ho!

Queen Nay, but Ophelia, —

Ophelia Pray you, mark.   35
White his shroud as the mountain snow, —

[Enter KING]

Queen Alas! look here, my lord.

Ophelia *Larded all with sweet flowers;*
Which bewept to the grave did not go
With true-love showers.   40

King How do you, pretty lady?

Ophelia Well, God 'ild you! They say the owl was a
baker's daughter. Lord! we know what we are,
but know not what we may be. God be at your table!

King Conceit upon her father.   45

Ophelia Pray you, let's have no words of this; but
when they ask you what it means, say you this:
To-morrow is Saint Valentine's day,
All in the morning betime,
And I a maid at your window,   50
To be your Valentine:
Then up he rose, and donn'd his clothes
And dupp'd the chamber door;
Let in the maid, that out a maid
Never departed more.   55

King Pretty Ophelia!

Ophelia Indeed, la! without an oath, I'll make
an end on 't:
By Gis and by Saint Charity,
Alack, and fie for shame!   60
Young men will do 't, if they come to 't;
By Cock they are to blame.
Quoth she, before you tumbled me,

---

27. *imports:* is the meaning of.

38. *Larded:* garnished.

40. *true-love showers:* the tears of his true love.

42. *'ild:* yield, reward.

42–43. *They say . . . daughter:* An allusion to the legend that a baker's daughter was turned into an owl for hooting at her mother in scorn when the latter gave Christ a larger piece of bread than the daughter thought necessary.

45. *Conceit upon:* she thinks of.

46. *of:* about.

48. *Saint Valentine's day:* February 14. The old belief was that the first man seen by a maid on that day was destined to be her husband, and vice versa.

49. *betime:* early.

53. *dupp'd:* opened.

59. *Gis:* euphemism for Jesus.

62. *Cock:* euphemism for God

You promis'd me to wed:
(He answers) So would I ha' done, by yonder sun,   65
An thou hadst not come to my bed.

King How long hath she been thus?

Ophelia I hope all will be well. We must be patient:
but I cannot choose but weep, to think they
should lay him i' the cold ground. My brother shall   70
know of it: and so I thank you for your good counsel.
Come, my coach! Good-night, ladies; good-night,
sweet ladies; good-night, good-night. *[Exit]*

King Follow her close; give her good watch, I
pray you. *[Exit HORATIO]*   75
O! this is the poison of deep grief; it springs
All from her father's death. O Gertrude, Gertrude!
When sorrows come, they come not single spies,
But in battalions. First, her father slain;
Next, your son gone; but he most violent author   80
Of his own just remove: the people muddied,
Thick and unwholesome in their thoughts and whispers,
For good Polonius' death; and we have done but greenly,
In hugger-mugger to inter him: poor Ophelia
Divided from herself and her fair judgment,   85
Without the which we are pictures, or mere beasts:
Last, and as much containing as all these,
Her brother is in secret come from France,
Feeds on his wonder, keeps himself in clouds,
And wants not buzzers to infect his ear   90
With pestilent speeches of his father's death;
Wherein necessity, of matter beggar'd,
Will nothing stick our person to arraign
In ear and ear. O my dear Gertrude! this,
Like to a murdering-piece, in many places   95
Gives me superfluous death. *[A noise within]*

Queen   Alack! what noise is this?

[Enter a Gentleman]

King Where are my Switzers? Let them guard the door.
What is the matter?

Gentleman   Save yourself, my lord;
The ocean, overpeering of his list,

81. *muddied:* confused and stirred up.

83. *greenly:* foolishly; without using mature judgment.

84. *hugger-mugger:* secret haste.

86. *pictures:* men only to the eye.

87. *containing:* holding us.

89. *keeps . . . clouds:* shrouds himself in gloomy aloofness.

90. *wants:* lacks.

    buzzers: gossipers.

92–94. *Wherein necessity . . . ear and ear:* Without any knowledge of the truth of the matter, they do not hesitate to accuse me.

95. *murdering-piece:* cannon loaded with grapeshot.

96. *superfluous:* one bullet would have been sufficient.

97. *Switzers:* Swiss mercenaries acting as royal bodyguard.

99. *overpeering of his list:* looking over a rim or a boundary.

Eats not the flats with more impetuous haste   100
Than young Laertes, in a riotous head,
O'erbears your officers. The rabble call him lord;
And, as the world were now but to begin,
Antiquity forgot, custom not known,
The ratifiers and props of every word,   105
They cry, 'Choose we; Laertes shall be king!'
Caps, hands, and tongues, applaud it to the clouds,
'Laertes shall be king, Laertes king!'

Queen How cheerfully on the false trail they cry!
O! this is counter, you false Danish dogs!   110

King The doors are broke. *[Noise within]*

[Enter LAERTES, armed; Danes following]

Laertes Where is the king? Sirs, stand you all without.

Danes No, let's come in.

Laertes   I pray you, give me leave.

Danes We will, we will. *[They retire without the door]*

Laertes I thank you: keep the door. O thou vile king!   115
Give me my father.

Queen   Calmly, good Laertes.

Laertes That drop of blood that's calm proclaims me bastard,
Cries cuckold to my father, brands the harlot
Even here, between the chaste unsmirched brows
Of my true mother.

King   What is the cause, Laertes,   120
That thy rebellion looks so giant-like?
Let him go, Gertrude; do not fear our person:
There's such divinity doth hedge a king,
That treason can but peep to what it would,
Acts little of his will. Tell me, Laertes,   125
Why thou art thus incens'd. Let him go, Gertrude.
Speak, man.

Laertes   Where is my father?

King   Dead.

Queen   But not by him.

King Let him demand his fill.

---

100. *Eats not the flats:* floods not the lowlands.

101. *in a riotous head:* with a force of rioters.

103. *as:* as if.

104–105. *Antiquity . . . word:* ignoring prerogative and tradition, which sanction and support every decision.

110. *counter:* on the false trail (a hunting term); treason.

117–118. *That drop . . . father:* I cannot remain calm and be a true son to my father.

122. *fear:* fear for.

123. *There's such . . . a king:* A king is surrounded by divine protection as if by a hedge .

124. *peep:* look over, but not break through.

125. *Acts little of his will:* is little able to carry out its desires.

Laertes How came he dead? I'll not be juggled with.   130
  To hell, allegiance! vows, to the blackest devil!
  Conscience and grace, to the profoundest pit!
  I dare damnation. To this point I stand,
  That both the worlds I give to negligence,
  Let come what comes; only I'll be reveng'd   135
  Most throughly for my father.

King   Who shall stay you?

Laertes My will, not all the world:
  And for my means, I'll husband them so well,
  They shall go far with little.

King   Good Laertes,
  If you desire to know the certainty   140
  Of your dear father's death, is't writ in your revenge,
  That, swoopstake, you will draw both friend and foe,
  Winner and loser?

Laertes None but his enemies.

King   Will you know them then?

Laertes To his good friends thus wide I'll ope my arms;   145
  And like the kind life-rendering pelican,
  Repast them with my blood.

King   Why, now you speak
  Like a good child and a true gentleman.
  That I am guiltless of your father's death,
  And am most sensibly in grief for it,   150
  It shall as level to your judgment pierce
  As day does to your eye.

Danes *[Within]*   Let her come in.

Laertes How now! what noise is that?
  [Re-enter OPHELIA]
  O heat, dry up my brains! tears seven times salt,
  Burn out the sense and virtue of mine eye!   155
  By heaven, thy madness shall be paid by weight,
  Till our scale turn the beam. O rose of May!
  Dear maid, kind sister, sweet Ophelia!
  O heavens! is 't possible a young maid's wits
  Should be as mortal as an old man's life?   160
  Nature is fine in love, and where 'tis fine

134. *both . . . negligence:* I care not for this world or the next.

138. *husband:* use thriftily.

142. *swoopstake:* in a clean sweep.

146. *life-rendering pelican:* The pelican was supposed to feed its young with its own blood.

150. *sensibly:* feelingly.

151. *level:* true, as a carpenter's level.

155. *sense and virtue:* sensitiveness to light and power of sight.

157. *turn the beam:* overbalance the scale.

161. *fine:* delicate.

It sends some precious instance of itself
After the thing it loves.

Ophelia *They bore him barefac'd on the bier;*
Hey non nonny, nonny, hey nonny;   165
And in his grave rain'd many a tear; —
Fare you well, my dove!

Laertes Hadst thou thy wits, and didst persuade revenge,
It could not move thus.

Ophelia *You must sing, a-down a-down,*   170
And you call him a-down-a.
O how the wheel becomes it! It is the false steward
that stole his master's daughter.

Laertes This nothing's more than matter.

Ophelia There's rosemary that's for remembrance;   175
pray, love, remember: and there is pansies, that's
for thoughts.

Laertes A document in madness, thoughts and
remembrance fitted.

Ophelia There's fennel for you, and columbines;   180
there's rue for you; and here's some for me; we may
call it herb of grace o' Sundays. O! you must wear
your rue with a difference. There's a daisy; I would
give you some violets, but they withered all when my
father died. They say he made a good end, —   185
For bonny sweet Robin is all my joy.

Laertes Thought and affliction, passion, hell itself,
She turns to favour and to prettiness.

Ophelia
And will a' not come again?
And will a' not come again?   190
No, no, he is dead;
Go to thy death-bed,
He never will come again.
His beard was as white as snow
All flaxen was his poll,   195
He is gone, he is gone,
And we cast away moan:

162.   *instance:* token; in this case, her sanity.

172.   *wheel:* Perhaps she imagines herself seated at a spinning wheel; or she may be referring to a little dance.

       the false steward: the title of the ballad.

174.   *This nothing's more than matter:* This nonsense is more moving than sense.

175–185.   The distribution of herbs and flowers was an old funeral custom, and Ophelia imagines herself giving her father proper burial. Each flower carries a meaning (see Commentary).

178.   *document:* lesson.

181.   *rue:* a symbol of repentance.

Ophelia is compared with violets throughout the play.

188.   *favour:* charm.

195.   *poll:* head.

God ha' mercy on his soul!
And of all Christian souls I pray God. God be wi'ye!

[Exit]

Laertes Do you see this, O God?　　　　　　　　　　200

King Laertes, I must commune with your grief,
Or you deny me right. Go but apart,
Make choice of whom your wisest friends you will,
And they shall hear and judge 'twixt you and me.
If by direct or by collateral hand　　　　　　　　　205
They find us touch'd, we will our kingdom give,
Our crown, our life, and all that we call ours,
To you in satisfaction; but if not,
Be you content to lend your patience to us,
And we shall jointly labour with your soul　　　　　210
To give it due content.

Laertes　　　　　　　Let this be so:
His means of death, his obscure burial,
No trophy, sword, nor hatchment o'er his bones,
No noble rite nor formal ostentation,
Cry to be heard, as 'twere from heaven to earth,　　215
That I must call 't in question.

King So you shall;
And where the offence is let the great axe fall.
I pray you go with me. *[Exeunt]*

201.　*commune:* share.

205.　*collateral:* i.e., as an accessory.

206.　*touch'd:* implicated.

212.　*obscure burial:* Remember that Polonius was chief minister to the king. Ordinarily a man of his high rank would be given an ostentatious funeral.

213.　*hatchment:* coat of arms hung over the tomb of a deceased knight.

214.　*formal ostentation:* public ceremony.

COMMENTARY

The mood in the castle is largely one of sadness and resigned bewilderment. Ophelia has lost her mind, and Hamlet has been sent away to England. Ophelia's madness personifies the discord and dismay in Claudius's mind and in Claudius and Gertrude's household. Gertrude feels the need to avoid Ophelia, probably because she feels partly responsible for Polonius's death.

Genuine madness

The description of Ophelia's madness, coupled with Horatio's persuasion, compels Gertrude to see Hamlet's former love. Ophelia enters calling for "the beauteous majesty of Denmark" (21). She may be referring to Gertrude, but perhaps she seeks Hamlet, whom she still must love. She begins to sing a tune with verses that alternate subjects between love, sex, and death.

Ophelia's mention of the owl who was a baker's daughter refers to an old tale about a baker's shop that was visited by Jesus. When Jesus asked for some bread, the mistress of the bakery put some dough into the oven, but her daughter cut it in two, giving Christ a smaller portion than the mother would have preferred. The dough in the oven began to expand to more than twice its size and the baker's daughter cried out "Hoo, hoo, hoo." Jesus turned her into an owl for her wickedness.

Perhaps Ophelia feels that she is wicked because she was not honest with Hamlet. She may even feel that she drove Hamlet mad. Her bawdy verses, surprising from the daughter of a lord, must have been songs that she overheard other girls singing at school or in the kitchen, garden, or laundry. Hamlet's crude insults at the play made her feel common, and now she acts as if she is a loose woman. Ophelia's speeches contain references to ballads, folk tales, and ancient rural customs and ceremonies that center on marriage and funeral rites.

The king enters the scene unobtrusively. "Pretty Ophelia" is his way of saying what words cannot express (56). He wonders how this change could have happened. Ophelia babbles on about her father and her brother, and then she says goodnight as if she is leaving a party, bidding goodnight to the "sweet ladies" (73).

A court in turmoil

As Claudius feared, rumors have been spreading about Hamlet's departure and Polonius's unceremonious funeral. Laertes has returned from France for his father's funeral, and he has many questions concerning Polonius's death. Everyone seems quick to place the blame for the old man's murder on the king and the queen. Claudius has hired Swiss mercenaries to act as his bodyguards because he can no longer trust his own army.

A gentleman enters and warns Claudius that a mob is at the gates. The mob wants Laertes to be king and demands entrance to the palace. Laertes enters and challenges Claudius. Like Fortinbras and Hamlet, Laertes now has his father's murder to avenge. Laertes implies that Claudius is responsible for the murder of Polonius.

To Claudius's credit, he stands his ground against Laertes's accusations and displays remarkable courage. Perhaps he can do so because his conscience is clear regarding Polonius's death. The confrontation is interrupted by the appearance of Ophelia. Laertes cannot contain his shock and disbelief at

Ophelia in Her Madness, *artist unknown.*
Stock Montage/SuperStock

her appearance. "O rose of May," he cries, "is't possible a young maid's wits / Should be as mortal as an old man's life?" (157, 159–160).

But Polonius's death alone is not responsible for driving Ophelia mad. As Claudius has surmised, the source of Ophelia's dismay is the fact that Polonius died at the hands of her former lover. Ophelia has lost the two men who guided her course in a patriarchal society. Everything she once believed in has disappointed or deserted her. Ophelia sings distractedly and carries flowers, mocking the wedding ceremonies that she had expected to celebrate someday.

Laertes's second loss

Laertes is moved beyond tears by Ophelia's behavior. Ophelia's ballads, although coming from her disturbed mind, contain elements of truth. She distributes her flowers in a disjointed ceremony understood only to herself. She gives fennel and columbines, representing flattery and unfaithfulness, to Claudius. Rue stands for sorrow and repentance, daisies stand for falseness, and violets, which have all "withered" and died, stand for faithfulness (184).

The king approaches Laertes, who desperately needs a target for his anger. The murder of Polonius was not his doing, Claudius tells Laertes. The king promises to do everything in his power to bring justice to bear on the crime against Polonius.

Laertes questions the manner of his father's secretive burial. Polonius was, after all, the chief minister to the king. Ordinarily, a man of his rank would be given an elaborate funeral. Laertes asks why his father was given "[n]o noble right nor formal ostentation" (214). Claudius agrees that Laertes should have some answers, and he promises the young man that justice will be served.

Act IV, Scene 6

Horatio receives a letter from Hamlet. In it, Hamlet describes his adventures at sea and his separation from Rosencrantz and Guildenstern.

ACT IV, SCENE 6
Another room in the same.

[Enter HORATIO and a Servant]

Horatio What are they that would speak with me?

Servant Sailors, sir: they say they have letters
for you.

Horatio Let them come in. *[Exit Servant]*
I do not know from what part of the world   5
I should be greeted, if not from Lord Hamlet.

[Enter Sailors]

First Sailor God bless you, sir.

Horatio Let him bless thee too.

Second Sailor He shall, sir, an't please him.
There's a letter for you, sir; — it comes from the   10
ambassador that was bound for England; — if your
name be Horatio, as I am let to know it is.

Horatio *[Reads] Horatio, when thou shalt have
overlooked this, give these fellows some means to the
king: they have letters for him. Ere we were two*   15
*days old at sea, a pirate of very war-like appointment
gave us chase. Finding ourselves too slow of sail, we
put on a compelled valour; in the grapple I boarded
them. On the instant, they got clear of our ship, so I
alone became their prisoner. They have dealt with*   20
*me likes thieves of mercy, but they knew what they
did; I am to do a good turn to them. Let the king
have the letters I have sent; and repair thou to me
with as much haste as thou wouldst fly death. I have
words to speak in thine ear will make thee dumb, yet*   25
*are they much too light for the bore of the matter.
These good fellows will bring thee where I am.*

NOTES

9.   *an't:* if it.

14.   *overlooked:* looked over, read.

      means: access.

16.   *appointment:* equipment.

18.   *compelled valour:* bravery that stems from
necessity.

21.   *thieves of mercy:* merciful thieves.

21–22. *but they knew what they did:* They knew who I
was (so treating me well was to their advantage).

26.   *much . . . matter:* He hasn't strong enough words
to express himself; his words are too light.

Rosencrantz and Guildenstern hold their course for
England: of them I have much to tell thee. Farewell.
He that thou knowest thine,   30
Hamlet.
Come, I will give you way for these your letters;
And do't the speedier, that you may direct me
To him from whom you brought them. *[Exeunt]*

COMMENTARY

This brief scene provides valuable information about Hamlet's adventures since he left Elsinore bound for England. Horatio receives a letter at the hands of two sailors. One of the sailors tells Horatio that the letter has come from a Danish ambassador bound for England, but as Horatio reads, he understands that the letter is from Hamlet.

Hamlet writes about his escapades at sea, where pirates accosted his ship. As soon as they were within reach, Hamlet boarded their ship and fled from his companions, Rosencrantz and Guildenstern. The last time Hamlet saw them they were on their way to England. He asks Horatio to make sure that the letters he has sent reach the king. Then he asks Horatio to join him.

The question raised here is whether or not Hamlet knew about the pirates before he left. The circumstances of his escape are almost too coincidental. He had confided his suspicions to Gertrude in Act III, Scene 4, and his remarks to Claudius in Act IV, Scene 3 suggested a self-confidence that springs from being well-prepared.

Somehow, Hamlet had his own plan for escape when he departed for England. He did not trust Rosencrantz and Guildenstern. He seemed certain that Claudius meant to kill him, and he would not have agreed to go with the two men if he had not already made plans for an escape.

In any case, Hamlet is coming back home with much news for Horatio. Hamlet's quick action is indicative of his new self-assurance and determination. As noted in the commentary for Act IV, Scene 4, he is forever altered from his former contemplative self.

Act IV, Scene 7

Claudius skillfully brings Laertes into his confidence. Messengers arrive, bringing unexpected news of Hamlet's return. Claudius tells Laertes to challenge the prince to a duel. Laertes agrees and suggests that he use a sword dipped in potent poison to ensure Hamlet's death. Claudius agrees. Gertrude enters with the news that Ophelia has drowned.

ACT IV, SCENE 7
Another room in the same.

[Enter KING and LAERTES]

King Now must your conscience my acquittance seal,
  And you must put me in your heart for friend,
  Sith you have heard, and with a knowing ear,
  That he which hath your noble father slain
  Pursu'd my life.

Laertes   It well appears: but tell me   5
  Why you proceeded not against these feats,
  So crimeful and so capital in nature,
  As by your safety, wisdom, all things else,
  You mainly were stirr'd up.

King   O! for two special reasons;
  Which may to you, perhaps, seem much unsinew'd,   10
  But yet to me they are strong. The queen his mother
  Lives almost by his looks, and for myself, —
  My virtue or my plague, be it either which, —
  She's so conjunctive to my life and soul,
  That, as the star moves not but in his sphere,   15
  I could not but by her. The other motive,
  Why to a public count I might not go,
  Is the great love the general gender bear him;
  Who, dipping all his faults in their affection,
  Would, like the spring that turneth wood to stone,   20
  Convert his gyves to graces; so that my arrows,
  Too slightly timber'd for so loud a wind,
  Would have reverted to my bow again,
  And not where I had aim'd them.

Laertes And so have I a noble father lost;   25
  A sister driven into desperate terms,
  Whose worth, if praises may go back again,

NOTES

1. *my acquittance seal:* confirm my innocence.

6. *feats:* acts.

7. *capital:* deserving death.

9. *mainly:* strongly.

10. *unsinew'd:* weak.

14. *conjunctive:* closely united.

15. *but:* except.

    sphere: orbit.

17. *count:* account, trial.

18. *general gender:* common people.

20. *spring . . . stone:* a reference to mineral springs that petrify wood.

21. *Convert . . . graces:* regard his fetters as honorable rather than disgraceful; make a martyr of him.

22. *Too timber'd:* made of wood that is too light.

26. *terms:* conditions.

27. *if praises . . . again:* if one may praise her for what she used to be.

Stood challenger on mount of all the age
For her perfections. But my revenge will come.

King Break not your sleeps for that; you must not think   30
That we are made of stuff so flat and dull
That we can let our beard be shook with danger
And think it pastime. You shortly shall hear more;
I lov'd your father, and we love ourself,
And that, I hope, will teach you to imagine. —   35
[Enter a Messenger]
How now! what news?

Messenger   Letters, my lord, from Hamlet:
This to your majesty; this to the queen.

King From Hamlet! who brought them?

Messenger Sailors, my lord, they say; I saw them not:
They were given me by Claudio, he receiv'd them   40
Of him that brought them.

King   Laertes, you shall hear them.
Leave us. *[Exit Messenger]*
[Reads] High and mighty, you shall know I am set
naked on your kingdom. To-morrow shall I beg
leave to see your kingly eyes; when I shall, first   45
asking your pardon therunto, recount the occasions
of my sudden and more strange return. — Hamlet.
What should this mean? Are all the rest come back?
Or is it some abuse and no such thing?

Laertes Know you the hand?

King   'Tis Hamlet's character. 'Naked,' 50
And in a postscript here, he says, 'alone.'
Can you advise me?

Laertes I'm lost in it, my lord. But let him come!
It warms the very sickness in my heart,
That I shall live and tell him to his teeth,   55
'Thus diddest thou.'

King   If it be so, Laertes,
As how should it be so? how otherwise?
Will you be rul'd by me?

Laertes   Ay, my lord;
So you will not o'er-rule me to a peace.

28–29. *Stood . . . perfections:* stood out above all others of her age in perfection.

44. *naked:* destitute.

49. *abuse:* deception, plot.

50. *character:* handwriting.

King To thine own peace. If he be now return'd,   60
  As checking at his voyage, and that he means
  No more to undertake it, I will work him
  To an exploit, now ripe in my device,
  Under the which he shall not choose but fall;
  And for his death no wind of blame shall breathe,   65
  But even his mother shall uncharge the practice
  And call it accident.

Laertes   My lord, I will be rul'd;
  The rather, if you could devise it so
  That I might be the organ.

King   It falls right.
  You have been talk'd of since your travel much,   70
  And that in Hamlet's hearing, for a quality
  Wherein, they say, you shine; your sum of parts
  Did not together pluck such envy from him
  As did that one, and that, in my regard,
  Of the unworthiest siege.

Laertes   What part is that, my lord?   75

King A very riband in the cap of youth,
  Yet needful too; for youth no less becomes
  The light and careless livery that it wears
  Than settled age his sables and his weeds,
  Importing health and graveness. Two months since   80
  Here was a gentleman of Normandy:
  I've seen myself, and serv'd against the French,
  And they can well on horseback; but this gallant
  Had witchcraft in 't, he grew unto his seat,
  And to such wondrous doing brought his horse,   85
  As he had been incorps'd and demi-natur'd
  With the brave beast; so far be topp'd my thought,
  That I, in forgery of shapes and tricks,
  Come short of what he did.

Laertes   A Norman, was 't?

King A Norman.   90

Laertes Upon my life, Lamord.

King   The very same.

Laertes I know him well; he is the brooch indeed
  And gem of all the nation.

61. *checking at:* swerving aside from; a term in hawking.

63. *device:* plans.

66. *uncharge the practice:* acquit us of plotting.
practice: strategem.

69. *organ:* instrument.
It falls right: It fits in with my plan.

72. *your sum of parts:* all your accomplishments together.

75. *Of the unworthiest siege:* the least worthy of high praise.

78. *livery:* dress.

79. *his sables and his weeds:* dignified robes.

80. *Importing health:* denoting well-being.
since: ago.

83. *can well:* can do well.

86. *incorps'd and demi-natur'd:* an integral part of the body.

87–89. *so far . . . he did:* He surpassed my wildest imagination.

88. *forgery:* construction, invention.

92. *brooch:* jewel, highly esteemed.

King He made confession of you,
  And gave you such a masterly report   95
  For art and exercise in your defence,
  And for your rapier most especially,
  That he cried out, 'twould be a sight indeed
  If one could match you; the scrimers of their nation,
  He swore, had neither motion, guard, nor eye,   100
  If you oppos'd them. Sir, this report of his
  Did Hamlet so envenom with his envy
  That he could nothing do but wish and beg
  Your sudden coming o'er, to play with him.
  Now, out of this, —

Laertes   What out of this, my lord?   105

King Laertes, was your father dear to you?
  Or are you like the painting of a sorrow,
  A face without a heart?

Laertes   Why ask you this?

King Not that I think you did not love your father,
  But that I know love is begun by time,   110
  And that I see, in passages of proof,
  Time qualifies the spark and fire of it.
  There lives within the very flame of love
  A kind of wick or snuff that will abate it,
  And nothing is at a like goodness still,   115
  For goodness, growing to a plurisy,
  Dies in his own too-much. That we would do,
  We should do when we would, for this 'would' changes,
  And hath abatements and delays as many
  As there are tongues, are hands, are accidents;   120
  And then this 'should' is like a spendthrift sigh,
  That hurts by easing. But, to the quick o' the ulcer;
  Hamlet comes back; what would you undertake
  To show yourself your father's son in deed
  More than in words?

Laertes   To cut his throat i' the church.   125

King No place indeed should murder sanctuarize;
  Revenge should have no bounds. But, good Laertes,
  Will you do this, keep close within your chamber.
  Hamlet return'd shall know you are come home;

---

94.   *made confession of you:* spoke about you.

99.   *scrimers:* fencers.

102.   *envenom:* poison.

104.   *sudden:* soon.

107.   *painting:* imitation.

111.   *passages of proof:* proven by events.

112.   *qualifies:* diminishes.

114.   *snuff:* accumulation of smoldering wick that caused the candle to smoke and burn less brightly.

115.   *still:* always.

116.   *plurisy:* excess.

117–118.   *That we . . . when we would:* We ought to do things when the desire is new and strong.

121.   *spendthrift:* wasteful. It was generally supposed that sighing was bad for the blood.

122.   *quick o' the ulcer:* the heart of the matter.

126.   *sanctuarize:* give sanctuary to a murderer.

128.   *close:* out of sight.

We'll put on those shall praise your excellence,   130
And set a double varnish on the fame
The Frenchman gave you, bring you, in fine, together,
And wager on your heads: he, being remiss,
Most generous and free from all contriving,
Will not peruse the foils; so that, with ease   135
Or with a little shuffling, you may choose
A sword unbated, and, in a pass of practice
Requite him for your father.

Laertes I will do 't;
And, for that purpose, I'll anoint my sword.
I bought an unction of a mountebank,   140
So mortal that, but dip a knife in it,
Where it draws blood no cataplasm so rare,
Collected from all simples that have virtue
Under the moon, can save the thing from death
That is but scratch'd withal; I'll touch my point   145
With this contagion, that, if I gall him slightly,
It may be death.

King   Let's further think of this;
Weigh what convenience both of time and means
May fit us to our shape. If this should fail,
And that our drift look through our bad performance   150
'Twere better not assay'd; therefore this project
Should have a back or second, that might hold,
If this should blast in proof. Soft! let me see;
We'll make a solemn wager on your cunnings:
I ha 't: 155
When in your motion you are hot and dry, —
As make your bouts more violent to that end, —
And that he calls for drink, I'll have prepar'd him
A chalice for the nonce, whereon but sipping,
If he by chance escape your venom'd stuck,   160
Our purpose may hold there. But stay! what noise?
[Enter QUEEN]
How now, sweet queen!

Queen One woe doth tread upon another's heel,
So fast they follow: your sister's drown'd, Laertes.

Laertes Drown'd! O, where?   165

130. *put on those shall praise:* employ certain persons to praise.

132. *fine:* short.

133. *remiss:* careless.

134. *generous:* noble.

     contriving: plotting.

135. *foils:* special fencing swords with blunted or shielded points.

137. *unbated:* unblunted.

     pass of practice: a treacherous thrust or a warming-up exercise.

140. *unction:* ointment.

     mountebank: quack doctor.

142. *cataplasm:* poultice.

143. *simples:* herbs.

144. *Under the moon:* To be most effective, herbs are gathered by moonlight.

146. *gall:* scratch, draw blood.

148–149. *Weigh . . . shape:* consider ways and means for best carrying out our plans.

150. *our drift . . . performance:* by bungling, reveal our purpose.

151. *assay'd:* tried.

153. *blast in proof:* It might blow up in our faces when we try it.

     Soft: wait a minute.

159. *chalice:* cup.

     nonce: occasion.

160. *stuck:* thrust.

Queen There is a willow grows aslant a brook.
  That shows his hoar leaves in the glassy stream;
  There with fantastic garlands did she come,
  Of crow-flowers, nettles, daisies, and long purples,
  That liberal shepherds give a grosser name,   170
  But our cold maids do dead men's fingers call them:
  There, on the pendent boughs her coronet weeds
  Clambering to hang, an envious sliver broke,
  When down her weedy trophies and herself
  Fell in the weeping brook. Her clothes spread wide,   175
  And, mermaid-like, awhile they bore her up;
  Which time she chanted snatches of old lauds,
  As one incapable of her own distress,
  Or like a creature native and indu'd
  Unto that element; but long it could not be   180
  Till that her garments, heavy with their drink,
  Pull'd the poor wretch from her melodious lay
  To muddy death.

Laertes   Alas! then, she is drown'd?

Queen Drown'd, drown'd.

Laertes Too much of water hast thou, poor Ophelia,   185
  And therefore I forbid my tears; but yet
  It is our trick, nature her custom holds,
  Let shame say what it will; when these are gone
  The woman will be out. Adieu, my lord!
  I have a speech of fire, that fain would blaze,   190
  But that this folly douts it. *[Exit]*

King   Let's follow, Gertrude.
  How much I had to do to calm his rage!
  Now fear I this will give it start again;
  Therefore let's follow. *[Exeunt]*

167. *hoar:* gray.

170. *liberal:* free-spoken.

172. *coronet weeds:* garlands of flowers.

173. *envious sliver:* malicious branch.

177. *lauds:* hymns of praise.

178. *incapable:* insensible.

179. *indu'd:* endowed, belonging to.

182. *lay:* song.

187. *our trick:* our fashion.

188. *these:* referring to tears, for which he apologizes.

189. *The woman will be out:* The woman in me will be gone.

191. *douts:* extinguishes; literally, do out.

COMMENTARY

This scene continues where Scene 5 ended. In a heart-to-heart talk, Claudius continues to pull Laertes into his web. He tries to comfort and reassure Laertes, but his ulterior motives are apparent. He needs to bring Polonius's son into his confidence so he can goad Laertes into turning his anger and desire for vengeance towards Hamlet. If the prince is already dead, as Claudius hopes, then he can poison Laertes's mind against him. If the prince is not dead yet, Claudius will have a guaranteed ally in Laertes. He uses several skillful devices to accomplish this, including declarations of friendship and common enmity, candor about his most intimate affairs, and, of course, flattery.

Creating an ally

Claudius bemoans the fact that he fully recognizes the destruction that Hamlet has caused and yet cannot respond adequately because he is married to Hamlet's mother. Gertrude "[l]ives almost by his looks," and Claudius claims to love her so much that he cannot bear to see her hurt (12). Claudius tells Laertes that he loved Polonius, too — probably as much as Laertes did (34).

Ophelia by Sir John Everett Millais, 19th century.
Tate Gallery, London/ET Archive, London/SuperStock

Before Claudius can explain further, messengers enter with the letters from Hamlet, one addressed to the king and another to the queen. Claudius cannot believe this turn of events. He opens his letter and reads it out loud. Hamlet's salutation is blatantly insulting. He addresses Claudius as "High and mighty" (43). Hamlet is returning to Denmark and will have an audience with the king. After giving himself time to think of another strategy with which he might fight the threat of Hamlet, Claudius skillfully manipulates Laertes's grief to draw the grieving man into another scheme against Hamlet.

Claudius slanders Hamlet and tells Laertes that the prince is the rightful target of Laertes's revenge. The king and Laertes have a common enemy in Hamlet, and Claudius assures Laertes that Hamlet's crime will not go unpunished. He must now make sure that Laertes will be waiting to kill Hamlet upon his return.

Laertes cannot think clearly. He is angry, to be certain, but his desire for revenge outweighs any capacity for reason or logic. He does not try to decipher Claudius's plan or his intentions in bringing Laertes into his confidence. Claudius uses Laertes's confusion and instability to lure him into killing Hamlet. Claudius is

Laertes's king, but he speaks to Laertes like a father when he asks, "Will you be rul'd by me?" (57). Laertes has just lost his father, and his sister is mad. He is hungry to restore some feeling of belonging, and he answers Claudius affirmatively: "Ay, my lord" (58).

A duel until death

Now Claudius reveals his scheme. The king suggests that Laertes challenge Hamlet to a duel. Laertes is an excellent swordsman. The chances are good that he will defeat Hamlet and kill the prince. He will be blamed for Hamlet's death, and Claudius will regain the trust of Gertrude and the Danish people.

Laertes rises quickly to the bait. He tells Claudius that he has come into possession of a poison so potent that one scratch is enough to guarantee death. As the match proceeds, Claudius will offer a poisoned drink to Hamlet to ensure that should Laertes fail to kill the prince, the drink will finish the job. Claudius's love of elaborate evil and his impatience to be rid of Hamlet outweigh any caution the king might display. This scheme confirms Claudius's villainy.

The two men cement their plans. Claudius will outwardly wager on Hamlet, but the wager he really hopes to win has higher stakes. If he feels any hesitation, he does not show it. Laertes's desire for revenge consumes him and overwhelms any sense of honor.

Gertrude interrupts their vicious plans to deliver even more tragic news to Laertes: Ophelia has drowned. The poetic beauty of Gertrude's lines makes us think kindly of the queen (166–183). Ophelia went down to the brook to gather flowers. Singing bits of her favorite tunes, she entered the water. Although she floated for a little while, eventually her clothes became soaked and they dragged her under.

Laertes can barely respond. His grief is now too much to bear, and he leaves the room. Gertrude and Claudius, worried about Laertes's ability to withstand this latest news, follow him.

Notes

CLIFFSCOMPLETE

HAMLET
ACT V

Hamlet *[T]here's a special providence in the fall of a sparrow. If it be now, 'tis not to come; if it be not to come, it will be now; if it be not now, yet it will come: the readiness is all. Since no man has aught of what he leaves, what is 't to leave betimes?*

Act V, Scene 1

This graveyard scene includes dialogue between two men who are preparing a grave for Ophelia, a discussion between one of the gravediggers and Hamlet, and Ophelia's funeral. Laertes and Hamlet fight at Ophelia's gravesite.

ACT V, SCENE 1
A churchyard.

[Enter two Clowns, with spades and mattock]

First Clown Is she to be buried in Christian burial
that wilfully seeks her own salvation?

Second Clown I tell thee she is: and therefore
make her grave straight: the crowner hath sat on
her, and finds it Christian burial.   5

First Clown How can that be, unless she drowned
herself in her own defence?

Second Clown Why, 'tis found so.

First Clown It must be *se offendendo;* it cannot
be else. For here lies the point: if I drown myself   10
wittingly it argues an act; and an act hath three
branches; it is, to act, to do, and to perform: argal,
she drowned herself wittingly.

Second Clown Nay, but hear you, goodman
delver, —   15

First Clown Give me leave. Here lies the water;
good: here stands the man; good: if the man go to
this water, and drown himself, it is, will he, nill he, he
goes; mark you that? but if the water come to him,
and drown him, he drowns not himself: argal, he   20
that is not guilty of his own death shortens not his
own life.

Second Clown But is this law?

First Clown Ay, marry, is't; crowner's quest law.

Second Clown Will you ha' the truth on 't? If this   25
had not been a gentlewoman she should have been
buried out o' Christian burial.

NOTES

s.d.   *Clowns:* countrymen. The word indicates that these
       roles were played by comic actors.

1.   *in Christian burial:* in consecrated ground. People
       who committed suicides were buried in unhallowed
       ground.

4.   *straight:* straightaway.

       crowner: coroner.

5.   *finds . . . burial:* brings in a verdict that she should
       have a Christian burial.

9.   *se offendendo:* in self-defense.

11.   *wittingly:* knowingly, on purpose.

12.   *argal:* therefore.

15.   *delver:* digger.

18.   *will he, nill he:* willy-nilly, whether he wishes or not.

24.   *quest:* inquest.

First Clown Why, there thou sayest; and the more
pity that great folk should have countenance in this
world to drown or hang themselves more than their   30
even Christian. Come, my spade. There is no ancient
gentlemen but gardeners, ditchers, and grave-makers;
they hold up Adam's profession.

Second Clown Was he a gentleman?

First Clown A' was the first that ever bore arms.   35

Second Clown Why, he had none.

First Clown What! art a heathen? How dost thou
understand the Scripture? The Scripture says, Adam
digged; could he dig without arms? I'll put another
question to thee; if thou answerest me not to the   40
purpose, confess thyself —

Second Clown Go to.

First Clown What is he that builds stronger than
either the mason, the shipwright, or the carpenter?

Second Clown The gallows-maker; for that frame   45
outlives a thousand tenants.

First Clown I like thy wit well, in good faith; the
gallows does well, but how does it well? it does well to
those that do ill; now thou dost ill to say the gallows
is built stronger than the church: argal, the gallows   50
may do well to thee. To 't again; come.

Second Clown Who builds stronger than a mason, a
shipwright, or a carpenter?

First Clown Ay, tell me that, and unyoke.

Second Clown Marry, now I can tell.   55

First Clown To 't.

Second Clown Mass, I cannot tell.

[*Enter HAMLET and HORATIO at a distance*]

First Clown Cudgel thy brains no more about it, for
your dull ass will not mend his pace with beating;
and, when you are asked this question next, say,   60
'a grave-maker:' the houses that he makes last till

---

28. *thou sayest:* You said it; that's the truth.

29. *countenance:* permission.

31. *even:* fellow.

33. *hold up:* support, keep it going.

35. *arms:* a coat of arms, the prerogative of gentlemen.

41. *confess thyself:* The proverb continues with "and be hanged." (This is why the second clown interrupts.)

54. *unyoke:* consider your day's work done.

57. *Mass:* by the mass.

doomsday. Go, get thee to Yaughan; fetch me a
stoup of liquor.
[Exit Second Clown. First Clown digs, and sings]
In youth, when I did love, did love,
Methought it was very sweet, 65
To contract o' the time, for-a my behove,
O! methought there was nothing meet.

Hamlet Has this fellow no feeling of his business,
that he sings at grave-making?

Horatio Custom hath made it in him a property of 70
easiness.

Hamlet 'Tis e'en so; the hand of little employment
hath the daintier sense.

First Clown
But age, with his stealing steps,
Hath claw'd me in his clutch, 75
And hath shipped me intil the land,
As if I had never been such.

[Throws up a skull]

Hamlet That skull had a tongue in it, and could sing
once; how the knave jowls it to the ground, as
if it were Cain's jaw-bone, that did the first murder! 80
This might be the pate of a politician which this ass
now o'er-reaches, one that would circumvent God,
might it not?

Horatio It might, my Lord.

Hamlet Or of a courtier, which could say, 'Good 85
morrow, sweet lord! How dost thou, good lord?'
This might be my Lord Such-a-one, that praised my
Lord Such-a-one's horse, when he meant to beg it,
might it not?

Horatio Ay, my lord. 90

Hamlet Why, e'en so, and now my Lady Worm's
chapless, and knocked about the mazzard with a
sexton's spade. Here's fine revolution, an we had the

62. *Yaughan:* probably the name of a tavern-keeper near the Globe.

63. *stoup:* flask.

67. *meet:* suitable, proper.

70–71. *Custom . . . easiness:* Habit has made him indifferent to his occupation.

76. *Intil:* into.

79. *knave:* rude fellow.

jowls: bumps.

80. *Cain's jaw-bone:* the jawbone of an ass, with which Cain is supposed to have killed Abel.

81. *politician:* plotter, schemer.

82. *o'er-reaches:* gets the better of.

circumvent: get around.

88. *beg:* borrow.

92. *chapless:* jawless.

mazzard: slang for head (literally, drinking bowl).

93. *revolution:* turn of fortune.

an: if.

trick to see 't. Did these bones cost no more the
breeding but to play at loggats with 'em? mine   95
ache to think on 't.

First Clown
A pick-axe, and a spade, a spade,
For and a shrouding sheet;
O! a pit of clay for to be made
For such a guest is meet.   100

[Throws up another skull]

Hamlet There's another; why may not that be the
skull of a lawyer? Where be his quiddities now, his
quillets, his cases, his tenures, and his tricks? why
does he suffer this rude knave now to knock him about
the sconce with a dirty shovel, and will not tell him   105
of his action of battery? Hum! This fellow might be
in 's time a great buyer of land, with his statutes,
his recognizances, his fines, his double vouchers, his
recoveries; is this the fine of his fines, and the recovery
of his recoveries, to have his fine pate full of fine   110
dirt? will his vouchers vouch him no more of his
purchases, and double ones too, than the length and
breadth of a pair of indentures? The very conveyance
of his land will hardly lie in this box, and must
the inheritor himself have no more, ha?   115

Horatio Not a jot more, my lord.

Hamlet Is not parchment made of sheep-skins?

Horatio Ay, my lord, and of calf-skins too.

Hamlet They are sheep and calves which seek out
assurance in that. I will speak to this fellow. Whose   120
grave's this, sir?

First Clown Mine, sir.
O! a pit of clay for to be made
For such a guest is meet.

Hamlet I think it be thine, indeed; for thou liest in't. 125

First Clown You lie out on 't, sir, and therefore it is not
yours; for my part, I do not lie in 't, and yet it is
mine.

94. *trick:* skill.

95. *loggats:* skittles or ninepins, a British game in which a ball is bowled at nine wooden pins.

102. *quiddities:* subtle distinctions, hairsplitting.

103. *quilets:* quibbles.

    tenures: titles to property.

    tricks: legal tricks, technicalities.

105. *sconce:* a slang word for head (literally, block-house).

107. *statutes:* bonds.

108. *recognizances:* obligations.

    fines: conveyances.

    vouchers: witnesses.

109. *recoveries:* transfers.

    fine: end.

113. *pair of indentures:* agreements in duplicate.

    conveyance: documents recording purchase.

114. *box:* coffin.

115. *inheritor:* possessor.

120. *assurance:* a pun on conveyance of property by deed and security.

    that: parchment.

Hamlet Thou dost lie in 't, to be in 't and say it is
thine; 'tis for the dead, not for the quick; therefore   130
thou liest.

First Clown 'Tis a quick lie, sir; 'twill away again
from me to you.

Hamlet What man dost thou dig it for?

First Clown For no man, sir.   135

Hamlet What woman, then?

First Clown For none, neither.

Hamlet Who is to be buried in 't?

First Clown One that was a woman, sir; but, rest her
soul, she's dead.   140

Hamlet How absolute the knave is! we must speak
by the card, or equivocation will undo us. By the
Lord, Horatio, these three years I have taken note of
it; the age is grown so picked that the toe of the peasant
comes so near the heel of the courtier, he galls   145
his kibe. How long hast thou been a grave-maker?

First Clown Of all the days i' the year, I came to 't that
day our last King Hamlet overcame Fortinbras.

Hamlet How long is that since?

First Clown Cannot you tell that? every fool can tell   150
that; it was the very day that young Hamlet was born;
he that is mad, and sent into England.

Hamlet Ay, marry; why was he sent into England?

First Clown Why, because he was mad: he shall
recover his wits there; or, if he do not, 'tis no great   155
matter there.

Hamlet Why?

First Clown 'Twill not be seen in him there; there
the men are as mad as he.

Hamlet How came he mad?   160

First Clown Very strangely, they say.

Hamlet How strangely?

132. *quick:* living.

141. *absolute:* exact, literal.

142. *by the card:* precisely.

      equivocation: double meaning, ambiguity.

144. *picked:* refined.

145–146. *galls his kibe:* steps on (scrapes) his heel.

First Clown Faith, e'en with losing his wits.

Hamlet Upon what ground?

First Clown Why, here in Denmark; I have been   165
sexton here, man and boy, thirty years.

Hamlet How long will a man lie i' the earth ere he
rot?

First Clown Faith, if he be not rotten before he
die, — as we have many pocky corses now-a-days, that   170
will scarce hold the laying in, — he will last you some
eight year or nine year; a tanner will last you nine
year.

Hamlet Why he more than another?

First Clown Why, sir, his hide is so tanned with his   175
trade that he will keep out water a great while,
and your water is a sore decayer of your whoreson
dead body. Here's a skull now; this skull hath lain
you i' the earth three-and-twenty years.

Hamlet Whose was it?   180

First Clown A whoreson mad fellow's it was: whose
do you think it was?

Hamlet Nay, I know not.

First Clown A pestilence on him for a mad rogue;
a' poured a flagon of Rhenish on my head once. This   185
same skull, sir, was, sir, Yorick's skull, the king's
jester.

Hamlet This!

First Clown E'en that.

Hamlet Let me see. — *[Takes the skull]* — Alas!   190
poor Yorick. I knew him, Horatio; a fellow of
infinite jest, of most excellent fancy; he hath borne me
on his back a thousand times; and now, how
abhorred in my imagination it is! my gorge rises at it.
Here hung those lips that I have kissed I know not   195
how oft. Where be your gibes now? your gambols?
your songs? your flashes of merriment, that were
wont to set the table on a roar? Not one now, to
mock your own grinning? quite chapfallen? Now

170.	*pocky:* pock-marked, sore-covered corpses.
171.	*you:* The use of "you" and "your" in these speeches by the clown is in a general or indefinite, rather than personal, sense.
177.	*sore:* severe.
	whoreson: worthless (literally, bastard) .
194.	*gorge:* stomach (literally, throat).
196.	*gibes:* jests.
199.	*chapfallen:* a pun — it literally means jawless and figuratively means downcast.

get you to my lady's chamber, and tell her, let her   200
paint an inch thick, to this favour she must come;
make her laugh at that. Prithee, Horatio, tell me
one thing.

Horatio What's that, my lord?

Hamlet Dost thou think Alexander looked o' this   205
fashion i' the earth?

Horatio E'en so.

Hamlet And smelt so? pah! *[Puts down the skull]*

Horatio E'en so, my lord.

Hamlet To what base uses we may return, Horatio!   210
Why may not imagination trace the noble
dust of Alexander, till he find it stopping a
bung-hole?

Horatio 'Twere to consider too curiously, to
consider so.   215

Hamlet No, faith, not a jot; but to follow him
thither with modesty enough, and likelihood to lead
it; as thus: Alexander died, Alexander was
buried, Alexander returneth into dust; the
dust is earth; of earth we make loam, and why   220
of that loam, whereto he was converted, might they
not stop a beer-barrel?
Imperious Caesar, dead and turn'd to clay,
Might stop a hole to keep the wind away:
O! that that earth, which kept the world in awe,   225
Should patch a wall to expel the winter's flaw.
But soft! but soft! aside: here comes the king.
[Enter KING, QUEEN, LAERTES, and a coffin with Lords
attendant and Priest]
The queen, the courtiers: who is that they follow?
And with such maimed rites? This doth betoken
The corse they follow did with desperate hand   230
Fordo its own life; 'twas of some estate.
Couch we awhile, and mark.

[Retiring with HORATIO]

Laertes What ceremony else?

201. *favour:* appearance.

213. *bung-hole:* a hole in a keg of beer.

214. *too curiously:* too precisely.

217–218. *with modesty . . . lead it:* without exaggeration and within the bounds of all probability.

220. *loam:* a mixture of sand and clay used to make plaster.

225. *earth:* Caesar.

226. *flaw:* fierce wind.

229. *maimed:* curtailed.

      betoken: indicate.

231. *Fordo:* destroy.

      estate: high rank.

232. *Couch:* lie concealed.

Hamlet   That is Laertes,
A very noble youth: mark.

Laertes Where ceremony else?   235

First Priest Her obsequies have been as far enlarg'd
As we have warrantise: her death was doubtful,
And, but that great command o'ersways the order,
She should in ground unsanctified have lodg'd
Till the last trumpet; for charitable prayers,   240
Shards, flints, and pebbles should be thrown on her;
Yet here she is allow'd her virgin crants,
Her maiden strewments, and the bringing home
Of bell and burial.

Laertes Must there no more be done?

First Priest   No more be done: 245
We should profane the service of the dead,
To sing sage requiem, and such rest to her
As to peace-parted souls.

Laertes   Lay her i' th' earth;
And from her fair and unpolluted flesh
May violets spring! I tell thee, churlish priest,   250
A ministering angel shall my sister be,
When thou liest howling.

Hamlet   What! the fair Ophelia?

Queen Sweets to the sweet: farewell! *[Scattering flowers]*
I hop'd thou shouldst have been my Hamlet's wife;
I thought thy bride-bed to have deck'd, sweet maid,   255
And not have strew'd thy grave.

Laertes   O! treble woe
Fall ten times treble on that cursed head
Whose wicked deed thy most ingenious sense
Depriv'd thee of. Hold off the earth awhile,
Till I have caught her once more in mine arms.   260
[Leaps into the grave]
Now pile your dust upon the quick and dead,
Till of this flat a mountain you have made,
To o'ertop old Pelion or the skyish head
Of blue Olympus.

Hamlet   *[Advancing]* What is he whose grief
Bears such an emphasis? whose phrase of sorrow   265

237.   *warrantise:* authority.

238.   *but that . . . the order:* if the king had not used his authority to override the rule of the church.

240.   *for:* instead of.

241.   *shards:* broken earthenware.

242.   *crants:* wreaths.

243.   *maiden strewments:* flowers strewn on a girl's grave.

248.   *peace-parted:* departed in peace.

250.   *churlish:* rude.

258.   *most ingenious sense:* intelligence.

263.   *skyish:* reaching in the sky.

263–264.   Pelion and Olympus are mountains in Greece. Hamlet mentions another mountain, Ossa, in line 293.

Conjures the wandering stars, and makes them stand
Like wonder-wounded hearers? this is I,
Hamlet the Dane. *[Leaps into the grave]*

Laertes   The devil take thy soul! *[Grapples with him]*

Hamlet Thou pray'st not well.
I prithee, take thy fingers from my throat;   270
For though I am not splenetive and rash
Yet have I in me something dangerous,
Which let thy wisdom fear. Away thy hand!

King Pluck them asunder.

Queen   Hamlet! Hamlet!

All Gentlemen, —

Horatio   Good my lord, be quiet.   275

[The Attendants part them, and they come out of the grave]

Hamlet Why, I will fight with him upon this theme
Until my eyelids will no longer wag.

Queen O my son! what theme?

Hamlet I lov'd Ophelia: forty thousand brothers
Could not, with all their quantity of love,   280
Make up my sum. What wilt thou do for her?

King O! he is mad, Laertes

Queen For love of God, forbear him.

Hamlet 'Swounds, show me what thou'lt do:
Woo't weep? woo't fight? woo't fast? woo't tear thyself?   285
Woo't drink up eisel? eat a crocodile?
I'll do't. Dost thou come here to whine?
To outface me with leaping in her grave?
Be buried quick with her, and so will I:
And, if thou prate of mountains, let them throw   290
Millions of acres on us, till our ground,
Singeing his pate against the burning zone,
Make Ossa like a wart! Nay, an thou'lt mouth,
I'll rant as well as thou.

Queen   This is mere madness:
And thus a while the fit will work on him;   295
Anon as patient as the female dove,

266. *wandering stars:* planets.

      stand: stand still.

267. *wonder-wounded:* overcome with wonder.

271. *splenetive:* full of spleen, hot-tempered.

283. *forbear him:* pay no attention to him, make
      allowances for him.

285. *Woo't:* colloquial and familiar form of wilt thou.

286. *eisel:* vinegar.

288. *outface:* put to shame, outdo.

292. *the burning zone:* the sun.

293. *Ossa:* mountain in Greece (see lines 263–264).

294. *mere:* utter.

When that her golden couplets are disclos'd,
His silence will sit drooping.

Hamlet   Hear you, sir;
What is the reason that you use me thus?
I lov'd you ever: but it is no matter;   300
Let Hercules himself do what he may,
The cat will mew and dog will have his day. *[Exit]*

King I pray you, good Horatio, wait upon him. *[Exit
    HORATIO]*
[To LAERTES] Strengthen your patience in our last
    night's speech;
We'll put the matter to the present push.   305
Good Gertrude, set some watch over your son.
This grave shall have a living monument:
An hour of quiet shortly shall we see;
Till then, in patience our proceeding be. *[Exeunt]*

297.   *couplets:* The dove lays only two eggs.

         disclos'd: hatched.

305.   *present push:* immediate test.

307.   *a living monument:* an enduring memorial.

COMMENTARY

This scene contains three distinct movements: the witty exchanges of the gravediggers, Hamlet's meditation on death, and the funeral of Ophelia. The gravediggers are pragmatic and comical, bringing much-needed relief to the audience, which has just learned of the tragic death of Ophelia and is anticipating a revenge scene. The contrast between this and the previous scene allows the audience to step back and gain new perspective on the tragic events that are propelling the action forward.

The gravediggers

The "clowns," as the gravediggers are known, work in a world of death, but they are amazingly alive and their honest approach to life and death is refreshing. They are oblivious to the poisonous and corrupting effects of court intrigue, although the lives of the nobles provide an interesting and never-ending source of gossip and distraction for the workmen. The gravediggers discuss the question of Ophelia's burial in Christian ground. In Shakespeare's time, suicide, like murder, was considered a mortal sin. As a result, people who took their own lives were buried in unconsecrated ground (land not blessed by a priest) just like murderers and excommunicates. They could not lie in the same graveyard as people who died in grace.

The rumors circulating in and around Elsinore suggest that Ophelia killed herself. Still, she is being allowed a Christian burial. The gravediggers decide that if Ophelia had been a commoner, this exception to the rule would not have been allowed. The age-old complaint of the poor rings familiar: The rich have privileges that poor people do not enjoy. Birth and wealth provide power and create the true distinctions between the classes.

As Hamlet returns to Elsinore, he comes upon the gravediggers at work. He cannot help stopping to listen to their dialogue, musing at their ability to chat and sing even while they dig a grave and work among bones. The song of the first gravedigger is an amusing jumble of half-remembered verses from a mediocre poem by Lord Vaux called "The Ancient Lover Renounceth Love."

Hamlet and Horatio in the Cemetery *by Eugene Delacroix, 19th century. Musee de Louvre, Paris/ET Archive/SuperStock*

Horatio, who must have gone to meet the prince and travel with him back to the castle, accompanies Hamlet. Hamlet's now subdued demeanor stands in stark contrast to his earlier self. Horatio, on the other hand, has never changed; he is as constant as the North Star. In response to Hamlet's observation, Horatio tells the prince that gravediggers are used to seeing death and they have become insensitive to it: "Custom hath made it in him a property of / easiness" (70–71).

A meditation on death

Hamlet is fascinated and continues to watch the workmen. He muses over the skulls and bones, wondering to whom they belonged in life, and he quietly speculates on the equality and inevitability of death. His discussion with the gravedigger reveals Hamlet's thoughts. He has been appalled and revolted by the moral corruption of the living, and now he is soothed and even amused by the universality of physical corruption in the dead.

Hamlet is intrigued by the gravedigger's riddles, and the ensuing conversation is peppered with the humor and the wisdom of the common man. The worker tells the prince that he has been a gravedigger since the day that the old king killed old Fortinbras, the same year young Hamlet was born. This timeline would make Hamlet about 30, although most actors play him as a younger man. The gravedigger tells Hamlet that the prince has been sent to England to "recover his wits" (155). However, he says, in England no one will notice the prince's madness because the English are all witless themselves. This line surely garnered significant laughter from Shakespeare's English audience.

The unearthing of the skull of Yorick, the court jester during Hamlet's youth, elicits an amazed reaction from the prince. He tells Horatio about the jester, giving a complimentary and loving eulogy on the man's relationship to Hamlet as a young boy. He imagines Yorick alive and contemplates the lifeless bones in his hand. This passage shows that Hamlet's ordeals have not made him forget about the people in his life who loved him. He is not without pity. Hamlet asks Horatio about Alexander the Great. Could it be that even Alexander, the military genius and brilliant leader, now looks and smells like Yorick, the court jester? If this is the fate of every man, then what is life but a journey into dust? Death eliminates the differences between people. The hierarchical structure of society is illusory and ultimately crumbles into dust, just like these bones.

The funeral procession

A procession arrives and interrupts Hamlet's digressions. The procession appears to be a court funeral, and Hamlet wonders who has died. He and Horatio hide themselves and watch. Hearing Laertes's objections to the abbreviated funeral services, Hamlet realizes that they have come to bury Ophelia. His grief and shock reveal the depth of his feelings for her. Gertrude's flower ritual evokes Ophelia's youth and Gertrude's now lost hopes for a wedding between Ophelia and Hamlet.

Laurence Olivier directed and starred in the 1948 film version of Hamlet.
Everett Collection

This scene marks the end of the flower imagery in the play and, as such, it accentuates Ophelia's tragedy. With her goes the last of Hamlet's youth and Hamlet's dreams. At the grave, Laertes openly curses Hamlet, whom he blames for Ophelia's madness and death. He jumps into the grave and pulls Ophelia's body close for one last embrace.

Hamlet cannot hide his feelings any longer, and he reveals his presence to the assembly. Interestingly he announces himself as if he were king: "[T]his is I, / Hamlet the Dane" (267–268). He jumps in after Laertes, who drops Ophelia's body and tackles Hamlet. The sequence that follows is quick, heated, and full of action as Hamlet and Laertes fight. The queen calls after Hamlet, happy to see him alive but frightened for his safety. She must want to run to her son, but instinct holds her back.

Claudius calls for attendants (probably soldiers) to pull Laertes and Hamlet apart as the two men continue to try to outdo each other. The argument finally subsides with Hamlet's departure after he insists that he loved Ophelia more than "forty thousand brothers" (279). His declarations of love have come too late to help Ophelia. After his behavior toward her, the assertions sound a little too frantic and insistent. One can well imagine why Laertes does not want to hear this from Hamlet.

The fight dies down and Hamlet, sounding bewildered, cannot understand why Laertes is so angry with him. Laertes says nothing. Claudius asks Gertrude to look after her son, and he takes this opportunity to speak to Laertes. As Gertrude reminds the mourners of Hamlet's madness, so the king reminds Laertes of the plans they made the previous night.

Act V, Scene 2

Claudius sends Osric to Hamlet with Laertes's challenge to a duel. Hamlet accepts. Before the court, Laertes and Hamlet duel. Claudius drops a poisoned pearl into a cup of wine intended for Hamlet. Gertrude drinks the wine and dies. Laertes and Hamlet are both cut by Laertes's poison-tipped weapon and are doomed to die as well. Before Hamlet dies, he kills Claudius. Fortinbras enters, and Horatio reveals the events that have occurred.

ACT V, SCENE 2
A hall in the castle.

[Enter HAMLET and HORATIO]

Hamlet So much for this, sir: now shall you see the other;
  You do remember all the circumstance?

Horatio Remember it, my lord?

Hamlet Sir, in my heart there was a kind of fighting
  That would not let me sleep; methought I lay   5
  Worse than the mutines in the bilboes. Rashly, —
  And prais'd be rashness for it, let us know,
  Our indiscretion sometimes serves us well
  When our deep plots do pall; and that should teach us
  There's a divinity that shapes our ends,   10
  Rough-hew them how we will.

Horatio   That is most certain.

Hamlet Up from my cabin,
  My sea-gown scarf'd about me, in the dark
  Groped I to find out them, had my desire,
  Finger'd their packet, and in fine withdrew   15
  To mine own room again; making so bold —
  My fears forgetting manners — to unseal
  Their grand commission; where I found, Horatio,
  O royal knavery! an exact command,
  Larded with many several sorts of reasons   20
  Importing Denmark's health, and England's too,
  With, ho! such bugs and goblins in my life,
  That, on the supervise, no leisure bated,
  No, not to stay the grinding of the axe,
  My head should be struck off.

Horatio   Is't possible?   25

NOTES

6. *mutines:* mutineers.

bilboes: fetters.

7. *let us know:* let us acknowledge.

8–9. *Our . . . pall:* Sometimes it is to our advantage, when our deeply laid plans fall flat (pall), to act on the spur of the moment without weighing the consequences.

10–11. *There's a . . . we will:* No matter how crudely we begin our designs, Fate steps in to put the finishing touches on them.

13. *sea-gown:* a skirted garment with short sleeves, worn by seamen.

scarf'd: wrapped.

14. *them:* Rosencrantz and Guildenstern.

15. *Finger'd:* stole.

20. *Larded:* fattened.

several sorts: different kinds.

21. *Importing:* concerning.

22. *bugs:* terrors, nightmares.

in my life: in my continued existence.

23. *supervise:* reading, first glance over the letter.

bated: allowed.

Hamlet Here's the commission: read it at more leisure.
But wilt thou hear me how I did proceed?

Horatio I beseech you.

Hamlet Being thus be-netted round with villainies, —
Ere I could make a prologue to my brains   30
They had begun the play, — I sat me down,
Devis'd a new commission, wrote it fair;
I once did hold it, as our statists do,
A baseness to write fair, and labour'd much
How to forget that learning; but, sir, now   35
It did me yeoman's service. Wilt thou know
The effect of what I wrote?

Horatio   Ay, good my lord.

Hamlet An earnest conjuration from the king,
As England was his faithful tributary,
As love between them like the palm should flourish,   40
As peace should still her wheaten garland wear,
And stand a comma 'tween their amities,
And many such-like 'As'es of great charge,
That, on the view and knowing of these contents,
Without debatement further, more or less,   45
He should the bearers put to sudden death,
Not shriving-time allow'd.

Horatio   How was this seal'd?

Hamlet Why, even in that was heaven ordinant.
I had my father's signet in my purse,
Which was the model of that Danish seal;   50
Folded the writ up in form of the other,
Subscrib'd it, gave 't th' impression, plac'd it safely,
The changeling never known. Now, the next day
Was our sea-fight, and what to this was sequent
Thou know'st already.   55

Horatio So Guildenstern and Rosencrantz go to 't.

Hamlet Why, man, they did make love to this employment;
They are not near my conscience; their defeat
Does by their own insinuation grow.

30. *prologue:* introductory speech.

33. *statists:* statesmen.

36. *yeoman's service:* good service. English yeomen made the most reliable soldiers.

41. *wheaten garland:* a symbol of prosperity.

42. *stand . . . amities:* provide a connecting link between their friendships.

43. *charge:* weight, import.

45. *debatement:* debating.

47. *Not . . . allow'd:* not giving them time even to confess their sins.

48. *ordinant:* provident.

50. *model:* copy.

51. *writ:* writing.

52. *Subscrib'd . . . impression:* signed and sealed it.

53. *changeling:* literally, an elf-child substituted for a human one.

56. *go to 't:* as we might say, have had it.

57. *they did . . . employment:* they asked for it.

58. *They . . . conscience:* Their death is not on my conscience.

defeat: destruction.

59. *insinuation:* intervention, meddling.

'Tis dangerous when the baser nature comes   60
Between the pass and fell-incensed points
Of mighty opposites.

Horatio   Why, what a king is this!

Hamlet Does it not, thinks't thee, stand me now upon —
He that hath kill'd my king and whor'd my mother,
Popp'd in between the election and my hopes,   65
Thrown out his angle for my proper life,
And with such cozenage — is 't not perfect conscience
To quit him with this arm? and is 't not to be damn'd
To let this canker of our nature come
In further evil?   70

Horatio It must be shortly known to him from England
What is the issue of the business there.

Hamlet It will be short: the interim is mine;
And a man's life's no more than to say 'One.'
But I am very sorry, good Horatio,   75
That to Laertes I forgot myself;
For, by the image of my cause, I see
The portraiture of his: I'll court his favours:
But, sure, the bravery of his grief did put me
Into a towering passion.

Horatio   Peace! who comes here?   80

[Enter OSRIC]

Osric Your lordship is right welcome back to Denmark.

Hamlet I humbly thank you, sir. *[Aside to HORATIO]*
Dost know this water-fly?

Horatio *[Aside to HAMLET]* No, my good lord.

Hamlet *[Aside to HORATIO]* Thy state is the more   85
gracious; for 'tis a vice to know him. He hath much
land, and fertile: let a beast be lord of beasts, and
his crib shall stand at the king's mess; 'tis a chough;
but, as I say, spacious in the possession of dirt.

Osric Sweet lord, if your lordship were at leisure, I   90
should impart a thing to you from his majesty.

Hamlet I will receive it, sir, with all diligence of spirit.
Put your bonnet to his right use; 'tis for the head.

60–62.	*'Tis . . . opposites:* It is dangerous for inferiors to get between the thrusting blades and sword points of angry and mighty opponents.
63.	*Does . . . upon:* Don't you think it is now my duty?
65.	*Popp'd . . . hopes:* prevented me from being elected king as I had hoped.
66.	*angle:* fishing tackle.
	my proper life: my very life.
67.	*cozenage:* treachery.
68.	*To quit him:* to pay him back.
68–70.	*and is 't . . . evil:* Will I not risk eternal damnation if I allow this destructive element (canker) in our life (nature) to accomplish any more harm?
73–74.	*It will . . . 'One':* There is no great hurry; it takes only a second to kill a man.
77–78.	*For, by the . . . of his:* I realize his duty and feelings are like mine.
79.	*bravery:* bravado.
s.d.:	*Enter OSRIC:* Osric is an example of the fashionable affected courtier of Shakespeare's own time.
83.	*water-fly:* an insect without apparent purpose.
85–86.	*Thy . . . gracious:* You are better off.
87–88.	*let a beast . . . mess:* Even if a man is beastly, if he has money, he'll be welcome at the king's table.
88.	*chough:* a chatterer.
89.	*spacious . . . dirt:* a possessor of much land.
94.	*Put . . . head:* Although Elizabethans wore their hats indoors, removing head covering was customary when in the presence of superiors.

Osric I thank your lordship, 'tis very hot.   95

Hamlet No, believe me, 'tis very cold; the wind is northerly.

Osric It is indifferent cold, my lord, indeed.

Hamlet But yet methinks it is very sultry and hot for my complexion.   100

Osric Exceedingly, my lord; it is very sultry, as 'twere, I cannot tell how. But, my lord, his majesty bade me signify to you that he has laid a great wager on your head. Sir, this is the matter, —

Hamlet I beseech you, remember —   105

[HAMLET moves him to put on his hat]

Osric Nay, good my lord; for mine ease, in good faith. Sir, here is newly come to court Laertes; believe me, an absolute gentleman, full of most excellent differences, of very soft society and great showing; indeed, to speak feelingly of him, he is the   110 card or calendar of gentry, for you shall find in him the continent of what part a gentleman would see.

Hamlet Sir, his definement suffers no perdition in you; though, I know, to divide him inventorially would dizzy the arithmetic of memory, and yet but   115 yaw neither, in respect of his quick sail. But, in the verity of extolment, I take him to be a soul of great article; and his infusion of such dearth and rareness, as, to make true diction of him, his semblable is his mirror; and who else would trace him, his umbrage,   120 nothing more.

Osric Your lordship speaks most infallibly of him.

Hamlet The concernancy, sir? why do we wrap the gentleman in our more rawer breath?

Horatio Is 't not possible to understand in another   125 tongue? You will do 't, sir, really.

Hamlet What imports the nomination of this gentleman?

Osric Of Laertes?

98.	*indifferent:* fairly.
99–100.	*for my complexion:* for a person of my complexion or temperament.
106–107.	*for . . . faith:* a polite phrase of the time.
108.	*absolute:* perfect.
109.	*differences:* marks of distinction.
	soft: polite.
109–110.	*great showing:* distinguished appearance.
110.	*feelingly:* with proper appreciation.
111.	*card . . . gentry:* the model or guide of good breeding.
112.	*continent:* container.
	part: qualities.
	would see: would wish to see.
113–121.	In this speech, Hamlet outdoes Osric with extravagant language.
113–114.	*perdition in you:* loss in your speech.
114–116.	*though . . . sail:* It would strain our memories to attempt to list all his fine qualities, and even if we did so our description would be clumsy compared with his excellence.
116–117.	*in . . . extolment:* to praise him truly.
117–118.	*of great article:* of a long list of accomplishments.
118.	*infusion . . . rareness:* rare spirit.
119.	*to make . . . of him:* to speak truly of him.
119–120.	*his semblable is his mirror:* only his mirror can give the true picture of him.
120.	*umbrage:* shadow.
123.	*concernancy:* How does all this concern us?
123–124.	*why do we . . . breath?:* Why do we so inadequately discuss this most cultivated gentleman?
125–126.	*Is 't . . . tongue?:* Horatio asks Osric if it is not possible for him to understand his own affected, extravagant language when spoken by another; and he urges Osric to try harder.
127–128.	*What . . . gentleman?:* Why have you named this gentleman?

Horatio His purse is empty already; all's golden words   130
are spent.

Hamlet Of him, sir.

Osric I know you are not ignorant —

Hamlet I would you did, sir; in faith, if you did, it
would not much approve me. Well, sir.   135

Osric You are not ignorant of what excellence
Laertes is —

Hamlet I dare not confess that, lest I should compare
with him in excellence; but, to know a man well,
were to know himself.   140

Osric I mean, sir, for his weapon; but in the
imputation laid on him by them in his meed, he's
unfellowed.

Hamlet What's his weapon?

Osric Rapier and dagger.   145

Hamlet That's two of his weapons; but, well.

Osric The king, sir, hath wagered with him six
Barbary horses; against the which he has imponed, as
I take it, six French rapiers and poniards, with
their assigns, as girdle, hangers, and so: three of the   150
carriages, in faith, are very dear to fancy, very
responsive to the hilts, most delicate carriages, and of
very liberal conceit.

Hamlet What call you the carriages?

Horatio I know you must be edified by the margent,   155
ere you had done.

Osric The carriages, sir, are the hangers.

Hamlet The phrase would be more germane to the
matter, if we could carry cannon by our sides; I
would it might be hangers till then. But, on; six   160
Barbary horses against six French swords, their assigns,
and three liberal-conceited carriages; that's the
French bet against the Danish. Why is this
'imponed,' as you call it?

135. *approve:* commend.

141. *his weapon:* his skill with his weapon.
142. *imputation:* reputation.
       meed: pay, service.
143. *unfellowed:* without equal.

148. *imponed:* staked.
149. *poniards:* daggers.
150. *assigns:* appurtenances.
       hangers: straps by which the rapier was hung from the girdle.
       and so: and so on.
151. *dear to fancy:* pleasing to one's fancy.
151–152. *very responsive to:* a good match for
153. *very liberal conceit:* fanciful design.
155–156. *I know . . . had done:* Horatio says that he knew Hamlet would have to consult the margin notes to be able to understand Osric.
158. *germane:* appropriate.

Osric The king, sir, hath laid, sir, that in a dozen   165
passes between yourself and him, he shall not exceed
you three hits; he hath laid on twelve for nine, and it
would come to immediate trial, if your lordship would
vouchsafe the answer.

Hamlet How if I answer no?   170

Osric I mean, my lord, the opposition of your
person in trial.

Hamlet Sir, I will walk here in the hall; if it
please his majesty, 'tis the breathing time of day
with me; let the foils be brought, the gentleman   175
willing, and the king hold his purpose, I will win
for him an I can; if not, I will gain nothing but my
shame and the odd hits.

Osric Shall I re-deliver you e'en so?

Hamlet To this effect, sir; after what flourish your   180
nature will.

Osric I commend my duty to your lordship.

Hamlet Yours, yours. *[Exit OSRIC]* He does well
to commend it himself; there are no tongues
else for 's turn.   185

Horatio This lapwing runs away with the shell on
his head.

Hamlet He did comply with his dug before he
sucked it. Thus has he — and many more of the same
bevy, that I know the drossy age dotes on — only got   190
the tune of the time and outward habit of encounter,
a kind of yesty collection which carries them through
and through the most fond and winnowed opinions; and
do but blow them to their trial, the bubbles are out.

[Enter a Lord]

Lord My lord, his majesty commended him to you by   195
young Osric, who brings back to him, that you attend
him in the hall; he sends to know if your pleasure
hold to play with Laertes, or that you will take
longer time.

---

166. *him:* Laertes

167. *he:* Laertes.

twelve for nine: In a match of twelve bouts (instead of the usual nine), Laertes will win by at least three up.

169. *vouchsafe the answer:* condescend to participate in the encounter.

174. *breathing time:* time of exercise.

179. *re-deliver:* report.

180. *flourish:* fanfare, fancy wording.

180–181. *To this . . . nature will:* Horatio knows how impossible it would be for Osric to make a report in plain language.

183. *Yours, yours:* at your service.

186–187. *This lapwing . . . his head:* Horatio compares Osric to a young bird that, in its rush to be hatched, runs off with part of its shell on its head.

188. *comply:* exchange courtesies.

dug: breast.

188–189. *He did . . . sucked it:* He was a courtier from the time he was born.

190. *drossy:* frivolous.

191. *tune of the time:* fashionable jargon.

encounter: address, compliment.

192. *yesty collection:* frothy collection of catchwords.

193. *fond:* foolish.

winnowed: with the good sifted out.

194. *do but . . . are out:* If you try to get any sense out of their speech, you are wasting your time. (Nothing remains after the froth has been blown off.)

195. *commended him to you:* sent his regards to you.

Hamlet I am constant to my purposes; they follow   200
the king's pleasure: if his fitness speaks, mine is
ready; now, or whensoever, provided I be so able
as now.

Lord The king, and queen, and all are coming
down.   205

Hamlet In happy time.

Lord The queen desires you to use some gentle
entertainment to Laertes before you fall to play.

Hamlet She well instructs me. *[Exit Lord]*

Horatio You will lose this wager, my lord.   210

Hamlet I do not think so; since he went into
France, I have been in continual practice; I shall
win at the odds. But thou wouldst not think how
ill all's here about my heart; but it is no matter.

Horatio Nay, good my lord, —   215

Hamlet It is but foolery; but it is such a kind of
gain-giving as would perhaps trouble a woman.

Horatio If your mind dislike any thing, obey it;
I will forestal their repair hither, and say you are
not fit.   220

Hamlet Not a whit, we defy augury; there's a special
providence in the fall of a sparrow. If it be
now, 'tis not to come; if it be not to come, it will be
now; if it be not now, yet it will come: the readiness
is all. Since no man has aught of what he leaves,   225
what is 't to leave betimes?
Let be.

*[Enter KING, QUEEN, LAERTES, Lords, OSRIC, and
Attendants with foils, &c]*

King Come, Hamlet, come, and take this hand
from me.

[The KING puts the hand of LAERTES into that of HAMLET]

Hamlet Give me your pardon, sir; I've done you wrong;   230
But pardon 't, as you are a gentleman.
This presence knows, and you must needs have heard,

---

201. *his fitness speaks:* he says it is convenient to him.

206. *In happy time:* Good.

207–208. *gentle entertainment:* kindly treatment.

217. *gain-giving:* misgiving.

219. *repair:* coming.

221. *augury:* omens.

222. *it:* death.

226. *betimes:* early.

232. *presence:* assembled court.

How I am punish'd with a sore distraction.
What I have done
That might your nature, honour and exception 235
Roughly awake, I here proclaim was madness.
Was't Hamlet wrong'd Laertes? Never Hamlet:
If Hamlet from himself be ta'en away,
And when he's not himself does wrong Laertes,
Then Hamlet does it not; Hamlet denies it. 240
Who does it then? His madness. If 't be so,
Hamlet is of the faction that is wrong'd;
His madness is poor Hamlet's enemy.
Sir, in his audience,
Let my disclaiming from a purpos'd evil 245
Free me so far in your most generous thoughts,
That I have shot mine arrow o'er the house,
And hurt my brother.

Laertes   I am satisfied in nature,
Whose motive, in this case, should stir me most
To my revenge; but in my terms of honour 250
I stand aloof, and will no reconcilement,
Till by some elder masters, of known honour,
I have a voice and precedent of peace,
To keep my name ungor'd. But till that time,
I do receive your offer'd love like love, 255
And will not wrong it.

Hamlet   I embrace it freely;
And will this brother's wager frankly play.
Give us the foils. Come on.

Laertes   Come, one for me.

Hamlet I'll be your foil, Laertes; in mine ignorance
Your skill shall, like a star i' the darkest night, 260
Stick fiery off indeed.

Laertes   You mock me, sir.

Hamlet No, by this hand.

King Give them the foils, young Osric. Cousin Hamlet,
You know the wager?

Hamlet   Very well, my lord;
Your Grace hath laid the odds o' the weaker side. 265

235. *exception:* resentment.

245. *purpos'd evil:* intentional wrong.

247. *That:* in that, as if.

248. *nature:* natural affection.

250–254. *but in my . . . ungor'd:* I refuse a reconciliation until I have received the assurances of men of experience and honor that I may do so without risking the loss of my honorable reputation.

259. *foil:* sword, fencing weapon; also might be a pun on the other meaning of foil — the tinsel backing of a jewel to make it show more brilliantly.

261. *Stick fiery off:* stand out brightly.

King I do not fear it; I have seen you both;
   But since he is better'd we have therefore odds.

Laertes This is too heavy; let me see another.

Hamlet This likes me well. These foils have all a length?

Osric Ay, my good lord. *[They prepare to play]*   270

King Set me the stoups of wine upon that table.
   If Hamlet give the first or second hit,
   Or quit in answer of the third exchange,
   Let all the battlements their ordnance fire;
   The king shall drink to Hamlet's better breath;   275
   And in the cup an union shall he throw,
   Richer than that which four successive kings
   In Denmark's crown have worn. Give me the cups;
   And let the kettle to the trumpet speak,
   The trumpet to the cannoneer without,   280
   The cannons to the heavens, the heavens to earth
   'Now the king drinks to Hamlet!' Come, begin;
   And you, the judges, bear a wary eye.

Hamlet Come on, sir.

Laertes   Come, my lord. *[They play]*

Hamlet   One.

Laertes   No.

Hamlet   Judgment.

Osric A hit, a very palpable hit.

Laertes   Well; again.   285

King Stay; give me drink. Hamlet, this pearl is thine;
   Here's to thy health. Give him the cup.

[Trumpets sound; and cannon shot off within]

Hamlet I'll play this bout first; set it by awhile.
   Come — *[They play]* Another hit; what say you?

Laertes A touch, a touch, I do confess.   290

King Our son shall win.

Queen   He's fat, and scant of breath.
   Here, Hamlet, take my napkin, rub thy brows;
   The queen carouses to thy fortune, Hamlet.

267. *better'd:* may mean either improved by training or considered better.

269. *likes:* pleases.

   have . . . length: are all of the same length.

273. *quit in answer:* score a return hit.

276. *union:* a large pearl.

279. *kettle:* kettledrum.

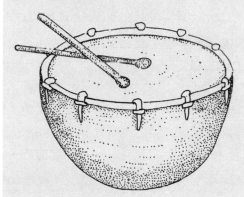

The kettledrum announces the start of the duel.

285. *palpable:* evident.

286. *this pearl is thine:* The king poisons the wine with a fake pearl containing poison.

291. *fat:* out of condition, sweaty.

292. *napkin:* handkerchief.

Hamlet Good madam!

King   Gertrude, do not drink.

Queen I will, my lord; I pray you, pardon me.   295

King *[Aside]* It is the poison'd cup! it is too late.

Hamlet I dare not drink yet, madam; by and by.

Queen Come, let me wipe thy face.

Laertes My lord, I'll hit him now.

King   I do not think 't.

Laertes *[Aside]* And yet 'tis almost 'gainst my conscience.   300

Hamlet Come, for the third, Laertes. You but dally;
I pray you, pass with your best violence.
I am afeard you make a wanton of me.

Laertes Say you so? come on. *[They play]*

Osric Nothing, neither way.   305

Laertes Have at you now.

[LAERTES wounds HAMLET; then, in scuffling, they
  change rapiers, and HAMLET wounds LAERTES]

King   Part them! they are incens'd.

Hamlet Nay, come, again. *[The QUEEN falls]*

Osric   Look to the queen there, ho!

Horatio They bleed on both sides. How is it, my lord?

Osric How is it, Laertes?

Laertes Why, as a woodcock to mine own springe, Osric;   310
I am justly kill'd with mine own treachery.

Hamlet How does the queen?

King   She swounds to see them bleed.

Queen No, no, the drink, the drink, — O my dear Hamlet!
The drink, the drink; I am poison'd. *[Dies]*

Hamlet O villainy! Ho! let the door be lock'd: 315
Treachery! seek it out. *[LAERTES falls]*

Laertes It is here, Hamlet. Hamlet, thou art slain;
No medicine in the world can do thee good;

301.   *dally:* play.

302.   *pass:* thrust.

303.   *make . . . me:* merely trifle with me.

310.   *springe:* snare.

In thee there is not half an hour of life;
The treacherous instrument is in thy hand,   320
Unhated and envenom'd. The foul practice
Hath turn'd itself on me; lo! here I lie,
Never to rise again. Thy mother's poison'd.
I can no more. The king, the king's to blame.

Hamlet The point envenom'd too! —   325
Then, venom, to thy work. *[Stabs the KING]*

All Treason! treason!

King O! yet defend me, friends; I am but hurt.

Hamlet Here, thou incestuous, murderous, damned Dane,
Drink off this potion; — is thy union here?   330
Follow my mother. *[KING dies]*

Laertes   He is justly serv'd;
It is a poison temper'd by himself.
Exchange forgiveness with me, noble Hamlet:
Mine and my father's death come not upon thee,
Nor thine on me! *[Dies]*   335

Hamlet Heaven make thee free of it! I follow thee.
I am dead, Horatio. Wretched queen, adieu!
You that look pale and tremble at this chance,
That are but mutes or audience to this act,
Had I but time, — as this fell sergeant, death,   340
Is strict in his arrest, — O! I could tell you —
But let it be. Horatio, I am dead;
Thou liv'st; report me and my cause aright
To the unsatisfied.

Horatio   Never believe it;
I am more an antique Roman than a Dane: 345
Here's yet some liquor left.

Hamlet   As thou'rt a man,
Give me the cup: let go; by heaven, I'll have 't.
O God! Horatio, what a wounded name,
Things standing thus unknown, shall live behind me.
If thou didst ever hold me in thy heart,   350
Absent thee from felicity awhile,
And in this harsh world draw thy breath in pain,
To tell my story. *[March afar off, and shot within]*
                    What war-like noise is this?

321. *practice:* trick.

325. *The point envenom'd:* The swordtip has poison on it.

332. *temper'd:* mixed.

334. *come not upon thee:* lie not at your door.

336. *make thee free:* acquit thee.

338. *chance:* fatal occurrence.

339. *mutes or audience:* silent spectators.

340. *fell:* dread.

344. *the unsatisfied:* those who do not know the truth.

345. *antique Roman:* The ancient Roman was ever ready to commit suicide when confronted with calamity.

348. *wounded name:* tarnished reputation.

Osric Young Fortinbras, with conquest come from Poland,
To the ambassadors of England gives　　　　　　　　355
This war-like volley.

Hamlet　　　　　　O! I die, Horatio;
The potent poison quite o'er-crows my spirit:
I cannot live to hear the news from England,
But I do prophesy the election lights
On Fortinbras: he has my dying voice;　　　　　360
So tell him, with the occurrents, more and less,
Which have solicited — The rest is silence. *[Dies]*

Horatio Now cracks a noble heart. Good-night, sweet prince,
And flights of angels sing thee to thy rest!
Why does the drum come hither? *[March within]*　　365

[Enter FORTINBRAS, the English Ambassadors, and Others]

Fortinbras Where is this sight?

Horatio　　　　　　　　　　What is it ye would see?
If aught of woe or wonder, cease your search.

Fortinbras This quarry cries on havoc. O proud death!
What feast is toward in thine eternal cell,
That thou so many princes at a shot　　　　　370
So bloodily hast struck?

First Ambassador　　　The sight is dismal;
And our affairs from England come too late:
The ears are senseless that should give us hearing,
To tell him his commandment is fulfill'd,
That Rosencrantz and Guildenstern are dead.　　375
Where should we have our thanks?

Horatio　　　　　　　　　　Not from his mouth,
Had it the ability of life to thank you:
He never gave commandment for their death.
But since, so jump upon this bloody question,
You from the Polack wars, and you from England,　　380
Are here arriv'd, give order that these bodies
High on a stage be placed to the view;
And let me speak to the yet unknowing world
How these things came about: so shall you hear
Of carnal, bloody, and unnatural acts,　　　　385
Of accidental judgments, casual slaughters;

357.　*o'er-crows:* triumphs over.

359.　*election:* as king of Denmark.

360.　*voice:* support.

361–362.　*occurrents . . . solicited:* the great and small occurrences which have incited me.

368.　*quarry:* heap of slain.
　　cries on: proclaims.
　　havoc: indiscriminate slaughter.

369.　*toward:* being prepared.

379.　*jump:* exactly.
　　question: matter.

382.　*stage:* elevated platform.

385.　*carnal:* lustful.

386.　*accidental judgments:* mistakes of judgment.
　　casual: chance.

Of deaths put on by cunning and forc'd cause,
And, in this upshot, purposes mistook
Fall'n on the inventors' heads; all this can I
Truly deliver.   390

Fortinbras Let us haste to hear it,
And call the noblest to the audience.
For me, with sorrow I embrace my fortune;
I have some rights of memory in this kingdom,
Which now to claim my vantage doth invite me.   395

Horatio Of that I shall have also cause to speak,
And from his mouth whose voice will draw on more:
But let this same be presently perform'd,
Even while men's minds are wild, lest more mischance
On plots and errors happen.

Fortinbras   Let four captains   400
Bear Hamlet, like a soldier, to the stage;
For he was likely, had he been put on,
To have prov'd most royally: and, for his passage,
The soldiers' music and the rites of war
Speak loudly for him.   405
Take up the bodies: such a sight as this
Becomes the field, but here shows much amiss.
Go, bid the soldiers shoot.

*[A dead march. Exeunt, bearing off the bodies;
after which a peal of ordnance is shot off]*

---

387.   *put on:* instigated

394.   *rights of memory:* rights that have not been forgotten altogether.

395.   *vantage:* opportunity.

397.   *whose . . . more:* whose support will cause others to give you their support.

398.   *this same:* the action of placing the bodies.

400.   *On:* on top of.

402.   *put on:* put to the test, made king.

403.   *passage:* passing

COMMENTARY

After such a long build-up, the ending of the play seems peculiarly sudden, which emphasizes the tragic nature of the story. After becoming familiar with these characters, we are not fully prepared for them to die. In a revenge tragedy, however, there is no other choice.

Hamlet and Horatio have returned to the castle and are engaged in a dialogue about Hamlet's adventures at sea. This kind of opening is called *in media res*, which means "in the middle of." Hamlet is already in the middle of his story when this scene opens.

Hamlet tells Horatio that the night before the pirates attacked the ship bound for England, he was restless and unable to sleep. His uneasiness prompted him to go to where Rosencrantz and Guildenstern slept and open the packet of letters that the king had commissioned them to take to England. The letters confirmed Hamlet's suspicions; the king had arranged for him to be killed in England. Hamlet daringly rewrote the letters, replacing his name with those of Rosencrantz and Guildenstern. They would deliver the letters of execution, but they would be the victims instead of Hamlet. They would not be allowed any "shriving-time" — no chance to confess or repent their sins (47). Hamlet sealed the new letter using his father's ring.

Hamlet suffers no pangs of guilt at his forgery; Rosencrantz and Guildenstern got what they deserved. As for his uncle, who has "kill'd my king and whor'd my mother, / Popp'd in between the election and my hopes," Hamlet will move against him soon (64–65). He tells Horatio that he does hold one regret: He wishes he had not behaved so violently toward Laertes at Ophelia's graveside. He can relate to what Laertes is feeling, but the shock of Ophelia's death put Hamlet "[i]nto a towering passion" (80).

Laertes's challenge

Osric, a gentleman from the court, enters with a challenge from Laertes. Osric, like Polonius, provides a target for Hamlet's disdain of flattering courtiers. Hamlet baits the messenger and toys with him, emphasizing the point that Osric, like the rest of the court, cannot be taken seriously. He is nothing more than a carrier of the degenerative disease that is slowly destroying Elsinore.

The king has wagered six Barbary horses on Hamlet against Laertes's wager of six French rapiers and daggers. The two men are to play 12 bouts. Hamlet accepts the king's terms and soon receives the message that the king and Laertes are waiting for Hamlet's arrival. Horatio warns Hamlet that he will lose, but Hamlet objects, telling Horatio that he is well-prepared and, in any case, his destiny is at hand. He will not buckle under the pressure of fear.

Hamlet tells Horatio that "there's a special providence in the fall of a sparrow" (221–222). He means that God has a divine plan for everyone and everything, no matter how seemingly insignificant. God works through his creatures, particularly man, to keep the universe in order. Hamlet knows that his fate is already determined; if he doesn't fight today, he will have to fight eventually. The two men go to join the already assembled court.

Before Hamlet selects his weapon, he approaches Laertes and offers him an apology for his outburst at Ophelia's funeral. Interestingly, Hamlet places the blame for his behavior on his "madness" (236). Because he claims that his actions were beyond his ability to control, he tells Laertes that he should not be judged for what he said or did. Laertes accepts the apology on the surface, but he reminds Hamlet that he has wounded Laertes's honor. Laertes must refuse this apology until he is sure that by accepting it he does not lose his reputation.

Although the truth remains unspoken, Laertes needs to revenge Polonius's murder and Ophelia's madness

and death. Nothing less than a fight to the end can satisfy Laertes's honor now. Nevertheless, Laertes's speech is notably stilted. Perhaps he is already beginning to regret his impetuous agreement with the king.

The duel

The two combatants select their weapons. Laertes is no match for Hamlet, though both men are skilled swordsmen and the action is exciting. Hamlet wins the first two bouts and draws the third. It becomes obvious that it will be difficult for Laertes to regain the lost ground. The king moves to pick up the chalice of wine. Hamlet strikes at Laertes, and Osric calls it "very palpable hit" (285). The king decides that the time is right to drop the poisoned pearl into the wine and offer it to Hamlet.

Gertrude leaves her place and approaches Hamlet to wipe his brow. Unexpectedly, she picks up the poisoned cup of wine and, before Claudius can stop her, she drinks. The king and Laertes stand in conspiratorial silence. The duel continues. Hamlet and Laertes, monitored closely by Osric and the king, cross blades. Laertes wounds Hamlet and they scuffle. In the confusion, somehow they exchange weapons and Hamlet wounds Laertes. Both men are now poisoned.

A scene from the 1996 film directed by Kenneth Branagh.
Everett Collection

Meanwhile, the poisoned wine that Gertrude drank has taken effect, and the queen falls. She cries out to Hamlet, warning him of the king's treachery before she dies. Echoing Polonius's words to Ophelia, Laertes confesses to Hamlet that "as a woodcock to mine own springe" the trap he set for Hamlet has trapped him as well (310). He tells Hamlet that they are both dying and "the king's to blame" (324). Hamlet orders the doors locked; he does not want to give Claudius a chance to escape or call for help. Hamlet rushes forward to the now powerless Claudius and kills him.

The entire play has moved toward this act of revenge. Laertes and Hamlet exchange forgiveness as they had exchanged weapons only moments before; but this time, the exchange is made in peace. The king, the queen, and Laertes lie dead. Hamlet is dying and turns to his most loyal friend — the only person who has never disappointed him — Horatio. He asks Horatio to accurately "report me and my cause" (342).

Alex Jenning, Diana Quick, and Paul Freeman in the 1997 Royal Shakespeare Company production. Clive Barda/PAL

Horatio compares himself to an "antique Roman," a reference that was easily understood by Shakespeare's audience (345). Romans customarily ran on their swords, killing themselves rather than living defeated and in dishonor. Horatio is telling Hamlet that he will follow him in death. But Hamlet will not allow Horatio to die. Horatio must once again act as Hamlet's messenger.

A deadly scene

The sound of guns alerts the court to the imminent arrival of Fortinbras, who has successfully conquered the Poles. Before Hamlet dies, he gives his vote to Fortinbras in the election that must now be held. Looking at Horatio, Hamlet succumbs to the poison and dies. Because revenge was considered to be a form of murder, the act could be justified only if the revenger died after the revenge was carried out. Shakespeare addresses the expectations of his Early Modern audience with Hamlet's death.

Fortinbras enters and asks the assembly what has happened. Horatio, true to his word, informs Fortinbras that he will explain everything, but first he asks that the bodies be placed high on a stage. Fortinbras does as Horatio has asked, commanding four captains to carry Hamlet's body "like a soldier" to the stage (401).

All three men who sought revenge for their fathers' deaths have now achieved it. Hamlet and Laertes have died for their revenge, but Fortinbras, without taking an active role, has avenged his father and will live on as king.

Hamlet's heroism is not truly appreciated until the end of the play. The audience comes to a realization of the true nature of Hamlet's dilemma along with the development of the character himself. By writing the tragedy this way, Shakespeare allows the audience to build its understanding of the play as slowly as Hamlet evolves in his understanding of his course of action. We grow along with Hamlet. We begin to feel what he is feeling. This parallel allows the audience to have an intimacy with the hero that is rarely achieved in the theatre. Ultimately, the audience recognizes the value of the life that has been lost.

Notes

CLIFFSCOMPLETE REVIEW

Use this CliffsComplete Review to gauge what you've learned and to build confidence in your understanding of the original text. After you work through the review questions, the problem-solving exercises, and the suggested activities, you're well on your way to understanding and appreciating the works of William Shakespeare.

IDENTIFY THE QUOTATION

Identify the following quotations by answering these questions:

* Who is the speaker of the quotation?
* What does the quotation reveal about the speaker's character?
* What does the quotation tell us about other characters within the play?
* Where does the quotation occur within the play?
* What does the quotation show us about the themes of the play?
* What significant imagery do you see in the quotation, and how do these images relate to the overall imagery of the play?

1. There's fennel for you, and columbines;
   there's rue for you; and here's some for me;
   we may call it herb of grace o' Sundays.
   O! you must wear your rue with a difference.
   There's a daisy; I would give you some violets,
   but they withered all when my father died.

2. Why, as a woodcock to mine own springe, Osric;
   I am justly kill'd with mine own treachery.

3. Good-night, sweet prince,
   And flights of angels sing thee to thy rest!

4. Let my disclaiming from a purpos'd evil
   Free me so far in your most generous thoughts,
   That I have shot mine arrow o'er the house,
   And hurt my brother.

5. Madness in great ones must not unwatch'd go.

6. The lady doth protest too much methinks.

7. Thrift, thrift, Horatio! the funeral bak'd meats
   Did coldly furnish forth the marriage tables.
   Would I had met my dearest foe in heaven
   Or ever I had seen that day, Horatio!

8. Neither a borrower, nor a lender be;
   For loan oft loses both itself and friend,
   And borrowing dulls the edge of husbandry.

9. Alas! poor Yorick. I knew him, Horatio; a
   fellow of infinite jest, of most excellent fancy;
   he hath borne me on his back a thousand
   times.

10. Sweets to the sweet: farewell!

11. Something is rotten in the state of Denmark.

12. O! my offence is rank, it smells to heaven;
    It hath the primal eldest curse upon 't.
    A brother's murder!

TRUE / FALSE

1. T F Hamlet is thrilled that his mother remarries.

2. T F Rosencrantz and Guildenstern are true friends to Hamlet.

3. T F Hamlet is a patron of drama.

4. T F Ophelia is really in love with Horatio.

5. T F Hamlet goes mad because his mother has married his uncle.

6. T F Polonius is a lonely old man who cannot stand to lose control of his children's lives.

7. T F Hamlet can hardly wait to kill his uncle so that he can be king.

8. T F Hamlet is convinced that Horatio is a liar.

9. T F Elsinore is a castle in Denmark.

10. T F Polonius sends Reynaldo to Paris to bring Laertes home.

11. T F Hamlet plays the king in "The Mousetrap."

12. T F Gertrude knows that Claudius killed the old king.

13. T F Fortinbras avenges his father's death.

14. T F Ophelia cannot be buried in Christian ground because she might have committed suicide.

15. T F Hamlet is a true Renaissance prince.

MULTIPLE CHOICE

1. What type of play is *Hamlet*?
   a. History
   b. Tragedy
   c. Pastoral
   d. Folio

2. What is Hamlet's relationship with Ophelia at the play's beginning?
   a. They are schoolmates.
   b. They are cousins.
   c. They are in love.
   d. They have not met.

3. Who poses a military threat to King Claudius at the play's beginning?
   a. Fortinbras
   b. Old Norway
   c. Poland
   d. Hamlet

4. In what country does the play take place?
   a. England
   b. Germany
   c. Denmark
   d. Norway

5. Which of the following sees the ghost of Hamlet's father first?
   a. Marcellus
   b. Claudius
   c. Horatio
   d. Hamlet

6. Approximately how much time has passed between the death of King Hamlet and the remarriage of Gertrude to Claudius?

   a. Six months

   b. Two weeks

   c. Two months

   d. One year

7. What is Hamlet trying to decide in his "To be" soliloquy?

   a. If the ghost of his father is real.

   b. If his life is worth living.

   c. If he should murder Claudius in order to become king.

   d. If he should confront Gertrude about her rash remarriage.

8. What is the main plot function that the players serve?

   a. They help Hamlet determine if his father's ghost is telling the truth.

   b. They distract Hamlet from his grief, which gives Claudius enough time to arrange for Hamlet's murder.

   c. They instruct Gertrude regarding the true nature of her former husband's death.

   d. They distract the court while Fortinbras's troops surround Elsinore.

9. Why doesn't Hamlet kill Claudius after the play, before going to his mother's chamber?

   a. He fears for Gertrude's health if she loses another husband.

   b. He doesn't want Claudius to be able to repent his sins before dying.

   c. He wants an audience when he exacts his revenge.

   d. He knows Claudius's guards are nearby.

10. Why does the apparition appear in Gertrude's chamber?

   a. To prove to Gertrude that Hamlet is not mad.

   b. To warn Gertrude that Claudius is a murderer.

   c. To show Gertrude that she is forgiven for remarrying so quickly.

   d. To protect Gertrude from Hamlet's excessive anger.

11. Why is Hamlet sent to England?

   a. Gertrude fears someone will harm Hamlet for killing Polonius.

   b. Claudius knows that Hamlet is insane.

   c. Claudius wants the King of England to have Hamlet killed.

   d. Ophelia tells the queen that Laertes has sworn to kill Hamlet.

12. Who aids in Hamlet's escape from the ship?

   a. Horatio

   b. Gertrude

   c. The King of England

   d. Pirates

13. Who tells Hamlet that Laertes has challenged him to a duel?

   a. Claudius

   b. Osric

   c. Horatio

   d. Laertes

14. How does Laertes die?

   a. Hamlet stabs him with a poisoned rapier.

   b. He stabs himself in a moment of regret for having tricked Hamlet.

   c. He drinks from Claudius's poisoned cup.

   d. Fortinbras kills him to revenge his father's death.

15. Who survives at the end of the play?

    a. Ophelia

    b. Gertrude

    c. Rosencrantz and Guildenstern

    d. Horatio

FILL IN THE BLANKS

1. Horatio: But, soft! behold! lo! where it comes again.

I'll cross it, though it blast me. Stay, _____!

2. King: Now Hamlet, where's _____?

Hamlet: At supper.

3. Polonius: At such a time I'll loose my daughter to him;

Be you and I behind an _____ then.

4. Hamlet: Ay, so, God be wi' ye! Now I am alone.

O! what a _____ and _____ slave am I.

5. Laertes: This nothing's more than matter.

Ophelia: There's rosemary that's for _____;

pray, love, remember: and there's pansies, that's for _____.

6. Hamlet: O! that this too too solid _____ would _____,

thaw and resolve itself into a _____.

7. King: Though yet of Hamlet our dear _____ death

The memory be green.

8. Polonius: Neither a _____ nor a _____ be.

9. Hamlet: There are more things in _____ and _____, Horatio,

Than are dreamt of in your philosophy.

10. Hamlet: To be, or not to be: that is the _____.

DISCUSSION

Use the following questions to generate discussion.

1. Would Hamlet have made a good king? What aspects of his personality seem to indicate that he may have been a good ruler of Denmark? What aspects of his personality seem to indicate that he may have had difficulty leading a nation? Are there any other characters in the play who seem better suited to the position of king than Hamlet?

2. Keeping in mind the boundaries and expectations placed on women living in Early Modern England, consider the actions of Ophelia and Gertrude. Do you agree with Ophelia's decision to end her relationship with Hamlet? Did she have an alternative? What does her obedience to Polonius say about her character? Was Gertrude wrong to marry Claudius? What may have been her motivation(s) for doing so? What might her life have been like had she refused his advances?

3. Consider Hamlet's soliloquy in Act II, Scene 2, starting at line 553. Why is he so upset with himself at this moment in the play? Who does he contrast himself with? What does Hamlet say about his own personality here? Do you agree with his self-analysis? Why or why not?

4. Do you believe that Ophelia committed suicide? Or would argue that in her madness, she did not realize that she was in danger of drowning? What reasons do you have for forming either opinion?

5. When Hamlet asks Gertrude how she likes "The Mouse-trap," she answers, "The lady doth protest too much methinks" (III.2.234). What does Gertrude mean by this? Why would she have this criticism of the scene at hand?

6. Hamlet tells Ophelia, "God hath given you one face, and you make yourselves another" (III.1.145). Later, in the graveyard, he speaks to the skull of Yorick and says, "[T]ell her, let her paint an inch think, to this favour she must come" (V.1.200–201). What is Hamlet talking about in these two passages? What might these quotations tell us about Hamlet's opinion of women? Is he referring to Ophelia, to Gertrude, or to women in general?

7. Ophelia is a noblewoman, probably sheltered and educated to be a nobleman's wife. After she goes mad, the songs she sings are bawdy, common, and overtly sexual. How do you think she learned these songs? Why is she singing them in her madness? What do they say about the cause of her madness? What do they indicate about the effect of her madness?

8. The characters Rosencrantz and Guildenstern have become quite famous in the past few decades thanks to a play written by Tom Stoppard entitled *Rosencrantz and Guildenstern are Dead*. Consider what we know about these characters from their interactions with Hamlet, Claudius, and Gertrude. What is their function in the play? Are there any distinctions made between the two characters, or do they act entirely as one entity? What qualities do they display?

9. The introduction of the traveling players in Act II, Scene 2 is one of the happier moments in Hamlet's life as portrayed in this play. What does this scene tell us about Hamlet? Why has Shakespeare included this scene in the play? Consider also the opening to Act III, Scene 2.

Why does Shakespeare detail Hamlet's instructions to the players in this scene?

10. Does Hamlet change from the beginning of the play to the end? Consider, for example, how he finally exacts his father's revenge on Claudius. Is this action premeditated? Does the fact that Hamlet finally accomplishes his goal indicate a significant transformation of his personality? If so, how and when do you think that transformation occurred?

IDENTIFYING PLAY ELEMENTS

Find examples of the following elements in the text of *Hamlet*:

* **Soliloquy:** A monologue in which a character in a play is alone and speaking to him or herself. Soliloquies are used in *Hamlet* to let the audience know what Hamlet is thinking. They help the audience understand and relate to Hamlet's actions (or lack thereof).

* **Dramatic irony:** This is what occurs when the audience knows more than the characters on stage. Soliloquies are useful in creating dramatic irony. The audience is then able to anticipate what may happen, even though the characters onstage are taken by surprise.

* **Verbal irony:** This is a kind of wordplay that occurs when what a character actually means is very different from what is literally said.

* **Imagery:** Shakespeare uses this device in his plays and sonnets to evoke a certain image in relation to a character or a place. For example, Ophelia is compared to violets, the flower that symbolizes faithfulness.

* **Blank Verse:** Unrhymed iambic pentameter — lines of approximately ten syllables, where five syllables are clearly stressed. This was the most common verse form in English during Shakespeare's time.

* **Rhymed couplet:** A rhymed couplet consists of two consecutive *rhyming* lines of iambic pentameter.

* **Wordplay:** Hamlet frequently uses witty puns — words that have more than one meaning — and riddles to keep his distance from other characters, to keep other characters off balance, to make himself sound crazy, and to lend a comic atmosphere to a scene. Shakespeare often plays with words in his plays. This device forces the other characters, as well as the audience, to think about the real meaning of the lines and the actual attitude and motivations of the character.

* **Foreshadowing:** This is a device whereby a character or a situation informs the audience about something that will happen and allows the audience to anticipate an eventual outcome. One minor example is the dumb show in the play-within-the-play. The silent action in that show foreshadows what will happen in "The Mouse-trap."

* **Symbol:** A symbol is a person, place, or thing that figuratively represents, or symbolizes, something else. Symbols are often physical things that represent abstract ideas. For example, Yorick's skull symbolizes death in *Hamlet*.

ACTIVITIES

The following activities can serve as a springboard for further discussions and projects.

1. Create a newspaper that reports what has happened in the play *Hamlet*. Write interesting headlines, include stories dealing with the political and legal issues in the play, and include any non-news sections that you think are appropriate. (For example, you may want to include a society section, obituaries, an editorial page, and so on.)

2. Create a board game that deals with aspects of the play. Use whatever format that you would like. You can use dice, draw cards, spin a wheel, and so on to determine how to advance. Be sure that the game reflects the characters and plot points in the play. For example, a player who lands on "Hamlet is sent to England" may miss a turn, or one who lands on "Laertes poisons his sword" may move ahead two spaces.

3. Write the story of the play *Hamlet* from one of the character's points of view. Choose any of the characters, and feel free to make up information that would add depth to the story. But make sure that any information that you create does not conflict with what is contained in the play. Follow the play text carefully to determine which events the character you select would or would not know about. For example, Laertes would not know that Hamlet had seen a ghost, and he probably would not be aware of Hamlet's strange behavior because Laertes was away in Paris during most of the play.

4. Create a Web site about *Hamlet*. Consider carefully what content you want to include on your home page and what links you think are important to include. You can do this project alone or in small groups.

5. Write a report comparing the characters in *Hamlet* to historical figures or to people you know. Include as many reasons as possible to explain how the characters and the people you choose are similar. List any differences between them as well. For example, you might say that Polonius is like your best friend because they both constantly give advice, but your best friend is unlike Polonius because she would never send someone to spy on you.

6. Put together a group of students who enjoy performing or would like to give it a try. Stage the dumb show and the play-within-the-play. Compare the two performances, and discuss with the audience how the dumb show foreshadows what happens in "The Mouse-trap."

7. Write a report on the theme of revenge in *Hamlet*. Address issues such as the morality of revenge and the need for personal justice. Compare Hamlet's dilemma with those of Laertes and Fortinbras. How are their situations the same, and how do they differ? Is each man justified in his actions? Is it difficult or easy to understand how each must feel?

8. Stage a debate between Hamlet and Claudius. Address issues in a way that the audience will be able to see how effective or ineffective each man would be as king. After the debate, ask the audience to judge which man would be the better king. Consider some of the following questions: Is it ever necessary to make decisions that go against a leader's conscience for the greater good of the state? Are moral questions better left to the church? Are leaders obligated to base their choices on personal morality rather than on public opinion? Can a moral king be a strong king and make the difficult decisions that may be necessary to secure the well being of the state?

9. Watch the film *Rosencrantz and Guildenstern are Dead*. What does the film tell you about these two men? After seeing them from this new perspective, what do you think of them? Has your opinion of them changed? How does playwright Tom Stoppard's interpretation compare to Shakespeare's portrayal of them?

10. Design a lesson plan for elementary age students that helps them learn the story of Hamlet. How would you explain Hamlet's story to children in a way that they could understand? Consider the fact that you need a fairly short lesson so that the class does not feel overwhelmed. What would you leave out when teaching the play? What would become your primary focus? What are the difficulties you encounter when trying to simplify this very complicated story?

ANSWERS

Identify the Quotation

1. The speaker is Ophelia in Act IV, Scene 5, Lines 180–185. The listeners are Claudius, Gertrude, and Laertes. Violets are the symbol of faithfulness and are associated with Ophelia throughout the play.

2. The speaker is Laertes in Act V, Scene 2, Lines 310–311. Laertes has been scratched with his own poisoned rapier during a fencing contest with Hamlet.

3. The speaker is Horatio in Act V, Scene 2, Lines 363–365. The statement is directed at Hamlet's corpse.

4. Hamlet is the speaker in Act V, Scene 2, Lines 245–248, and the listener is Laertes. Hamlet is apologizing to Laertes and explaining that he killed Polonius accidentally.

5. Claudius is the speaker in Act III, Scene 1, Line 192. The listener is Polonius. Claudius indicates his concern about Hamlet's strange behavior.

6. The speaker is Gertrude in Act III, Scene 2, Line 234. Hamlet is the listener. Gertrude says this line to her son during "The Mouse-trap" in response to Hamlet's question, "Madam, how like you this play?" Gertrude says that the actress playing the queen in the play should not repeatedly insist that she would never remarry if her husband should die.

7. The speaker is Hamlet in Act I, Scene 2, Lines 180–183. Horatio is the listener. Hamlet uses sarcastic humor in an attempt to make sense of why his mother remarried so quickly after Hamlet's father's death.

8. The speaker is Polonius in Act I, Scene 3, Lines 75–77. The listener is Laertes. Laertes is leaving Elsinore and returning to Paris. His

father is giving Laertes departing advice on how to live and how to act. Polonius may be worried that his son is irresponsible with money, and he is reminding Laertes to be thrifty.

9. The speaker is Hamlet in Act V, Scene 1, Lines 189–193). The listener is Horatio. Hamlet is gazing upon the skull of a man that he knew when he was a child. He comes to the conclusion that death is inevitable, and in the end, death makes all people equal.

10. Gertrude is the speaker in Act V, Scene 1, Line 253. The statement is directed toward Ophelia, who is dead. Gertrude is at the young woman's funeral, lamenting that Ophelia did not live to be Hamlet's wife.

11. The speaker is Marcellus in Act I, Scene 4, Line 90. The listener is Horatio. Marcellus, Horatio, and Hamlet have just seen the ghost. During Shakespeare's time, ghosts were considered devilish apparitions that assumed the form of a dead person in order to lead his survivors into danger. The appearance of ghosts or other supernatural phenomena were also believed to be an indication of impending doom for the whole country.

12. Claudius is speaking to himself in Act III, Scene 3, Lines 37–39. This is the scene in which Claudius fully reveals his treachery and confirms to the audience that the ghost of Hamlet's father was in fact telling the truth. Claudius is not capable of repenting for his sins. He feels remorse, and he fears that he will be eternally damned for his actions, but he cannot bring himself to truly regret his actions.

True/False

(1) F (2) F (3) T (4) F (5) F (6) T (7) F (8) F (9) T (10) F (11) F (12) F (13) T (14) F (15) T

Multiple Choice

(1) b. (2) c. (3) a. (4) c. (5) a. (6) c. (7) b. (8) a. (9) b. (10) d. (11) c. (12) d. (13) b. (14) a. (15) d.

Fill in the Blank

(1) illusion (2) Polonius (3) arras (4) rogue, peasant (5) remembrance, thoughts (6) flesh, melt, dew (7) brother's (8) borrower, lender (9) heaven, earth (10) question

CLIFFSCOMPLETE RESOURCE CENTER

The learning doesn't need to stop here. CliffsComplete Resource Center shows you the best of the best: great links to information in print, on film, and online. And the following aren't all the great resources available to you; visit www.cliffsnotes.com for tips on reading literature, writing papers, giving presentations, locating other resources, and testing your knowledge.

BOOKS AND ARTICLES

Association of the Bar of the City of New York. *The Elsinore Appeal: People v. Hamlet.* Ed. Kevin Thomas Duffy. New York: St. Martin's Press, 1996.

This book is a report of the hypothetical trial of Prince Hamlet of Denmark. He has been convicted of six homicides: those of Claudius, Polonius, Laertes, Ophelia, and Rosencrantz and Guildenstern. Hamlet has already served 400 years of a life sentence, but now the American system of justice has agreed to reexamine his case on appeal. Good resource for anyone interested in law and literature.

Bloom, Harold, ed. *William Shakespeare: Modern Critical Views. The Tragedies.* Broomall, Pa.: Chelsea House, 1986.

This collection of critical essays represents a wide range of twentieth-century scholarship. Appropriate for advanced high school and college level students. Includes an index and a very useful bibliography.

Bradley, A.C. *Shakespearean Tragedy.* London: Macmillan, 1904.

These essays were originally delivered as lectures by the author, who was a professor of literature at Oxford University. The text is very scholarly and not an easy read. The collection describes and explains the genre of revenge-tragedy and helps to bring about a better understanding of the nature of plays such as *Hamlet.* Highly recommended, especially for college and graduate-level students.

Branagh, Kenneth. *Hamlet: By William Shakespeare.* New York: W.W. Norton, 1996.

This book describes the day-to-day decisions made on the set of Branagh's production of *Hamlet.* It includes the screenplay for the film, an introduction by Branagh, his diary on the set, and photographs. This title is a good companion piece for watching the film. Highly recommended for any level.

Dawson, Anthony B. *Hamlet in Performance.* Manchester: Manchester University Press, 1995.

This is an easy-to-read book and an excellent source of the theatrical history of performances of *Hamlet.* It includes stage history, film history, and translations. Excellent source for Shakespeare students as well as those interested in the theatre.

Doyle, John and Ray Lischner. *Shakespeare For Dummies.* Foster City: IDG Books Worldwide, Inc., 1999.

This guide to Shakespeare's plays and poetry provides summaries and scorecards for keeping track of who's who in a given play, as well as painless introductions to language, imagery, and other often intimidating subjects.

Irace, Kathleen, ed. *The First Quarto of 'Hamlet.'* Cambridge: Cambridge University Press, 1998.

This is a modern-spelling edition of the First (or so-called "bad") Quarto. The introduction describes the critical theories concerning the origin of this version of the play and provides a description of modern theatrical staging. It compares the First Quarto with the two more widely used texts — the Second Quarto and the Folio — and provides footnotes and explanations in-text for a better understanding of the early play. Highly recommended for anyone interested in the First Quarto or early theatrical texts.

Jenkins, Harold, ed. *Hamlet.* London:Metheun, 1982.

This version of the play has an introduction like no other. Professor Jenkins provides extensive historical information on Shakespeare's sources, contemporary plays with which *Hamlet* competed, publication history, and an in-depth analyses of the play. The text is replete with invaluable and useful footnotes that clarify Shakespeare's language and explain the use of imagery and allusion in the play. Highly recommended for college level.

Kliman, Bernice W. *Hamlet: Film, Television, and Audio Performance.* Rutherford, N.J.: Fairleigh Dickenson University Press, 1988.

A good guide to recorded versions of performances of *Hamlet*, this book is useful in film studies and for the examination of different kinds of technology applied in the play's production. Highly recommended for college level film, literature, or communications majors.

Mowat, Barbara, ed. *Hamlet.* New York: Washington Square Press, 1992.

This is part of a series of Shakespeare's plays compiled by the Folger Library in Washington, D.C. This edition of *Hamlet* contains clear explanatory notes on every other page. Each page of notes faces a page of the text of the play to make references accessible and easy to understand. Students of *Hamlet* may especially appreciate introductory sections within the book, including an introduction to the text, a history of the publication of Shakespeare's texts, coverage of Shakespeare's life, and a section on the theatrical environment in which he worked. Especially helpful for students is a section on Shakespeare's language. Recommended for high school and early college students.

Nesbit, E. *The Best of Shakespeare.* Oxford: Oxford University Press, 1997.

This author retold ten of Shakespeare's greatest stories in 1927. Her work was reprinted in 1997 with an introduction by Iona Opie and an afterword by Peter Hunt. The tales tell the stories at the heart of Shakespeare's plays with wit and humor. The book includes black-and-white photographs from modern productions on the English stage. Highly recommended for fifth through twelfth grade.

Newell, Alex. *The Soliloquies in Hamlet: The Structural Design.* Rutherford, NJ: Fairleigh Dickenson University Press, 1991.

The author's excellent explanation of the structure of soliloquies is helpful in understanding what they are, how they were written, and what function they serve in *Hamlet*. Highly recommended for upper-level high school and college.

Pennington, Michael. *Hamlet: A User's Guide.* New York: Limelight Editions, 1996.

A guide to acting *Hamlet*, this book takes the reader through the play scene by scene, discussing performance techniques while simultaneously providing valuable information on past performances of the play and acting methods. The author has been an actor for over 30 years, and that personal experience gives this book an "insider" quality. Good character study, especially recommended for theatre majors and high school students interested in production.

INTERNET

"The Hamlet home page."

www.hamlet.edmonton.ab.ca

This Web site will guide the user to many other links to interesting and helpful *Hamlet* Web pages. It is a good resouce for quick links.

"The Hamlet Navigator."

www.clicknotes.com/hamnavl/Hhome.html

This colorful and informative site provides summaries of the acts and scenes, gives notes on the characters, and explains themes and language.

"Falcon Education Link Home Page and Shakespeare Resource."

www.falconedlink.com/~falcon

The site provides thorough explanations and descriptions. It is a quick and enjoyable way to learn *Hamlet.*

"Hamlet Notes."

www.glen-net.ca/english/hamlet.html

This link can connect you to several other *Hamlet* sites, including discussions titled "Hamlet's Character," "Hamlet Discussion," and "Hamlet's Delay." The link called "To be or not to be" provides an excellent analysis of Hamlet's famous soliloquy.

"Introduction to *Hamlet.*"

www.ulg.ac.be/libnet/germa/hamleteng.htm

This page comes out of the University of Liège. It is very long but readable. In addition to the play, the site offers notes on Shakespeare and the themes and soliloquies in *Hamlet.* It also provides links to Shakespeare, *Hamlet*, and theatre sites.

"A Short Course on Shakespeare's *Hamlet.*"

http://server1/hypermart.net/hamlet

Just as the title suggests, this site provides a complete overview of *Hamlet.* The pictures are wonderful. Click on the "Course" link to access an online edition of *Hamlet* with more explanatory notes, questions and answers, and other study guides.

"Shakespeare Illustrated."

www.cc.emory.edu/ENGLISH

This site should appeal to anyone interested in art based on performances of *Hamlet.* It provides high quality reproductions of paintings from nineteenth-century Shakepearean productions. This is an excellent link to many beautiful artistic interpretations of Ophelia.

"Surfing with the Bard."

www.ulen.som/Shakespeare

Described as "Your Shakespeare classroom on the Internet," this site provides links to terrific *Hamlet* sites. There are seven different "Zones," each one carefully designed to make sure that you get the most out of all of Shakespeare's plays.

"Hamlet."

www.pathguy.com/hamlet

Designed by a pathologist with a passion for *Hamlet,* this is a colorful, informative, and always up-to-date site. It contains illustrations and explanations that bring *Hamlet* to life and explain the play in modern, conversational language.

FILMS

Discovering "Hamlet." Directed by Mark Olshaker. Narrated by Patrick Stewart. The Renaissance Theatre Company, 1990.

This film provides a glimpse into the processes that actors go through when they rehearse for a play and search for their own interpretations of character, motivation, and theme.

Hamlet. Directed by Kenneth Branagh. Performed by Kenneth Branagh, Julie Christie, Derek Jacobi, Kate Winslet. Castle Rock Entertainment, 1996.

Kenneth Branagh made the courageous decision not to shorten the Second Quarto / Folio text from which this film is adapted. He also decided not to modernize Shakespeare's language. Its 238-minute running time might deter some viewers, but the film is well worth the effort. It is set in nineteenth-century Denmark, giving the play a more modern feel. An excellent and complete film version.

Hamlet. Directed by Laurence Olivier. Performed by Laurence Olivier, Jean Simmons, Felix Aylmer, and Peter Cushing. Denham Studios, 1948.

This stark, abstract, deeply psychological black and white film was the recipient of four Academy Awards, including Best Picture and Best Actor. The film uses voiceovers for Hamlet's soliloquies instead of having the actor speak his lines aloud.

Hamlet. Directed by Tony Richardson. Performed by Nicole Williamson, Anthony Hopkins, Judy Parfitt, Mark Digham, and Marianne Faithful. Woodfall, 1969.

This is the first film version to use elements of the First Quarto in the script. This film is an adaptation of a theatrical production presented at the Roundhouse in London. Uniquely entertaining.

Hamlet. Directed by Franco Zeffirelli. Performed by Mel Gibson, Glenn Close, Alan Bates, Ian Holm, Paul Scofield, Helena Bonham-Carter. Warner Bros., 1990.

Zefferelli's realistic Elsinore and Danish coast lend this film a gutsy realism while still managing to capture the essence of *Hamlet*. The action never slows in this colorful, sumptuous film.

Rosencrantz and Guildenstern Are Dead. Directed by Tom Stoppard. Performed by Tim Roth and Gary Oldman. Buena Vista, 1990.

This movie, based on the play of the same name, is written from the perspective of Hamlet's two quirky, comical school chums. They find themselves in a situation that spins far beyond their understanding or ability to control. Their story weaves in and out of Shakespeare's play. However, Stoppard chooses to make the men and their dilemma a comedy rather than a tragedy. Highly entertaining.

Shakespeare: The Animated Tales, Hamlet. HBO/Random House, 1992.

This is part of a series of plays originally featured on HBO in the United States and BBC2 in Great Britain. Each play is a condensed, colorfully animated production designed to introduce children to Shakespeare. All of the films are closed-captioned. Recommended for grades 3 through 8.

AUDIOCASSETTES AND CD-ROMS

BBC Radio Presents Hamlet. Audiocassette (unabridged and abridged) and audio CD. Bantam Doubleday Dell Pub., 1993.

Kenneth Branagh leads a full cast with music and sound effects that help to bring this recorded version to life. A 24-page booklet provides some insight into each character, but there is no synopsis included.

Bookworm Shakespeare Series: Hamlet. CD-ROM. Bookworm. 1994.

This learning resource provides an extensive and in-depth examination of plot, language, and themes. Color-coded annotations throughout the text help to explain difficult passages. They also offer historical background information, scene summaries, character analysis, and discussions about the themes. Very useful and fun.

Hamlet. CD-ROM. Shakespeare Interactive Library. Cromwell Productions, 1998.

This is a multimedia seminar including video commentary by Professor Stanley Wells and Professor Russell Jackson of the Shakespeare Institute. The program investigates the text of the play, its characters, and its history. The CD has a search program, a synopsis, a biography of Shakespeare, and many other aids. It provides Internet links and can be used with Windows and Macintosh. Highly recommended.

CLIFFSCOMPLETE READING GROUP DISCUSSION GUIDE

Use the following questions and topics to enhance your reading group discussions. The discussion can help get you thinking — and hopefully talking — about Shakespeare in a whole new way!

DISCUSSION QUESTIONS

1. Throughout the Victorian era and in several modern productions, female actors (perhaps most notably Sarah Bernhardt) have played the role of Hamlet. How does this cross-gender casting of the role of Hamlet change the character's relationships and actions? If Hamlet is played by a female actor, should other characters — Ophelia, Gertrude, or Claudius — be cross-gender cast also?

2. A 1979 stage production of *Hamlet* featured two actors playing the role of Hamlet. One actor performed Hamlet's physical actions while the other actor stood in the middle of the stage motionless and recited Hamlet's lines. Throughout the production, the "physical" Hamlet was clearly crazed, and the "vocal" Hamlet was completely sane. How does this radical interpretation affect your understanding of the play? What does the play gain from this type of interpretation? What does it lose?

3. Throughout *Hamlet,* you can view many of the characters' actions as based on choice *(free will)* or based on fate *(destiny)*. Which of Hamlet's actions seem to come from free will? Which seem to come from destiny? What about the actions of Ophelia? Claudius? Gertrude? Polonius? What relationship between free will and destiny does Shakespeare suggest?

4. The character of Hamlet has been played by actors of both genders, many races, and many ages. He's been motivated to kill by insanity, political intrigue, love for his mother, love for his dead father, and nearly every social ill from corporate greed to the prevalence of violence in the media. Given all these interpretations, is it possible to ever figure out who Hamlet really is? How do you envision Hamlet? Why is the character open to so much interpretation? What might Shakespeare be saying in *Hamlet* about our ability to truly know each other?

5. *Hamlet* features a large cast of supporting characters. Why did Shakespeare include the characters of Rosencrantz and Guildenstern? Horatio? Osric? The players? What do these characters add to the play? How would the play be different if you took away each of these characters?

6. Shakespeare chose not to dramatize the death of Ophelia and instead has Gertrude describe the event in a monologue. During the last 200 years, numerous artists have attempted to paint, sketch, or sculpt Ophelia's suicide. Why do artists keep returning to this undramatized moment in *Hamlet?*

7. Film and stage productions of *Hamlet* that set the play in modern times sometimes struggle

with how to present scenes that include the ghost of Hamlet's father. While modern directors have the technical wizardry to make the ghost scenes impressive, most modern audience members don't believe in ghosts, and the end result can be more silly than scary or dramatically powerful. Some recent productions have tried to deal with this issue by cutting the character of the ghost altogether. Other productions have used audio recordings of the ghost's lines and had Hamlet pretend to see the ghost. How important is the character of the ghost? How necessary is it for an audience to see the ghost? What are the benefits of having the actor playing Hamlet pretend to see the ghost? What is the down side? How much of the ghost is in Hamlet's mind?

8. Several productions of *Hamlet* have cut Fortinbras's entrance at the end of the play and concluded the play with Horatio's final speech. How important is Fortinbras's final presence to the end of *Hamlet?* What are the pros and cons of ending the play with Horatio's eulogy?

9. Based on the work of psychoanalyst Sigmund Freud, most productions of *Hamlet* performed during the twentieth century have featured a bed in Hamlet and Gertrude's closet scene, even though Shakespeare's text does not specifically call for this piece of furniture. In some recent productions, the bed has been replaced by a couch and even a stool. How does the choice of one piece of furniture change our understanding of Hamlet and Gertrude's relationship? What piece of furniture would you use when staging the play?

10. Film and stage productions of *Hamlet* have been set in literally hundreds of different locations and historical time periods. Select a location or historical time period (Victorian England, World War II Europe, a modern corporate boardroom, a futuristic space colony, and so on) and suggest how you would stage the following:

* Hamlet encountering the ghost of his father
* Hamlet telling Ophelia to go to a nunnery
* Hamlet in the graveyard
* The final duel between Hamlet and Laertes
* The deaths of Gertrude, Claudius, and Hamlet

Index

continued

D

E

M

N

O

Notes

Notes

Notes

Notes

Notes

Notes